D1127791

Six California Kitchens

*A Collection of Recipes, Stories, and
Cooking Lessons from a Pioneer
of California Cuisine*

by Sally Schmitt
with Bruce Smith

photography by Troyce Hoffman
forewords from Thomas Keller and Cindy Pawlcyn

CHRONICLE BOOKS
SAN FRANCISCO

Text copyright © 2022 by Sally Schmitt

All photographs copyright © 2022 by Troyce Hoffman, except page 336 by Mariah Tauger. Archival photos and illustrations provided by Sally's family and friends with the exception of page 75 by Gerry Pickering, page 85 by Joseph Rychetnik, pages 242 and 244 by Kate Klein May, and page 339 by Brown W. Cannon III.

All rights reserved. No part of this book may be reproduced in any form without written permission from the publisher.

Page 351 constitutes a continuation of the copyright page.

Library of Congress Cataloging-in-Publication Data

Names: Schmitt, Sally, 1932- author. | Smith, Bruce (Food writer), author.
 | Hoffman, Troyce, photographer.
Title: Six California kitchens : a collection of recipes, stories, and cooking lessons
 from a pioneer of California cuisine / by Sally Schmitt with Bruce Smith ;
 photography by Troyce Hoffman.
Description: San Francisco : Chronicle Books, [2022] | Includes index.
Identifiers: LCCN 2021023787 | ISBN 9781797208824 (hardcover)
Subjects: LCSH: Cooking, American--California style. | Cooking--California.
 | Schmitt, Sally, 1932- | LCGFT: Cookbooks.
Classification: LCC TX715.2.C34 S33 2022 | DDC 641.59794--dc23
LC record available at https://lccn.loc.gov/2021023787

Manufactured in China.

Design by Byron Hoffman (Sally's grandson).
Food and prop styling by Sally Schmitt, Byron Hoffman, Troyce Hoffman (Sally's grandson), Karen Bates (Sally's daughter), Kathy Hoffman (Sally's daughter), Terry Schmitt (Sally's daughter), Debey Zito (Sally's daughter-in-law), Perry Hoffman (Sally's grandson), and Rita Bates (Sally's grandaughter).

10 9 8 7 6 5 4 3 2

Mom's Strawberry Shortcake

Mix and sift -
 2 c flour
 1/4 c sugar
 4 t b.p.
 1/2 t. salt
 few grains nutmeg
Work in ~~1/3~~ cube butter
add 1 egg well beaten and lastly
 1/2 c milk. ~~Pat into desired form.~~
 Drop -

Peach Shortcake

2 c cake flour	1/2 c sour milk or
1/2 t salt	buttermilk
3 t b.p.	2 c sliced fresh
1/2 t soda	peaches
1/4 c sugar	1/4 - 1/2 c sugar
1/2 c shortening	1 tsp cinnamon

Sift flour, salt, b.p., soda, and sugar.
Cut in shortening till resembles coarse
crumbs. Add buttermilk. Mix just
enough till dough follows fork around
the bowl. Pat out in greased 8" pan.
Bake at 425° 20 min. Split hot
shortcake. Fill and top with peaches sprinkle
with sugar and cinnamon. Serve with
cream. Serves 6-8.

Contents

First: My Mother's Kitchen:
Where It Started (1932 to 1948)

Second: The Vintage Cafe:
The Kitchen I Took Over (1967 to 1978)

Third: The Chutney Kitchen:
The Kitchen I Designed (1970 to 1978)

Fourth: The French Laundry:
Just up the Street (1978 to 1994)

Foreword by Thomas Keller

Sally Schmitt. Her name is revered at the French Laundry restaurant. Not just as our original cofounder, but as our original cook and guiding light. Her influence endures in so many ways. It was Sally who established the practice of inviting guests into the kitchen after a meal for a tour or a chat, a tradition that we carry on today. The prix fixe menu that we offer once a year to Yountville neighbors is the very menu that Sally used to serve.

Kind and generous, forthright, and unpretentious. A culinary pioneer but also a throwback, preparing dishes that evoked the most delicious versions of your favorite childhood meals. That is the Sally we all came to know. And that is the Sally who comes through in her first cookbook, *Six California Kitchens*, written from her home on the Apple Farm in Philo, California, where she is enjoying retirement with her family close by.

Flipping through these pages, I was transported back to 1992, the year I first laid eyes on the French Laundry. I knew almost immediately that I wanted it to be my future, that I could build on the foundation Sally and her husband, Don, had established. It took another two years before that dream began to come together, two years of struggle and setbacks as I strove to raise money to buy the restaurant, two years during which Sally and Don never lost faith in me. I owe them my undying gratitude.

I also owe them the restaurant's name. In 1978, they set up shop in the body of what had been an actual laundry. Sally operated from a minimalist kitchen that somehow reflected her cooking style, which was based on approachable French technique. There was nothing grandstanding about Sally's food. Her repertoire employed Gallic touches but also drew on cherished elements of Americana: tomato soup, braised oxtails, cranberry and apple kuchen. I have fond memories of standing at her green stove with its blue hood—uncommon colors for restaurant kitchens. Years later, when we remodeled the restaurant and I saw the work crew hauling off the blue hood, it struck me that they were removing a tangible link to the restaurant's history, to all the meals Sally cooked and all the memories she and Don helped create. I decided to paint the front door the same blue as that hood: the color now known as French Laundry Blue.

Sally has given us so much already. And now, she has gifted us with this book. Proud of her second-generation California roots, she describes her cooking as being informed by what was around her, by what was in season, fresh and carefully raised. We can all learn from Sally and her approach to food, to say nothing of her approach to life.

Thomas Keller is the chef and proprietor of the French Laundry, in Napa Valley, and Per Se, in New York, among other restaurants. He is the first and only American-born chef to hold multiple three-star ratings from the prestigious Michelin Guide, as well as the first American male chef to be designated a Chevalier of the French Legion of Honor, the highest decoration in France. Named America's Best Chef by *Time* magazine, Chef Keller led a team from the United States in 2017 to its first-ever gold medal in the Bocuse d'Or, the prestigious biannual competition that is regarded as the Olympics of the culinary world.

Foreword by Cindy Pawlcyn

When I set out to become a chef, Sally Schmitt was my hero. Later, when I opened my first restaurant, she was my mentor. I grew up in Minnesota, and Sally didn't know me then, or how important she was to me. I had always wanted to cook. I started doing catering when I was still in high school, and went on to graduate from the University of Wisconsin in hotel and restaurant management.

I was told many times by many people that it would be "impossible" for me to be a woman chef. Maybe I could work in a kitchen doing salads, or in a bakery, but that would be as close as I would ever get to being a real chef. Then, on a trip to California, my sister-in-law found an article in *Sunset* magazine about this woman chef, Sally Schmitt. She brought it back for me, and it was one of the best gifts I've ever received. It had a photo showing Sally in the herb garden at the French Laundry. Finally, I had proof! Here was a real woman chef. I cut it out and kept that photo in my wallet for years, holding on to it to quiet my fears as I worked toward the "impossible."

In 1980 I moved to Northern California and three years later opened my own restaurant, Mustards Grill, just up the road from the French Laundry, in Yountville. One day, shortly after we opened, Sally and Don walked in. I told Sally the story of how I had learned about her and how much she meant to me. It was the beginning of a long and valuable friendship.

When Sally and Don started the French Laundry, it became the place where the locals went to really enjoy themselves, eating, drinking, and just being with each other. The upstairs room was notorious for wild evenings of great fun—and often a bit of trouble. When I bring up those days with the old-timers, most just start a story, then smile and stop, saying, "Well, it was a bit wild back then, so maybe that's not for publication!" Darn! I try to get it out of them, and from the look in their eyes, I could tell it was a riot of fun.

Don would greet you at the door, making you feel like royalty, and then help you select the wine to match that night's menu. I can still taste Sally's lamb shanks. Oh, how I enjoyed her cooking! Her olive oil crust, her oxtails, and the Zanzibar duck were to live for! Her orzo, like other simple dishes, was memorable in its deliciousness, equal parts cream and butter with some black pepper. Like everything she cooked, it was made with love.

But most of all, Sally was always there to answer any questions and guide you in the right direction. She took no prisoners either. She is famous for saying, "You could do that, but I wouldn't." What she did do, what she achieved, made her important to me and to so many others. She did the "impossible" ahead of her time and on her own terms.

Cindy Pawlcyn is the chef and proprietor of the legendary Mustards Grill, named for the wild mustard flowers that grow in the Napa Valley. She not only grows her own organic vegetables at the restaurant, but also was an early advocate for using local sustainable produce and meats for her wine-country cuisine. She has partnered in the creation of over a dozen iconic San Francisco Bay Area restaurants, including Fog City Diner, Roti, and Tra Vigne, and authored five cookbooks, the James Beard Award–winning *Mustards Grill Napa Valley Cookbook*, *Fog City Diner Cookbook*, *Big Small Plates*, *Cindy Pawlcyn's Appetizers*, and *Cindy's Supper Club*.

Preface: My Six Kitchens

We all have a ladder to climb, and then descend. We first learn, then achieve, and finally share what our lives have been all about. My ladder was made up of six kitchens, all of them in California.

My first rung was my mother's kitchen. There I was taught the craft of cooking, which had been handed down through generations of my family. It was passed along to me with care and an emphasis on quality, and it was done gently, with love.

The second kitchen was my first commercial one. It was an established operation, but when I was abruptly thrust into it, I had to figure out how to make it work. So I used what I had learned in my mother's kitchen: quality, care, craft.

On the next rung up the ladder, I had the chance to design my kitchen and really cook in it for the first time, in my own restaurant, the Chutney Kitchen. I did it the way I wanted to, using what I'd learned, and I learned much from doing it.

When starting out, one never knows how high the ladder will reach. My husband, Don, and I reached the apex at the second restaurant we started together, the French Laundry, where we worked for sixteen years. They were magnificent years—cooking for others, sharing food, creating a welcoming atmosphere, striving for quality.

The steps down the ladder are about passing forth, sharing what one has learned and figured out. My years at the French Laundry were followed by fourteen wonderful years of teaching in my fifth kitchen, at the 30-acre [12-hectare] apple farm we had purchased. It was a time of expanding our community and sharing the joy of cooking, with hope, gentleness, and love.

And then, finally, in my sixth kitchen in the small cottage on the Northern California coast, where we had retired, I didn't cook for others; I cooked only for Don and myself. I had to learn to cook for two again, which was a pleasure in itself. These were sublime years, and I wish they could have gone on forever.

I am actually now in my seventh kitchen, the one I have not counted. My beloved husband died several years ago, and I cook for just myself now. I am still surrounded by my family, friends, former students, and customers, who all visit me. This matters. Now on the cusp of my ninetieth year, I live on the Apple Farm. I have a window I look out and can watch the change of seasons in the trees, the flowers, and the animals that pass by. I have a kitchen to cook in. And I have a desk for writing.

It is time that I do that, do what I have been thinking about for years: write down and share what I have learned—my recipes, my techniques, and my thoughts on cooking, quality, and craft after working in my six kitchens. It is also my story of climbing up, then back down, this glorious ladder.

Introduction: A California Girl

When it comes to food, I always was, and still am, a true California girl. I grew up in the 1930s outside a small town near Sacramento, surrounded by good food that was grown locally, much of it out of our garden or from our own animals. We always had unpasteurized milk from our cow, and when we saved up enough cream to make butter, it was my job to churn it. We gorged on vine-ripened tomatoes and Kentucky Wonder beans from the garden all summer long, and when the season peaked, we canned the leftovers for winter.

Our basement was filled with jars of canned apricots, nectarines, applesauce, green beans, tomatoes in every shape and form, and pickles. Since our freezer at home was tiny, just big enough for ice cubes and the occasional carton of ice cream, we rented a locker in town when Pa butchered our pig or male calf.

I think I got this sense of pride of place from my mother, a third-generation Californian. I recall hearing her complain when my father's Texas relatives took their first trip out to visit us, driving the whole way, and passing through the Central Valley at night. "Why, they didn't even see California!" she exclaimed. She had her revenge, however, by sending them out to taste, for the first time, olives freshly plucked from the tree.

In all of my six kitchens, I have been a California cook, making use of the food around me—in season, local, fresh, and carefully raised. I didn't really think I had a choice, since I didn't shop at supermarkets. I always welcomed what would turn up.

A friend would stop by and take a bag of chanterelles out of the trunk of her car. A local farmer would walk in through my kitchen door with a box of freshly picked tomatoes. Before dinner service, one of my staff would run out to grab a few Meyer lemons off the tree outside the French Laundry. And now, on a cool autumn afternoon, I can walk out of my home to see if there are any Gravenstein apples left at the farm stand on our apple farm.

I've always tried to keep it simple, which is why I've never felt the need to use a food processor or microwave. Instead, I've had good sharp knives, pots and pans, a big chopping block, a wooden spoon, and a whisk. I've always loved to work with my hands. It's what cooking is all about.

But most important, I try to allow the food to be just what it is, but also, to let it be the best it can be.

opposite: Sally Kelsoe at age eleven.

Chronology

1932   February 28, Sally Kelsoe is born in Roseville, California.

1935   *My Better Homes and Gardens Lifetime Cook Book* is published.

1936   *The Joy of Cooking*, by Irma S. Rombauer, is published.

1937   Sally's parents move the family to a farm a few miles outside of Roseville.

1947   *Let's Cook It Right*, by Adelle Davis, is published.

1952   Sally graduates from the University of California, Davis, with a degree in home economics.

1953   Sally and Don marry.

       C. A. Swanson and Sons produces their first TV Brand Frozen Dinner, a Thanksgiving meal consisting of turkey, cornbread dressing, frozen peas, and sweet potatoes. It sells for 98¢.

1956   Alan Hooker opens the Ranch House in Ojai.

1960   *French Provincial Cooking*, by Elizabeth David, is published.

1961   *Mastering the Art of French Cooking*, by Julia Child, Louisette Bertholle, and Simone Beck, is published.

1963   *The French Chef* debuts on WGBH.

1966   Alfred Peet open Peet's Coffee, Tea & Spices in Berkeley, California.

1967   Sally and Don come to Yountville, where Don manages the historic winery turned shopping arcade, Vintage 1870, and Sally runs the Vintage Cafe (until 1978).

       The Cheese Board opens in Berkeley.

       The first compact microwave is introduced into the American market.

       Arlo Guthrie, at age twenty, records his hit song "Alice's Restaurant."

1970   Don and Sally open the Chutney Kitchen in Yountville (remaining until 1977). Sally begins her Friday Night prix fixe dinners.

       The French Menu Cookbook, by Richard Olney, is published.

       The Tassajara Bread Book, by Edward Espe Brown, is published.

       General Mills introduces Hamburger Helper.

       Diet for a Small Planet, by Frances Moore Lappé, is published.

       The Random House Dictionary defines the word *chef* as "a cook, esp a male head cook."

1971   Alice Waters opens Chez Panisse in Berkeley with a three-course dinner for $3.95.

1972   Narsai David opens Narsai's in the Berkeley Hills, overlooking San Francisco Bay.

       The Cheese Board Collective opens.

1973   Victoria Kroyer Wise opens the Pig by the Tail Charcuterie in Berkeley.

       The Moosewood Restaurant opens in Ithaca, New York, serving a vegetarian menu inspired by Frances Moore Lappé and Adelle Davis.

       The Cuisinart food processor is introduced to America at the National Housewares Exposition, in Chicago, and is priced at $140.

1974   Don and Sally purchase the French Laundry building in Yountville for $39,000.

       Sous vide cooking introduced into restaurant cooking at the Restaurant Troisgros in Roanne, France.

       The Taste of Country Cooking, by Edna Lewis, is published.

1976	"The Judgment of Paris," the blind tasting by French judges in France of California wines against the best of Burgundy and Bordeaux. To everyone's amazement, the American wines came in first.
1977	Don and Sally leave Vintage 1870 and go to work renovating the French Laundry building, turning it into a restaurant.
	The restaurant at the Domaine Chandon winery in Yountville opens.
1978	The French Laundry opens, with a hand-printed menu offering pasta with clam sauce, blanquette de veau, fresh asparagus, rice, green salad, cheese, rhubarb mousse, and coffee for $12.50.
	The French Laundry building is designated a National Historic Site.
	Ben Cohen and Jerry Greenfield open Ben and Jerry's Homemade Ice Cream in a converted gas station in Burlington, Vermont.
1979	Sally is on the cover of the September issue of *Napa Valley Magazine*, with a feature story inside about the restaurant.
1980	Bruce LeFavour opens Rose et LeFavour in St. Helena.
	Cook's Magazine begins publication.
1981	First Auction Napa Valley held, organized by Napa Valley Vintners.
1982	Wolfgang Puck opens Spago on the Sunset Strip in Los Angeles.
	Chez Panisse Menu Cookbook, by Alice Waters, is published.
1983	Cindy Pawlcyn, a Rose et LeFavour alum, opens Mustards Grill in Yountville.
	Joyce Goldstein, a Chez Panisse alum, opens Square One in San Francisco.
	Jeremiah Tower, another Chez Panisse alum, opens Stars in San Francisco.
	Jonathan Waxman opens Jams in New York City, taking California cuisine to the East Coast.
1984	Don and Sally purchase what will become the Apple Farm, outside of Philo, with daughter Karen Bates and her husband, Tim.
1985	Cindy Pawlcyn opens Fog City Diner in San Francisco.
1987	Judy Rodgers, a Chez Panisse alum, takes over as chef at Zuni Café, in San Francisco.
1988	McDonald's opens its 10,000th restaurant.
1992	Thomas Keller enters a contract to purchase the French Laundry.
1993	On December 19, Sally cooks her last dinner at the French Laundry.
1994	Thomas Keller takes over the French Laundry. Sally and Don move to the Apple Farm.
1995	Sally teaches the first class at the Apple Farm.
2005	Starbucks opens its 10,000th coffeehouse.
2007	Sally has a stroke.
	"Locavore" is the Oxford word of the year, having been coined two years before by the Berkeley chef Jessica Prentice.
2008	Don and Sally move to their cottage in Elk.
2011	*Modernist Cuisine*, by Maxime Bilet and Nathan Myhrvoid, is published.
2016	Don and Sally move back to their home at the Apple Farm.
2017	Don passes.
2021	Sally is still cooking.

Sally's Basics

A few notes and recommendations to make preparing my recipes easier. Also, please see Sally's Pantry (page 340) about the ingredients I use with some sources for them.

- When I call for butter in my recipes, it is salted butter.

- I prefer to make my own stock, (see Making Stock, page 328) and some of my recipes call for strong or weak chicken stock. For strong chicken stock, reduce regular stock by about a quarter. For weak chicken stock, dilute it with a third more water.

- The oil I use for cooking is a good olive oil from Sciabica Family Olive Oil in Modesto, California.

- I like to buy all my spices, seeds, and peppercorns whole and grind only the amount I need for a recipe. Several of them I heat first, using a little sesame seed toaster. I toast each type of seed or peppercorn separately because I've found they each take a different amount of time to reach full potency. The sesame seed toaster is just a very small, light-weight pan with a mesh lid that I can hold over the burner on my stove. A small frying pan will work just as well, and you don't need oil. Just put the seeds into the dry pan, hold it over medium heat, and keep it moving, stirring or shaking, until it becomes fragrant and starts to brown. When cooled down, you can use a spice grinder if you like, but I use (and highly recommend) a Japanese version of the mortar and pestle called a *suribachi*.

- Pepper is one of my favorite spices, and Tellicherry black peppercorns are my pepper of choice. I keep them whole until I need them, and never use them without toasting them first in the little sesame seed toaster. After they've cooled down, I'll grind a few peppercorns by hand in my suribachi.

- For salt, I stay with Diamond Crystal Kosher Salt. I've played with almost everything through the years, and there are so many different types, different grinds, flakes, ways of processing, and sourcing, but the one thing I've learned is that every time you try a new salt, you need to learn all over again how to use it.

- When I call for parsley in a recipe, I mean the flat-leaf type, also known as Italian parsley, which has more flavor than the more decorative curly-leaf variety.

- When I use raw onions, I like to take the bitterness out by first slicing or chopping them, depending on the recipe, and then dousing them with a few tablespoons of white vinegar. Drain them right away with a sieve, because if they soak too long, they will lose their delightful crunch.

- With whipping cream, I never sweeten it because it goes on top of what is already sweet. It actually adds moisture and richness to complement the sweetness. You want to get a heavy cream to whip, one that has a high butterfat content. Regular whipping cream has around 30 percent, which will work, but look for what is called heavy cream, or heavy whipping cream, which has between 36 and 38 percent butterfat. It will whip better, holds it shape better, and actually tastes better.

- My recipes reflect my minimalist approach to cooking tools. I use only two knives, a paring knife and a santoku (the Japanese version of a chef's knife). I don't have anything to plug in except my toaster and a blender to purée soups, pâtés, and sauces. I keep the blender in a drawer so the countertop can be free for actual cooking. I rather enjoy mixing things by hand with either a whisk or a wooden spoon.

ABOUT THE RECIPE FORMAT

- I have written these recipes the way I cooked and taught them over the past fifty years. Each instruction is paired to the ingredient(s) being used. I know that this is not the usual way for cookbooks, where you see all the instructions bundled together and the ingredients in a separate itemized list, which I suppose, is to make shopping easier. With my way of doing it, which is common in professional kitchens, it is easy to see what ingredients you'll be using by looking down the right side. You will find instructions to the left of each ingredient. This makes it easier to keep your place in the recipe, as you are not jumping back and forth between ingredients and instructions.

- I've listed for each recipe how many portions it makes, and how long it takes to prepare, but be aware that I aimed for the middle ground. The number SERVES will change if you are cooking for a hungry young person, or light eaters, or preparing the dish as one of several courses or a simple, one-plate meal. The PREP TIME is your time at the stove, the cutting board, the sink, while the COOK TIME is when you can relax on the sofa with a glass of wine, when your meal is safely in the oven, or on the stove. The TOTAL TIME is the time the recipe takes, prep and cooking time plus any related tasks, with the exception of letting something chill, freeze, gel, or rest, specified at the end of a recipe. You need to read the recipe carefully to figure out when you will actually be able to serve it, and I recommend you read it through at least three times before you start cooking. You will find that carefully visualizing each step will streamline the whole process, and prevent errors.

ABOUT RED MARGIN NOTES: My red Margin Notes are comments about the stories, recipes, and photos in the book, sometimes with a memory or observation from a friend or family member.

ABOUT BLUE MARGIN NOTES: My blue Margin Notes are suggestions, comments, and variations directly relating to the actual steps and ingredients of the recipes that I think might help you in preparing the dishes the way I would.

The cherrywood and pine hutch in the Apple Farm kitchen. It is full of our favorite things, a small part of our extensive collection of beautiful and useful items that appear throughout the book. Among them, our porcelain ducks, a handmade batter bowl, my first real antique—a Jaspé pitcher, striped soup bowls from France, a set of twelve dessert plates brought back from Norway—a gift from one of my mother's trips, an original Earl Thollander sketch, my very dear, little blue pitcher— for a bunch of violets or tiny rosebuds, a checkered pitcher from Moustier St. Marie, oval Mexican plates— very frequently used, dinner plates by Ukiah potters Hoyman-Browe, a wonderful polka-dot platter, and a large green pitcher from a thrift shop in Napa.

First: My Mother's Kitchen
Where It Started (1932 to 1948)

Our Homestead

As I think back to my childhood days, I realize that food has always taken center stage. In 1937, when I was five, my family moved from the small California town of Roseville, in the Sacramento Valley, into the countryside. I think it was less than 5 miles [8 kilometers] from town to the 2½ acres [1 hectare] of rolling land my parents bought, right next to an old almond orchard. Doing much of the finish work themselves, they built a simple ranch house for us and planted a vegetable garden for their kitchen use.

We raised potatoes, carrots, beans of all kinds, onions, lots of corn in the summertime, parsley, and of course, tomatoes, tomatoes, and more tomatoes. We didn't raise much lettuce because it was too hot in the valley, but we did grow cucumbers, which we pickled. My father planted his favorite roses and irises, which he was always proud to show at the country fair.

There were two old apricot trees on the property, both Royal Blenheim, which to this day I consider the king of all apricots. The trees were big enough so that we could string our Uncle Willy's US Navy hammock between them. When our mother wasn't stretched out in it reading a book, we would climb those trees, gorging ourselves on the ripe fruit, or try to dump each other out of the hammock. How we loved those trees!

There was also a black walnut, a guava, a persimmon, and several oak trees surrounding us. Lining our driveway was an abandoned row of muscat grapes. Getting full sunlight and little water, the vines gave us the most delicious, intensely flavored grapes, deep gold in color. Just outside our kitchen was a huge, very old weeping willow. Our father made a swing and hung it from a top branch. We could really go high, at least high enough to scare me. Then we played hide and seek in the tall grasses until the dark drove us inside.

We soon acquired chickens, a pig, and a Guernsey cow. Sometimes we raised rabbits, too, which we dined on for special occasions. The rabbits were my little brother's pets, so when we ate one, we made sure to call it chicken and hoped he wouldn't ask for a wing, which he never did. I longed for a horse, but my father believed in raising only animals for meat, and he ruled with a rather heavy hand.

My father felt lucky to have survived the Depression with a steady job at the railroad, and he was determined to support his growing family. When my brother and I were old enough to help, he sent us out to the vegetable garden to pull weeds, reminding us to "Be sure to get the roots." I also learned how to pick the beans, deadhead the roses, and change the sprinklers, while my father was at work in town. He would come home after a hard day, deposit his lunch pail on the porch, and go right into the vegetable garden, where he

previous page: Me (on the left), and my original teachers. Aunt Polly showing her gravy expertise, Aunt Saidie observing in the back, and my mother and Kay up front watching the action, circa 1950.

opposite: A family dinner at our homestead. Front and center, Aunt Polly, moving left around the table, me, mom, Aunt Saidie, sister Kay, brother Tag, nephew Terry, Uncle Bob, and Uncle Name (that's really what we called him).

remained until he was called in for dinner. If we hadn't done our chores, that was the time of reckoning.

It seems strange that my mother did such a good job of cooking some vegetables, but not others. Her green beans, which we called string beans, were always cooked to death. There was a running battle between my parents over those beans. My father planted way too many, which we had to harvest and also get rid of the surplus. We would take the extras to town for credit on our grocery bill, or deliver them to old friends in town who didn't have gardens. Meanwhile, my father insisted that we eat the old green beans first, so they wouldn't be wasted, while the young, tender ones grew old on the vine! My mother mixed them with a little onion and sometimes tomato and cooked them long and slow. They turned army green but were still tasty.

Years later, at our family table in Yountville, I served my father some tender, bright green beans, which I had blanched and then quickly sautéed in butter. He turned to my mother and said, "Why don't you ever cook beans this way?" We all held back our howls of laughter until he was out of hearing.

We loved mushrooms. I recall one excursion after a rain when we went mushroom gathering with my grandmother out to the last of the unfenced fields right outside the town. We gathered buckets of field mushrooms. It must have been an extraordinary crop, because it was so hard not to step on them! Back home, my mother sautéed them in butter and served them in large soup bowls, filled to the brim. That was our dinner and clearly a wonderful one, as I still can picture those big slices and black juices to this day.

Whenever we had fish, my mother cooked mustard potatoes, small red potatoes from our garden when we had them, or russets from the store when we didn't. Since my father was an avid fisherman, we had them often, and I never tired of them. My mother boiled them, rolled them in bacon fat and French's mustard (the only mustard we knew) and roasted them until the skins were crisp and the interiors creamy.

This, the tastes and the attitudes, the love of food and cooking, are what sent me forth into the world.

Our family eventually grew to six in all, I being the second in the lineup. My older brother, Bob, was born in 1929, and I was born in 1932. John, whom we always called Tag, followed in 1936, and Kay, the last of the brood, was born in 1941.

Mustard Potatoes

SERVES 6 / PREP TIME: 10 MIN / COOK TIME: 30 TO 45 MIN

Cooking these brings back a flood of good memories from my childhood. Any potato will work well here. If I have russets on hand, I cut them into chunks. Small red potatoes, like the ones I dug up out of our garden as a child, I keep whole. Yukon golds of any size are wonderful. And yes, these are wonderful served with fish, as my mother did.

Preheat the oven to 400°F [200°C].

Scrub and peel (or not) and cut into chunks if large. Transfer to a medium pot and cover with water:

2 lb [910 g] russet, small red, or Yukon gold potatoes

I find it hard to believe that I grew up before potato peelers were a common kitchen gadget, but my mother wasn't big on gadgets, and I'm not either. For so many tasks, including peeling a potato, a good knife is all you need.

Add:

A generous pinch of salt

Place over medium heat, cover, and cook until tender, about 15 minutes.

Drain and toss them with a mixture of:

**¼ cup [60 ml] olive oil or bacon fat, or [55 g] butter
About 2 Tbsp of Dijon mustard
Salt and coarsely ground black pepper**

I used to use French's, but my preference now is Dijon mustard.

Cover the pot and shake it briskly to distribute the seasoning. Transfer the potatoes to a gratin dish and roast in the oven until they are browned and crispy around the edges and tender inside, 15 to 30 minutes. They will hold nicely, if you aren't quite ready to serve them.

Lazy Housewife Pickles

MAKES ENOUGH TO FILL A 1 GAL [3.8 L] CONTAINER / TOTAL TIME: 15 MIN
EXCLUDING CURING TIME

This has always been my favorite pickle. Growing up, my mother would
gather the cucumbers over several days from our garden, just as they were
reaching the perfect size. As she picked them, she would add them to the
pickling brine in the big brown crock we kept in a cooler. When the crock was
full, it was carried down to our basement for storage.

And then we waited; my mother would never allow any of our summer
preserves to be opened until Thanksgiving. This made sense for a frugal
household, since by then we were more than ready for a change in our daily
fare, and the garden was sparse.

These days, I cheat. I put the pickles in our refrigerator and start using
them after 2 weeks, when they are still crisp. For a container, be sure to use
something that won't corrode: stoneware crocks and large glass jars work well.
If your lid is metal, you can cut a square of wax paper or parchment paper to
cover the top of the jar before screwing on the lid.

This is embarrassingly simple—thus the name! I love to pair these pickles
with our Duck Liver Pâté (page 180), but more often than not, I simply make
a pickle and cheese sandwich with mayonnaise on sourdough or any good,
sliced whole-grain bread.

Wash well:

**2 to 3 lb [910 g to 1.4 kg]
medium pickling cucumbers**

Dry them and wedge into a 1 gal [3.8 L] container.

Mix together:

**8 cups [2 L] apple cider vinegar,
plus more as needed
½ cup [100 g] sugar
½ cup [80 g] kosher salt
Scant ½ cup [65 g] dry mustard**

Pour the vinegar mix over the cucumbers. It should cover them completely.
If it falls short, simply add a little more vinegar. The cucumbers must be
completely submerged. If necessary, weight them down with a plate or a
small plastic bag filled with some of the brine and sealed tightly. Cover
and refrigerate.

After 2 weeks, pull out a pickle, slice it, and give it a try. If, like me, you
like yours a little crisp, it's time to start using them. They'll last as long
as your jar does.

Also called Kirby
cucumbers, pickling cukes
are shorter and have thinner
skins than the ones you
slice for your salad. They're
available in summer and
can be found at your local
farmers' market. I also love
to use Armenian cucumbers,
which my granddaughter
Rita grows, as they have a
very tender skin, too. Do
not try this recipe with those
supermarket cucumbers
wrapped in plastic; most
have been waxed to keep
in the moisture, which will
interfere with the pickling.
These days, there are many
exotic shapes, including
round lemon cucumbers
and long, thin Persians.
Grab them when you see
them; next week they won't
be there.

My First Kitchen

My first recollection of hands-on cooking is standing on a stool at my mother's stove, patiently stirring the chocolate pudding, and watching it carefully as it came to a full boil and turned into a deliciously thick dessert. The smell was intoxicating, as was my awareness that I was responsible for it. After that, I recall churning butter, grinding beef with our old hand-cranked machine, setting the table, and, of course, doing dishes. That sometimes required sitting outside in our sandbox, and scouring with sand a pan that my mother had managed to burn, leaving it with a thick, brownish-black crust of food. To give her credit, she didn't own any of the beautiful pans we have today. I recall a lot of thin aluminum pots, which got thinner with each disaster.

When I grew tall enough so that I did not need the stool, I was allowed to start the chocolate pudding from scratch, to brown the beef for the stew, and to put together the cookie dough. Since my father loved desserts, there was always a pie, cake, or cookies to finish off a dinner.

My first cake was a thrill, but it took a while before Mom thought I was ready for piecrust. Of course, I had been given the trimmings long before to roll, cut out with a cookie cutter, and sprinkle with sugar and cinnamon. Remarkably, even though the dough was over handled, after baking, the cookies were never tough. Later, I kept up this tradition with our children and grandchildren, who loved to shape them into animals.

As soon as I was ready, my mother put a paring knife in my hand, and I peeled potatoes. And when she thought I was ready for a larger knife, I was cutting vegetables by her side. She was always in the kitchen with me.

I learned first by helping her. She would stay there in the kitchen to instruct me as we went along. She was a teacher by training, and she was a good one. She was patient and knew how to present things. She always said that she wanted me to learn the right way to cook; I could make my own shortcuts only after I had learned it well.

I don't remember her cooking from cookbooks. She did have a *Better Homes and Gardens* loose-leaf binder, to which she would add recipes from friends and family. And there was a drawerful of notes and recipes, which she had cut out of newspapers and magazines. But she only used the baking and dessert recipes. She knew the basics by heart, and this is what she taught me.

The kitchen wasn't large, like old-fashioned farmhouse kitchens, where there was enough space for several people to work at one time. This was a modern kitchen from the mid-1930s, geared towards the housewife who did her own cooking without servants. It was, like the whole house, modest. We had one smallish refrigerator, an electric stove, and a drop-down ironing

opposite: Recipes evolve over time. Here is a good example of a page from my mother's recipe book, complete with personal notes and substitutions.

board in the kitchen wall next to the cooler. We also had a basement, where we stored all of our summer produce, packed in jars and ready for the winter table.

I remember the day I was given, for the first time, full responsibility for dinner. My mother sat in her rocker in the living room, reading her latest *Ladies Home Journal*. She was available to answer questions, but would not come into the kitchen to stand and look over my shoulder. She was such a good teacher!

My younger sister later pointed out that she really never learned to do the canning and pickling and slow cooking that I did, since when I left for college, my mother went back to teaching, and their lifestyle changed. Looking back on it now from some eighty-odd years' distance, I am so grateful that I had that time in the kitchen with my mother, learning early to cook simple, basic foods in such a gentle, caring way.

A cooler, also known as a California cooler, was the West Coast's alternative to a cellar as a place to store perishable foods such as fruits, vegetables, milk, butter, and cheese. Dating to the turn-of-the-last-century bungalows, it was a kitchen cabinet vented at the top and bottom with slatted shelves. This allowed warmer air to escape, making it a few degrees cooler than the rest of the kitchen, especially in the temperate climate of California.

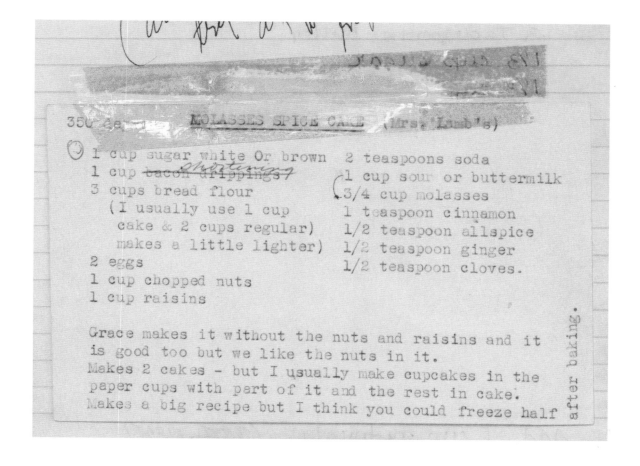

MOLASSES SPICE CAKE (Mrs. Lamb's)

350 4s

1 cup sugar white Or brown
1 cup bacon drippings~ *shortening*
3 cups bread flour
   (I usually use 1 cup
   cake & 2 cups regular)
   makes a little lighter)
2 eggs
1 cup chopped nuts
1 cup raisins

2 teaspoons soda
1 cup sour or buttermilk
3/4 cup molasses
1 teaspoon cinnamon
1/2 teaspoon allspice
1/2 teaspoon ginger
1/2 teaspoon cloves.

Grace makes it without the nuts and raisins and it is good too but we like the nuts in it.
Makes 2 cakes - but I usually make cupcakes in the paper cups with part of it and the rest in cake.
Makes a big recipe but I think you could freeze half

after baking.

Basic White Sauce

MAKES 2 CUPS [480 ML] / TOTAL TIME: 20 MIN

Since my inventive and frugal mother used her white sauce as a base for all sorts of concoctions, this was one of the very first things she taught me to make at a young age.

In a small saucepan over low heat, melt:

3 Tbsp butter

Stir in:

2 Tbsp all-purpose flour

Cook, stirring, until the mixture foams up and gets a tinge of brown.

Whisk in:

2 cups [480 ml] light cream or milk

Bring to a boil, stirring constantly. Lower the heat and simmer, stirring, until the sauce thickens. The whole process should take 5 to 10 minutes.

This is the base to work from. You can season the sauce with:

Salt and white pepper, preferably freshly ground

This is where white pepper really shines, but don't toast it before grinding, as that gives it an unpleasant flavor.

Now you have a good white sauce ready for anything. You can thin it, if necessary. I sometimes make it with half chicken stock and half milk or cream, and add a little good mustard.

I always make this sauce first, and set it, covered, on the back of the stove to let the flavors meld. It keeps just fine at room temperature until you're ready for it.

I learned later in life that this is one of the five classic French "mother sauces," as codified by the great French chef and cookbook author Auguste Escoffier. Though known as béchamel, I still call it my white sauce.

Often you will read that you should heat the cream or milk before adding it to the butter and flour. My mother taught me, though, that adding it cold prevents lumps, because the flour gets incorporated before it starts the thickening process. It also saves you from having to wash another pan!

VARIATION: I rarely make my white sauce without adding a touch of lemon in some form. The zest and juice of ½ lemon; or finely chopped preserved lemons, homemade (page 251) or store bought, are wonderful here. At the French Laundry, we called this variation Lemon Cream Sauce, as we always made it with half-and-half.

Mom's Potato Salad

SERVES 8 TO 10 / TOTAL TIME: 1 HOUR

This is the salad I learned to make from my mother. I grew up with it, and we made it often, always in large batches. This is best served while still warm, but if you have any left over, it will taste delicious the next day, cold from the fridge.

Peel and quarter lengthwise: **6 russet potatoes**

Transfer to a large pot and cover with water. Salt generously and bring to a boil. Lower the heat and simmer until the potatoes are fork-tender, about 15 minutes. It's rather tricky to get them just right. You want them tender, but not falling apart. Drain and spread out on a large baking sheet to cool.

Meanwhile, in a small saucepan with a lid, place: **3 eggs**

Cover with cold water. Bring to a boil and turn off the heat. Cover and let sit for 15 minutes. Drain, and fill the saucepan with cold water. One at a time, take out each egg, gently crack the eggshell, and return to the cold water. Let sit for 15 minutes. Cracking the shells lets a little water seep in, which makes them much easier to peel.

For the dressing, whisk together in a medium pitcher:

¼ cup [60 ml] apple cider vinegar
¼ cup [60ml] good olive oil
½ onion, minced
Salt and freshly ground black pepper

Then add, whisking until smooth:

½ cup [120 g] mayonnaise
½ cup [120 g] sour cream
1 Tbsp Dijon mustard

Peel and dice the cooled eggs and add to the dressing. Pour over the potatoes. With your hands, gently toss everything together.

If you have them available (ideally, from your garden), add:

A handful of chopped fresh parsley
A handful of minced fresh chives
A handful of chopped fresh dill

After Don and I were married, there was always a bit of a competition between my mother's and my mother-in-law's recipes for potato salad. Don's mother was famous for her version, which she always had ready for us when we made the long drive down the Central Valley to Visalia to visit her. We would arrive, sit in her kitchen nook, and feast on it with a couple of cold beers to dampen the travel dust. Hers was similar to my mom's, but she thinned the mayonnaise with condensed milk, which she kept on hand for her coffee. It was very good, but not as good as my mother's.

So, here is my mother's recipe, with no condensed milk.

Cheese Biscuit Dough Gods

MAKES 12 BISCUITS / PREP TIME: 10 MIN / COOK TIME: 25 MIN

This recipe for drop biscuits was passed down by my grandmother, who began making them before the turn of the last century. At the Apple Farm, they have become breakfast staples for our guests. Cruz Alvarado, through years of working with us, has become an expert at making these, her biscuits always turning out golden brown, plump, and crispy. She even discovered a shortcut: Grating the butter, cold from the refrigerator or freezer, with a box grater speeds up the process. No wonder she has become known as "the Cheese Biscuit Queen."

Preheat the oven to 400°F [200°C]. Line a baking sheet with parchment paper or grease it with butter.

In a large bowl, whisk together:	**2¼ cups [315 g] all-purpose flour** **1 Tbsp baking powder** **1 tsp salt**
With a pastry blender or your fingers, cut in:	**½ cup [110 g] cold butter, sliced**
When it resembles cornmeal, add and toss together:	**1 cup [80 g] coarsely grated sharp cheddar cheese**
Make a well in the center of the mixture. Pour in:	**1 cup [240 ml] cold half-and-half**

Using a fork, gently stir the dry ingredients into the cream until just incorporated and you have a nice stiff dough. Avoid overmixing, which toughens the biscuits. They should be very tender. Drop the dough by the forkful onto the prepared baking sheet, about ½ in [12 mm] apart.

Bake until they are nicely browned and crispy, about 25 minutes.

If they flatten out too much while baking, you have put in too much liquid or your mixture got too warm. Try holding back a little of the cream, only adding it if it is needed, or chilling the dry mixture.

Serve hot out of the oven with:	**Butter or honey butter** **Jam**

Leftovers can be stored in a plastic bag for 2 or 3 days at room temperature. Reheat in a hot oven for 10 minutes.

For some odd reason, my grandfather referred to his mule's droppings as dough gods. Since their shape reminded him of these biscuits, the family name for them was also "dough gods." My grandfather loved his mules, as well as the biscuits, so no one took the name as an insult. I believe my mother first added the cheese to the drop biscuits. But even with the cheese added, I used the original name until I started offering them in the 1970s to brunch customers at the Chutney Kitchen. I thought the explanation would be a little too cumbersome, so they became simply "cheese biscuits."

VARIATIONS: Try different cheeses and different sizes of biscuits. Once, at my son Johnny's Boonville Hotel, I was served tiny, one-bite biscuits, made with blue cheese and rosemary. They went perfectly with a glass of Champagne!

Mom's Simple Stew

SERVES 6 TO 8 / PREP TIME: 30 MIN / COOK TIME: 2 HOURS

In my early days, our livestock consisted of one cow and its yearly offspring, one pig, a flock of chickens, and a pen of rabbits. After my father butchered a calf or a pig, he never aged the meat, and I don't know exactly what the animals ate. Since the result wasn't dry-aged prime anything, my mother became an expert at long, slow cooking. The method was basically the same for all meats; only the vegetables and seasonings changed.

I learned this recipe for a simple stew from my mother. Near the end of the cooking time, she would add vegetables for a delicious, one-pot meal. Serve it with mashed potatoes or couscous to absorb those good juices.

Trim some of the fat from:

2 to 3 lb [910 g or 1.4 kg] shoulder of lamb, pork, beef, or goat

We use a lot of goat meat at the Apple Farm. We raise goats to make a fresh farmhouse cheese, and when you raise goats, there are always too many. We find that meat from the young goats, with its tenderness and mild flavor, is somewhere between beef and lamb, and it works well in most of our recipes.

Cut the meat into 2 in [5 cm] chunks.

Heat the fat trimmings in a Dutch oven over medium-high heat, rendering the fat. Remove the browned bits from the bottom of the pot, and if needed, add olive oil to make approximately 2 Tbsp fat.

Add the meat, in batches if necessary, to avoid crowding the pan.

Season generously with:

Salt and freshly ground black pepper

Cook the meat, undisturbed, until quite brown on the bottom (but not crusty); it will be easier to turn. Brown it all over, about 10 to 12 minutes. Remove the browned meat from the pan and set aside.

Add to the pan:

1 large onion, cut lengthwise into 8 wedges 6 to 8 garlic cloves, sliced lengthwise

Cook, stirring, while still at medium-high heat, until the onions are softened, about 5 minutes.

If the bottom of the pan is very brown and crusted, cover the pan with the lid, turn the heat off, and let rest for 5 minutes. You will find the crust has dissolved into the onions when you stir everything up.

Stir in:	**1 cup [240 ml] red or white wine**
	1 cup [240 ml] chicken stock

If you, like my mother, don't keep wine or stock on hand, add instead:	**3 Tbsp vinegar**
	2 cups [480 ml] water

Return the meat to the pan. Bring to a boil and lower the heat for a slow simmer. Cover and cook until the meat is fork-tender but still has a little bounce, 1½ to 2 hours.

Then, if desired, add:	**3 carrots or 2 parsnips and 2 Yukon gold potatoes, peeled and cut up into pleasing chunky shapes**

Turn up the heat to medium-high, cover, and cook until the vegetables are tender, about 10 to 15 minutes.

To remove some of the fat, pour off the juices into a large glass measuring cup. The fat will rise to the surface and can easily be skimmed off. But don't remove it all. Remember, the fat is full of flavor.

Taste the juices for salt and add more if needed. Pour the juices back over the meat and vegetables and reheat.

Serve, sprinkled with:	**A handful of coarsely chopped fresh parsley, chopped fresh thyme, minced fresh chives, or any combination**

Sweet Things

On the farm, our cow provided us with copious milk each day. While sitting in the refrigerator, the heavy cream floated to the top. When milk was called for, someone always asked, "Whose turn is it to skim the milk?" The cream seemed like a nuisance, but it was much loved when it came time to whip it for a chocolate cake, pour it over sliced peaches, or make ice cream. I think youth was a lot about dessert for us.

When my father came home from work, the first question out of his mouth was always, "What are we having for dinner?" We all knew that what he was really asking was, "What's the dessert going to be?" It could be anything from simple Jell-O with seasonal fruit to a special cake for a birthday celebration to a delicious pie, just because my mother felt like baking.

On hot days, he would bring home a block of ice from where he worked and crush it in a gunny sack to fill our old ice-cream machine. We took turns cranking it until the ice cream was almost done. Then one of us kids would sit on the machine for extra leverage and he would finish off the cranking. We often added fresh peaches, blackberries, or strawberries, but we liked our chocolate ice cream best. The process is all about using the best ingredients and the freshest cream.

below: Kathy's third birthday. From left at table, me, standing; oldest daughter, Kathy; my father, Henry Kelsoe; and younger daughter, Karen.

Double Chocolate Pudding

SERVES 6 / TOTAL TIME: 40 MIN

We left some of my mother's dessert recipes unchanged, because they were so good. Others evolved with time. This is my daughter Karen's version of the simple chocolate pudding recipe I once stirred over the stove. My mother would have cringed at the extravagance, but my father would have loved it!

In a large bowl, whisk together:

⅓ cup [25 g] cocoa powder
2 Tbsp cornstarch
A pinch of salt
1 cup [200 g] sugar

Whisk together in a small pitcher:

4 egg yolks
½ cup [120 ml] milk

In a medium, heavy-bottomed saucepan, scald:

½ cup [120 ml] heavy cream
2 cups [480 ml] milk

Slowly whisk the hot milk into the cocoa mix, followed by the egg mixture. Return to the saucepan, and over low heat, cook, stirring constantly with a wooden spoon, until slightly thickened, about 10 minutes. Do not allow to boil.

Push the custard through a fine-mesh sieve into a wide pitcher or clean bowl.

In two batches, stir in:

4 oz [115 g] semisweet or bittersweet chocolate, finely chopped

Continue stirring until melted, and stir in:

½ tsp vanilla extract

Divide the pudding among six to eight ramekins. Serve warm, at room temperature, or cover and refrigerate and serve cold.

Garnish with:

Softly whipped cream
Cocoa nibs

This is a perfect place to add a sprig of fresh chocolate peppermint from the garden.

The pudding will keep covered in the refrigerator for 1 or 2 days.

Almost My Mother's Pie

MAKES 1 TWO-CRUST 9 IN [23 CM] PIE / PREP TIME: 45 MIN
COOK TIME: 1 HOUR

I think the reason so many people are afraid of piecrusts these days is that there has been too much emphasis on making them perfectly. My mother's approach was pretty simple and straightforward, and I still use it, with a few tweaks. When my mother wanted to bake a pie, she simply took the ingredients out of the cooler, used water straight from the tap, and never questioned why she was doing it that way. She did it that way, of course, because her mother had done it that way before her, and my grandmother's pies were always delicious, with a crisp, flaky, and nicely browned crust.

Over the years, I have probably tried every new trick that I thought might improve my crust, but in the end, I have always just gone back to her no-nonsense approach. For the shortening I used Crisco at first, like my mother did, then switched to Fluffo. This was a shortening made, like Crisco, by Procter and Gamble, but it was the color of butter and made the crust a nice golden brown. It was all the rage in the 1960s. Then came the discovery that hydrogenated fat was unhealthy, so out went the Fluffo. And what came next? Good old butter. I miss my Fluffo, but I'm happy to trade a little flakiness for the added flavor.

In a large bowl, whisk together:

2 cups [280 g] all-purpose flour
1 tsp salt

Cut into slices and divide in half:

¾ cup [165 g] cold butter

With a pastry blender or your fingers, work half the butter into the flour until the mixture resembles cornmeal—this is for tenderness. Cut in the remaining half of the butter until the pieces are the size of large peas—this is for flakiness.

Have ready:

½ cup [80 ml] ice water

With a fork, stir most of the water into the dough (you may not need it all). Gather it into a ball. If it's not coming together, add a few more drops of water to the dry areas. Flatten into a disk and repair any cracks. Cover the dough loosely—I use a dish towel for this—and set it aside to rest while you prepare the fruit for the filling.

Preheat the oven to 425°F [220°C].

I think that to get a good piecrust, the most important thing is simply to do it often enough that you get the feel of it and lose the trepidation. There are abundant galettes and free-form pastries to try these days, both sweet and savory, which allow you to practice often.

In a large bowl, toss together:

4 cups [600 g] peeled and sliced apples, or 3 cups [500 g] berries, or 3 cups [450 g] sliced peaches
1 cup [200 g] sugar

Set aside the fruit and about a quarter of the dough for the top crust.

Sprinkle a pastry board and rolling pin with flour. Roll out the remaining dough into a circle about 15 in [38 cm] in diameter. Use the rolling pin to gently push the dough outward, working from the center to the edge, and rotating as you go. From time to time, lift the dough a bit to make sure it isn't sticking. If it is, sprinkle the board with a little more flour.

Transfer the dough to the pie pan by carefully folding it over your wrist or rolling pin and unfolding it into a 9 in [23 cm] pie pan.

Use your fingers to crimp the edges of the dough around the rim. Fill the crust with your fruit mixture.

Dot the fruit with:

2 Tbsp butter, cut into small pieces

For the top crust, roll the remaining dough into a circle about 8 in [20 cm] in diameter. Cut two or three slashes in the top crust to let the steam vent while the pie bakes. Transfer it carefully. It should fit loosely over the fruit, just inside the crimped edge of the bottom crust; as my mother liked to tell me, with a fruit pie, you want to see the fruit bubbling up around the rim.

In a small dish, mix together:

1 tsp sugar
¼ tsp ground cinnamon

Sprinkle over the top crust.

Bake for 15 minutes. Reduce the heat to 350°F [180°C] and continue baking until the juices bubble up around the edges, about 45 minutes more. Test the fruit with a skewer to make sure it's tender.

I usually use about 8 large apples in a pie; they will shrink as they cook, so you can pile them really high on your bottom crust. Some of our favorite apples are Gravenstein, Belle de Boskop, Sierra Beauty, and Bramley's Seedling. What they have in common is distinctive flavor and a good amount of acid.

Our favorite pies are apple, apricot, berry, and rhubarb. The amount of sugar needs to be adjusted depending on the sweetness and acidity of the fruit, but 1 cup is a good place to start.

Ginger Apple Upside-Down Cake

SERVES 12 / PREP TIME: 45 MIN / COOK TIME: 1 HOUR

I learned this from my mother. Her version was simpler, adapted from her standard gingerbread cake recipe, made with applesauce. I tweaked it a bit over the years, turning it upside down.

I have made this cake in all my kitchens; it is always a labor of love, and always worth the effort.

Preheat the oven to 325°F [165°C].

In a medium bowl, sift together and set aside:

2¼ cups [315 g] all-purpose flour
1 tsp baking soda
1 tsp ground ginger
1 tsp ground cinnamon
½ tsp salt

Peel and core:

2 or 3 apples

Cut them into quarters, and cut each quarter into four or five slices.
    Set aside three-quarters of the apple slices, including the prettiest ones, and finely chop the rest. Set aside the chopped apples.

For the apples, I prefer Philo Gold, a variety of Golden Delicious, but any good cooking apple—including Granny Smith, Jonathan, or a standard Golden Delicious—will do.

In a small saucepan, melt:

½ cup [110 g] butter

Line a 10 in [25 cm] cake pan with parchment to fit and pour in the butter.

Spread over the butter:

¾ cup [150 g] dark brown sugar

Use a fork to press the sugar down a little and even it out.
    Using all of the apple slices, make a circle of overlapping slices around the edges of the pan on the brown sugar mixture. Remember to think about how your design will look upside down. Pile the chopped apples into the center.

In a medium bowl, stir together:

1 cup [240 ml] sour milk
or buttermilk
¾ cup [240 g] dark molasses,
preferably blackstrap

To make sour milk, take 1 cup [240 ml] whole milk, add 1 Tbsp fresh lemon juice or cider vinegar, stir, and let sit for 5 minutes or so.

With an electric mixer at low speed, cream together in a large bowl:

½ cup [110 g] butter,
at room temperature
½ cup [100 g] granulated sugar
1 egg, lightly beaten

Recipe continues…

Add the dry ingredients, one third at a time, alternating with the liquid mixture. The batter will be rather stiff. Spoon into the prepared pan and carefully smooth out over the apples.

Bake until firm and springy to the touch, 50 to 60 minutes. Set on a rack and let cool for 10 to 15 minutes in the pan. Turn out the cake onto a rimmed plate, to catch any juices. Carefully pull the parchment back, not up, so that you don't disturb the apples.

It is best served warm with: **Softly whipped cream, or sour cream with apple cider syrup (see page 231) stirred into it**

The whipped cream should be soft enough to flow over the dessert, rather than just sit on top in a glob.

Little Aunt Saidie

"Little Aunt Saidie" and her husband, my beloved great uncle Johnny, lived with their son, Uncle Lem, who was gassed during the Great War and unable to work. Little Aunt Saidie was the sister-in-law of "Big Aunt Saidie," my great aunt. The reason for their nicknames was very evident if you were to see them side by side. Little Saidie wasn't quite five feet tall and had a humped back and soft frizzy white hair, which formed a halo around her tiny, sweet face. We all adored her. And unlike Big Saidie, she was a wizard in the kitchen!

From her I learned the ultimate way to present strawberry shortcake. She grew her own strawberries and counted on one basket per serving. She would crush and sugar them to perfection and set them aside until out of the oven came her scones, twice the normal size. She would split and butter each one before adding a large spoonful of berries, then replace the top of the scone, add lots more strawberries, and finish with a generous dollop of softly whipped cream. This was served in a wide soup bowl, and it was heaven!

Little Aunt Saidie and Uncle Johnny had a small, modest house beside the railroad tracks in Castella, just below Mt. Shasta. We didn't get there often, but our visits were memorable. I remember coming out for breakfast to the smell of trout sizzling in bacon fat on the wood stove. Uncle Lem had already been out fishing that morning on the Sacramento River, within easy walking distance of their house. It was all good food and good memories.

Thanks to Little Aunt Saidie, we have rules in our kitchen about making strawberry shortcake and other fruit shortcakes:

• Make your own shortcakes! Those spongy things they sell just don't do the job.

• Use plenty of fruit. Too much is better than too little!

• Top with softly whipped cream or Hot Cream Sauce (page 52).

• Try other kinds of fruit, such as peeled and sliced peaches, or whole raspberries or blackberries.

Strawberry Shortcake

MAKES 12 SHORTCAKES / TOTAL TIME: 40 MIN

Preheat the oven to 400°F [200°C]. Grease a baking sheet with butter or line it with parchment paper.

Prepare your fruit. In a medium bowl, combine:

4 cups [560 g] stemmed and quartered strawberries
¼ cup [50 g] sugar

You can vary the amount of sugar, depending on how ripe the fruit is; the riper the fruit, the less sugar you need.

In a large bowl, whisk together:

2¼ cups [315 g] all-purpose flour
½ cup [100 g] sugar
1 Tbsp baking powder
½ tsp freshly grated nutmeg
¼ tsp salt

Slice and add:

½ cup [110 g] cold butter

With a pastry blender or your fingers, work the butter into the flour mixture until it reaches the consistency of cornmeal.

A memory from Kathy Hoffman, my daughter: As kids, we would beg my grandma to make extra shortcakes for us to just eat plain, and I made extra for my kids, too.

In a glass measuring cup, lightly beat together:

1 egg
Enough cold light cream to total 1 cup [240 ml]

Add to the flour mixture, and stir with a fork, being careful not to overmix the dough. It should just hold together.

Drop the dough by the forkful onto the prepared baking sheet, about ½ in [12 mm] apart. Don't pat them. They should have a rough surface.

Bake until crispy and brown on top, about 15 minutes.

VARIATION: You can make these larger, forming eight instead of twelve shortcakes, and it becomes a perfect dish to feed a crowd. We often served this for brunch, and children especially loved it.

Split each shortcake, place the bottom half in a flat soup bowl, and, while still warm, butter generously with:

At least ½ cup [120 ml] butter, at room temperature and divided among the shortcakes

Pile on the fruit abundantly, cover loosely with the top half, and spoon more fruit over it all. Top with:

2 cups [480 ml] heavy cream, whipped to soft peaks

The shortcakes, stored in a plastic bag in the fridge, will keep for several days. Reheat in a 400°F [200°C] oven until crispy and hot in the middle, about 10 minutes.

Cleaning As You Go

When I look back at growing up on our small farm and working alongside my mother in the kitchen, I can't help but feel it was like a French *stage*, that tradition where novice cooks learn their craft by working alongside experienced chefs. I worked hard, really hard, during those years of growing up. I learned, and earned a lifetime of knowledge from my mother. And like the French *stage*, I didn't get paid! It's impossible to put a price on such a hands-on education, but I'd put it up against any of today's cooking schools.

What I didn't get from my mother, though, was the habit of neatness. I had to learn that for myself. When our family was expecting company at the farm for the holidays, only then would we launch into a frenzy of scrubbing, cleaning, and polishing. After our visitors left, we enjoyed a clean house for a while, but it didn't last.

It was only through managing my own kitchen that I finally learned the value of elbow grease, cleaning thoroughly each and every day, every time I finished a task. In my own restaurant kitchen, my motto was "work clean, work neat, and work carefully."

Although I had a dishwasher in the restaurant, I've never had one in any of our homes. I like washing dishes by hand, polishing my pots, handling my favorite bowls and cookware. It's part of the cooking process, cleaning as I go, and wrapping it all up at the end. Even though I didn't grow up this way, I now practice what I preach, and I cannot possibly exaggerate the value of cleaning up as you go.

A FEW POINTS

- Start the day clean. Don't have things piled up to be washed from the day or night before. Get it all done before you go to bed. It really saves time in the long run.

- Keep a large bowl in the sink with hot, soapy water, ready to wash your hands and small utensils.

- Wash your cooking pot right after using it.

- There's an art to washing dishes. The order matters: first glassware, second silverware, then plates and bowls, and finally the large utensils that might need some scrubbing.

- Wash with your fingers, not your eyes. But then, in a different light, holding the article up to check if it is truly clean never hurts.

- Never leave your knife out on the counter. Use it, wash it, wipe it dry, and put it away. Your knives will stay sharper if you do this.

- Do leave things out to dry; air drying is more sanitary than towel drying. But use a clean towel for the good stemware and silver to avoid water spots.

- Constantly wiping down your work area saves a lot of hard cleaning later.

Aunt Polly

My mother wasn't my only teacher. Aunt Polly, née Florence Polibitski, was from Milwaukee. When she was in her twenties, she came out to San Francisco and promptly stole the heart of my mother's older brother, Raymond, taking him away from his fiancée, Benita. She also confiscated Benita's favorite cookie recipe, which was clearly noted in her recipe book. Even though she was a party girl who loved Champagne cocktails, rum babas, and everything in between, she lived in a lovely, formal house in Oakland, where she would set a long, polished table that had high-backed carved chairs with needlepoint cushions.

After college, while working in Berkeley at Fraser's, the first contemporary home furnishings store in Northern California (a dream job), I lived with Polly and Raymond. By helping Polly with the meals, I learned a way of cooking and eating that was more formal and cosmopolitan than the meals I grew up with on the farm. Oh, and the salads she served, always in a big wooden bowl rubbed with garlic, filled with torn romaine lettuce, and tossed with good olive oil and vinegar. Sometimes she would add tiny bay shrimp as well. These salads met with nothing short of awe and adoration from me. The recipes that follow are still my favorites, over half a century later.

below: Aunt Polly pouring after-dinner coffee.

It was at the home of my Aunt Polly that I first encountered real San Francisco sourdough bread, often split, rubbed with garlic and olive oil, and toasted. My aunt always served it when we had cracked crab, which my uncle would pick up at the wharf in San Francisco on his way home from the office. They also introduced me to the lovely ritual of a glass of wine with dinner, often from Wente Brothers.

Stuffed Mushrooms

SERVES 6 TO 8 / PREP TIME: 25 MIN / COOK TIME: 15 MIN

I learned from my Aunt Polly to make this basic stuffing, which I have used not just for mushrooms but also eggplant and zucchini. Aunt Polly would serve them either as an appetizer or alongside the main course as both starch and vegetable. The beauty of the mushrooms is that they are simple and go well with a good piece of meat, such as Roast Leg of Lamb (page 142) or Steak with Three Peppercorns (page 196).

Preheat the oven to 400°F [200°C].

Brush or wipe clean:

16 very large white or brown cultivated mushrooms (or more if smaller)

Cut off the stems and chop coarsely. Set aside.

Tear or cut up:

6 to 8 slices good, slightly stale country-style white bread

Transfer to a food processor or blender and process until you have coarse crumbs. Measure and set aside 2 cups [80 g] and save the rest for another use.

Finely dice and set aside:

1 large or 2 medium white onions

In a medium skillet melt:

¾ cup [165 g] butter

Brush the mushroom caps lightly on both sides with some of the butter and arrange on a baking sheet, cup-side up.

Add the mushroom stems and onions to the pan, and sauté over medium heat until they soften and start to brown, about 5 to 8 minutes.

Stir in the bread crumbs and:

1 cup [240 g] sour cream
Salt and black pepper
Chopped fresh herbs, such as parsley, thyme, and tarragon

Spoon the mixture into the mushroom caps. Pile the stuffing high, because the mushrooms and stuffing will shrink as they cook.

Bake 10 to 15 minutes. Serve hot or warm.

Aunt Polly's Lamb Shanks

SERVES 4 / PREP TIME: 40 MIN / COOK TIME: 2½ TO 3 HOURS

This recipe has really withstood the passage of time. I made the lamb shanks in my earliest days of marriage, served them at all our restaurant ventures, and have been asked for the recipe by countless friends. When Aunt Polly was in her eighties, Don and I visited her in her high-rise apartment overlooking Lake Merritt in Oakland. She was living alone and still spunky enough to cook lamb shanks for herself for dinner. I was impressed! The lamb shanks can be cooked in the oven or on the stove top. I like to serve them with mashed potatoes or a small pasta.

If you plan to cook the lamb shanks in the oven, preheat to 325°F [165°C].

Trim the excess fat off:　　**4 medium lamb shanks**

Zest and juice of:　　**1 lemon**

Reserve the zest and rub the shanks generously with the juice.

Sprinkle and rub in:　　**Salt and freshly ground black pepper**

Let the shanks sit for 10 minutes.

Place a Dutch oven over medium heat and add:　　**3 Tbsp olive oil or butter**

When the oil is hot or the butter is melted, add:

1 large onion, slivered
2 garlic cloves, sliced
4 carrots, cut into matchsticks
4 celery stalks, cut into matchsticks

Sauté until limp and transfer to a bowl.

Add to the Dutch oven:　　**¼ cup [60 ml] olive oil**

Turn up the heat to medium-high and brown the lamb shanks on all sides, about 10 to 12 minutes total.

opposite: A dinner party in Aunt Polly's dining room. Her table expanded to easily accommodate a dozen or more people. This was in 1954 when the family gathered to celebrate Big Aunt Saidie's seventieth birthday. Don is on the far right, but I was in the hospital giving birth to our first child, Kathy.

Pour over them:	**1 cup [240 ml] red wine**
	2½ cups [600 ml] chicken stock
Season with:	**Salt and ground black pepper**

Return the vegetables to the pan, covering the shanks.

Add:	**8 to 12 sprigs mint**
	1 bay leaf

When using sprigs of an herb, the leaves will drop off during cooking, leaving only the stems for you to remove. If you prefer, though, you can pull the leaves off the stems before cooking and discard the stems.

Cover and cook in the oven or on the stove top over low heat until the shanks are very tender but not falling off the bone, 2½ to 3 hours. Pour the juices off into a heatproof measuring cup and skim off the fat. Taste and season the juices with more salt and freshly ground black pepper, if needed.

Add the reserved lemon zest to the juices, pour back over the shanks, and let sit at least 15 minutes. If necessary, reheat and serve the shanks with the juices.

Apple Cranberry Kuchen with Hot Cream Sauce

SERVES 8 TO 12 / PREP TIME: 30 MIN / COOK TIME: 40 MIN

One day Aunt Polly got out her binder of favorite recipes to share with me. I was soon to be married and to have a kitchen of my own with a hungry husband to cook for. A simple cake, full of cranberries, caught my eye. She flooded it with her very rich hot cream sauce, which added sweetness to counter the tart cranberries.

Later it became a frequent addition to the dessert counter at the French Laundry. When Aunt Polly finally came to dine there, we served this dessert. I told her that for years, I had been receiving rave reviews for the sauce. She surprised me by saying emphatically, "I don't remember that recipe!"

Preheat the oven to 350°F [180°C].

Peel, slice, and set aside:	**2 to 3 Philo Gold, Granny Smith, or other good baking apples**
With an electric mixer on medium speed, cream together in a large bowl:	**6 Tbsp [85 g] butter, at room temperature** **¾ cup [150 g] sugar**
Then add and beat in well:	**1 egg**
In a small bowl, whisk together:	**1½ cups [210 g] all-purpose flour** **2 tsp baking powder** **¼ tsp salt** **¼ tsp freshly grated nutmeg**
Add the dry ingredients into the butter and sugar, alternately with:	**½ cup [120 ml] milk or light cream**

Beat gently between additions to keep it tender.

Remove from the mixer and fold in:	**1 cup [130 g] fresh cranberries**

Recipe continues...

When Thomas Keller, who bought the French Laundry from us, wrote his wonderful *The French Laundry Cookbook* (1999), he presented us with the very first copy off the press. I was surprised to find he had my cranberry and apple kuchen recipe as the last recipe in the book, along with a lovely tribute. It was so much appreciated.

Make sure the cranberries are distributed evenly.

Spread out the batter in a 9 to 10 in [23 to 25 cm] buttered cake pan or cazuela. Arrange the apple slices, peeled side up, in a spoke pattern around the edge of the pan, pushing the slices into the batter until they stand up.

Fill the middle of the circle with:

1 cup [130 g] cranberries
½ cup [60 g] toasted chopped walnuts

Place a few extras around the edges.

Mix together:

1 Tbsp sugar
¼ tsp ground cinnamon

Sprinkle the cinnamon sugar over the batter. Bake the kuchen until firm to the touch, 40 minutes. Cool for 10 minutes.

Slice and pour over each portion:

Hot Cream Sauce (recipe follows)

HOT CREAM SAUCE

In a heavy medium saucepan (with enough room for your sauce to boil up, but not over) over medium heat, combine:

1 cup [220 g] butter, cut into chunks
1 cup [200 g] sugar
1 cup [240 ml] heavy cream

Cook, whisking the sauce, while the butter melts and the sauce comes to a boil. It will boil up and over the pot if you are not watching. Lower the heat and simmer until the sauce cooks down and thickens a little, 10 minutes. If it becomes too thick, add more cream or half-and-half. At the French Laundry, I usually started out with more cream, as we kept the sauce simmering while we served dessert. This is very potent stuff. Let your conscience be your guide!

My Aunt Polly's sauce became a must, not only for the Apple Cranberry Kuchen, but also for shortcakes, especially peach shortcake. In fact, it transformed any simple cake, even if it was a little stale, into a lovely dessert.

One night when I was serving it at the French Laundry, Julia Child burst into the kitchen and in her high, warbling voice asked, "My dear, what was in that sauce?" When I gave her the simple formula of equal parts butter, sugar, and heavy cream, she blurted out "Why, of course. Butter!"

VARIATION: For a less rich topping, combine ½ cup [120 ml] heavy cream with ½ cup [120 ml] apple cider syrup (see page 231) in a saucepan over low heat, and gently warm. Spoon a little over each serving.

From Home to Restaurant

My parents had always intended for me to become a teacher. It was an unspoken assumption. I suppose it was partially because my mother was a teacher. And at that time, there were few alternatives for women. By and large, the choice was to become a nurse, secretary, or teacher. And my mother had told me never to learn to type so that I wouldn't end up a secretary.

I left home when I was sixteen to attend the University of California, Davis, where I planned to study home economics. It was 1948, and I had graduated high school early. The Home Econ Department wasn't about cooking, though; it was all about the science of running a household. I actually learned more about cooking in my mother's kitchen and in high school than I did in college. Wonderful women at Davis taught sewing, interior design, bookbinding, color theory, the history of furniture, and nutrition, in both hands-on and theoretical classes. "Food classes" were actually more about learning practical chemistry, how pickling works, and the effect of acid on foods than they were about actual cooking.

It wasn't until my third year that I finally took my first teaching class, and I found it unbelievably boring and tedious. I couldn't bear to go further down that road, and I realized the simple truth: I did not want to be a teacher.

By this time, I had already taken all the basic requirements: math, English, and history, and I had finished all the requirements for the Home Econ degree. I only needed a few more units to graduate, but all the other elective courses at Davis were in agriculture, which didn't interest me. So for my last year, I transferred to UC Berkeley, where there were courses I wanted to take in music, drawing, and even logic.

Logic I failed. By this time, I had started writing to Don and was skipping classes, and when you missed one class in logic, you were lost. Even with that setback, I graduated in 1952, at the age of twenty, with a bachelor of science degree.

When I first arrived at Davis, I was one of about only two hundred women in a school with fifteen hundred students. So when I walked into that first welcoming dance, the men were all lined up to look over the new crop of girls. I had never dated in high school, but not because I didn't want to. For my senior prom, I had actually sat home and cried because no one had invited me to go, and girls didn't go by themselves in those days. So when I got to Davis, the social opportunities were just mind-blowing to me. One of the men I dated, Emil Schmitt, dropped me shortly after we began dating and took

up with my roommate. It was all for the best, however. I was invited to their wedding, where I met Emil's brother, Don.

After the ceremony, Don and I went to a party given by a friend of the groom. Then he drove me back to where I was staying, said goodbye, and disappeared, or so I thought. I still remember the day, shortly after I had returned to UC Davis, when I walked back to my residence after classes, and there, propped up against the bannister, was a little envelope with my name on it. My heart fluttered. I somehow knew that it was from him.

I had never seen his handwriting before, and he hadn't promised to write to me, but he did. He wrote a lovely letter telling me that even though he was studying at Berkeley, he had decided to join the Air Force. This was not long after the Korean War had begun. With American soldiers already fighting over there, he was afraid if he didn't enlist soon, he would be drafted into the army as a soldier. By enlisting in the Air Force, he would be able to go right into officer's training.

So I received this nice letter, and I wrote a letter back. There were more letters back and forth, but I didn't see him again until the fall, by which time I had transferred to Berkeley, and he was doing officer's training in Texas. He returned to Berkeley for the first football game, and to see me. The moment I looked out the window and saw him strolling down the walk toward my dorm, that was it for me. I went to the game with him, and it rained. We got drenched, but we had a date that night to go dancing. I came back to the dorm to change my soaking wet clothes and was sitting on my bed when one of the girls shouted into the hallway, "Come look at Sally. She's in love!" I didn't have to say anything.

Don came to see me again at Christmastime, and he drove me home to meet my parents. My older brother, Bob, and my cousin Terry were there for Christmas, and they teased me unmercifully. They had a recording of the Air Force song "Wild Blue Yonder," which they played over and over again. "Look," they would say, "he doesn't need wings. All he has to do is flap his ears." It was at that point, my mother said, that she knew he was the one, because I was so sure of my position that I didn't get mad about the teasing.

Yes, he was the one. I graduated in July 1952, and Don and I were married April of the following year. Our first child, Kathy, was born fifteen months later.

I loved being a housewife and mother. Those were my arts back then. I did them well, and we had a lovely home. It was spare, largely by choice, though we really had nothing when we started out. Our first dining table was made with a board held up by a couple of apple crates. But we gradually acquired furniture, carefully picking each piece. During the growing season, my father would always arrive with a trunkful of plants and seeds he thought we should have, and he'd help us plant them in our garden, for me to tend. I also sewed; I probably made three-quarters of the clothing my children and

opposite: Handwritten on the back of this 1953 snapshot: "Our favorite photo—3 days married— Carmel Beach—a sailor took it for us."

I knew from the start that Don and I weren't headed for a conventional life. Not long after we were married, I realized I was happiest with knife or spoon in hand, standing at the stove or butcher-block counter. So it didn't seem such a leap when I was eventually persuaded to take over my first restaurant kitchen. But before that, I was a home cook, a housewife, and a mother. I also liked doing crafts, including sewing. And Don and I were always involved in projects, working together to remodel the string of homes we lived in.

I wore. Little girls wore dresses to school in those days, so I had a hard time keeping up with it.

After we had the children, we couldn't afford to eat out, much less pay for a babysitter. Nor did we relish the idea of juggling children in a restaurant. Since I loved cooking, I would give dinner parties. With friends coming to dine, I could try out more elaborate dishes than I would cook for Don and the kids. Don had grown up in the Central Valley town of Visalia. His father was a butcher, and his mother, a no-nonsense housewife. He and our brood liked plain, basic fare, but I often added a few surprises.

I was into Adelle Davis in those days. Her groundbreaking book, *Let's Cook It Right* (1947), warned consumers about the dangers of additives, refined sugars, preservatives, and the pesticides used to grow food. So while everyone around me was living the dream with the latest packaged, frozen, or processed food sensation, I was substituting whole grain for white flour. And oh, my poor children were forbidden from drinking soda pop in the house. We saved candy for Christmas, when my family made old favorites, such as fudge, candied orange peel, and rocky road, always the first to disappear. Looking back on their diet now, the biggest thing I overlooked was how starch turns into sugar. I thought I was being so pure, but then I let my children eat Cheerios by the handful.

Even though I loved cooking, I never thought about going into the food world. There were no women chefs then. Plus, cooks were looked down upon in those days; there was no such thing as a celebrity chef. During this period, right after the World War II, most professional cooks were ex-servicemen who had learned their skills in mess hall kitchens, which did not usually lead to haute cuisine. I never dreamed I would end up in a restaurant kitchen as a woman chef.

My home cooking began, in a way, as an extension of my mother's. I made use of what I had learned from her, and treated her recipes as inspiration and reference. But soon I was branching out and trying new things, especially when guests were coming over. I remember cooking cannelloni for the first time. I had never heard of this Italian veal-filled pasta with three sauces, when I came across a recipe in *Sunset* magazine. I just went ahead and made it for a dinner party, and it was a smashing success. As with all new recipes, I followed all the steps carefully the first time. After that, I felt free to try variations. Some came out wonderful, and others, well, not so wonderful.

But no matter what I cooked, Don would always eat and smile. He was a wonderful person to cook for. He never sat down for dinner without thanking me and saying how much he appreciated what I had prepared. It was the encouragement I needed. So I went on experimenting with new recipes and

opposite, clockwise from top left: Me in my first kitchen, when Don was stationed at Travis Air Force Base, California; Don holding our first born, Kathy; our youngest child, Terry: Johnny, Karen, and Kathy helping with the cooking.

Our lives were a lot about babies, and I had a lovely time raising them. We didn't have any money, but we kept having babies. After Kathy came Karen, in 1955; our first son, Johnny, in 1957; then Eric, in 1963; and our youngest, our daughter Terry, was born in 1966. Don's mother would remind us that we weren't rich enough to have all these babies. My mother would counter that by declaring, "You don't afford babies, you just want and have them!"

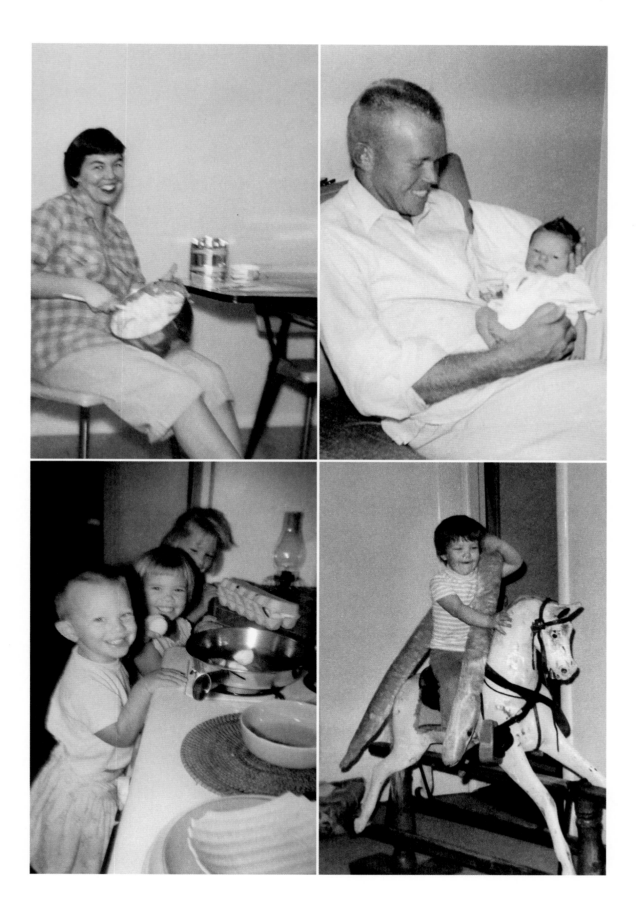

above: At the Chutney
Kitchen, me scolding my
youngest son, Eric, for his
choice of T-shirt. Actually,
it was his favorite T-shirt
back then.

techniques, sometimes combining elements of several recipes. My laboratory
courses at Davis came in handy.

So I was a home cook. And a good one, I think, looking back on it all. But,
as I was soon to find after we moved to Yountville, cooking for seven wasn't
the same as cooking for seventy. My home recipes couldn't be simply scaled
up, multiplying everything by ten. It doesn't work that way, especially with
seasoning. At home, I could spend all afternoon roasting a leg of lamb, and
still have time to bake a fresh apple pie. At the restaurants, though, I had to have
everything ready when the first customer arrived. It was a whole different way
of thinking about cooking. It took more planning, and much preparation, and
learning how to present food well on a plate. And it took working with others,
because it wasn't something that I could do alone, as in my home kitchen.

But the happiness was still there when I took on my first restaurant
kitchen, the joy of cooking good food in a place that was our own. But now
there were more people to appreciate it. Plus, there was the joy of working
with others who cared as much as I did. No, it was not the usual life, but it has
been a good one. A very good one at that.

Cauliflower Soufflé with Browned Butter

SERVES 6 TO 8 / PREP TIME: 30 MIN / COOK TIME: 30 MIN

During those early days of our married life, Don was often late coming home from his job at the bank, and the kids were always hungry around five. So I would feed them early, before Don got home, and then cook something special for us. This gave me the freedom to do something a bit exciting, something different, beyond what the kids would like. On Friday nights, I would plan a more festive dinner and have some music ready that we could listen to, or even dance a few steps around the living room. And there would be a bit of wine, maybe a half bottle. It was the equivalent of a night out for us, both affordable and special.

Those nights I wanted something that I could cook fast. Don would be so good playing with the children once he walked through the front door, romping around with them and wearing them out, and then he would put them to bed. This allowed me a few minutes in the kitchen to finish off what I was preparing for us that night.

I loved making soufflés for our Friday night dinners. The first one I learned to cook was a cheese soufflé from *Betty Crocker's Picture Cook Book*, and I didn't venture into more adventurous territory until Julia Child's first volume of *Mastering the Art of French Cooking* arrived in 1961. It was then I realized I could make a soufflé out of almost anything. So I did.

One of my favorite variations was a cauliflower soufflé with browned butter sauce, though I didn't come up with the idea until after I had started the French Laundry. We would serve it there as a first course, all by itself, especially during the winter months, when cauliflower was one of the few fresh vegetable choices.

Preheat the oven to 400°F [200°C].

Separate:	**6 eggs**
Put the egg whites in a large bowl and add:	**2 more egg whites**

Set aside the separated egg yolks and whites and make the browned butter.

In a small saucepan over low heat, melt:	**½ cup [110 g] butter**

Recipe continues...

Cook until the foam has subsided and there are brown flakes on the bottom of the pan, just a few minutes. Be careful not to burn it.

Add to the butter: **A squeeze of fresh lemon juice**

Stir and set aside to rest until the soufflé is finished.

Place a steamer basket in a medium   **2 cups [260 g] cauliflower florets**
saucepan and add water below it.
Bring to a boil and add:

Cover and steam for 5 minutes.   **¼ cup [10 g] finely chopped**
Drain the cauliflower, and when cool   **fresh parsley**
enough to handle, finely chop the
florets. Transfer to a medium bowl
and toss with:

Season with: **Salt and freshly ground**
                                          white pepper

In a large saucepan over low   **6 Tbsp [85 g] butter**
heat, melt:

Use a small amount of the butter to grease an 8 cup [2 L] soufflé dish.

Sprinkle the dish with: **½ cup [15 g] finely grated**
                                          Parmesan cheese

Turn the dish upside down and shake out any excess cheese.

To the remaining melted butter in   **4½ Tbsp [40 g] flour**
the pan, add and whisk in:

Cook, whisking, over medium heat until the butter turns slightly brown,
3 to 5 minutes.

Whisk in: **1½ cups [360 ml] half-and-half**
                                          ½ tsp salt
                                          ½ tsp freshly ground white pepper

Cook, whisking, until smooth and quite thick. Remove from heat and
gradually stir into the mixture the 6 egg yolks, one at a time.
   Fold in the cauliflower and parsley mixture. Taste for salt and add
more if needed.

Julia Child, in her wonderfully obsessive way, figured out the proportions you need for a basic soufflé. Thankfully she made it into a chart, taking the guesswork out of experimenting with different ingredients. The general proportions that Julia Child set out for a soufflé are:

For a 6 cup [1.4 L] mold:
2½ Tbsp butter
3 Tbsp all-purpose flour
1 cup [240 ml] liquid
4 egg yolks
5 egg whites, stiffly beaten
¾ cup of your ingredient of choice, such as [175 g] grated cheese, [100 g] flaked fish, or [about 115 g] finely chopped meat or vegetables
Salt to taste

For an 8 cup [2 L] mold:
3½ Tbsp butter
4½ Tbsp [40 g] all-purpose flour
1½ cups [360 ml] liquid
6 egg yolks
8 egg whites, stiffly beaten
1¼ cups of your ingredient of choice
Salt to taste

Mastering the Art of French Cooking, Volume 1 (New York: Knopf, 1961)

With a whisk or an electric mixer, beat the 8 egg whites until soft peaks form. It is really important not to overbeat the whites. Whisk a little of the beaten egg whites into the saucepan with the cauliflower base to lighten it. Then transfer the mixture to the bowl and gently fold it into the rest of the whites, just until incorporated. Don't worry if you see some white streaks.

Pour into the prepared soufflé dish and place on the middle rack of your oven. Set the timer for 25 minutes.

Tell everyone they better be seated! Check the soufflé after 25 minutes. When it's done, usually after 5 more minutes, it will be puffed up and browned on top, but still slightly jiggly in the center.

Present it to the table and then take it back to the kitchen to serve. Use a very large spoon to dish it out so that each serving stands up on the plate. Each one should have a bit of the browned top.

If it is underdone in the middle when you dip into it, just announce that that's the French way of making a soufflé!

Drizzle each serving with browned butter and serve warm. It needs no additional garnish. Anything more would distract from its simple elegance.

Soufflés have to be served fresh out of the oven. We would always have everyone seated before the soufflé was ready, then bring it to the table to show it off before serving it. It could be very dramatic!

Second: The Vintage Cafe
The Kitchen I Took Over (1967 to 1978)

Uprooting the Family

Our move in 1967 to the small Napa Valley town of Yountville was an enormous leap into the unknown. Our children, five in all, ranged in age from a one-year-old infant to a fourteen-year-old teenager. And we were leaving behind my husband Don's secure nine-to-five job as an appraiser with full benefits at the bank he worked for—all this for an unknown, unsecured future. It was a gamble at best, but we were ready to take it. It was all very exciting!

For years, we had been yearning to head to Northern California, wanting to leave behind the conservative, staid Central Valley city of Fresno. So when the opportunity arrived, we didn't think twice about dropping out of the corporate world and moving up to the Napa Valley. Besides, we loved the idea of doing something together that would involve our family as well. We were still young and full of energy and big ideas. We had both come from happy, healthy, loving families with moderate incomes. We had no aversion to hard work and had a bit of experience as "fixer-uppers." And so we leapt into what would become the turning point of our lives. We just didn't know that food and cooking were going to be such an essential part of it.

previous: There was everything we needed at the Vintage Cafe: the soda fountain in back, the Michelob beer tap up front, our Chemex pots, and the espresso maker—the first one in Napa Valley.

below: Our family outside Vintage 1870. In back, left to right, Kathy, Terry, Sally, and Don; in front, Johnny, Karen, and Eric.

Yountville

The little town of Yountville was to be our new home and livelihood for the next thirty years. When you stood in the middle, if you turned your head west, there were the Mayacamas Mountains; turn to the east, and you saw the Stag's Leap rock outcropping looming up over the narrow valley floor. The town was really in the center of the Napa Valley, which was only 30 miles [48 kilometers] long, and at its widest, just 5 miles [8 kilometers] across. The days could be hot, but usually cooled off by nightfall. There were vineyards and wineries, with more and more being added every year, as rows of grapes replaced the prune orchards and grazing lands.

There was good history here, too. The town was named for George C. Yount, the first person to plant grapes in the Napa Valley. And the beautiful, century-old complex of brick buildings Don was going to manage had been the largest pre-Prohibition winery in the valley. In front of it was the first brick train station on the Napa Valley Railroad, built in 1868. It ran from south of Napa all the way up the valley to the hot springs at Calistoga. In this beautiful old former train station was the café that I was to take over.

There was little culture here in the sixties, but it was just an hour's drive to the enlightenment and sophistication of San Francisco. Ever since the highway had passed the town by, its economy had become dependent on the veterans' home, set on the hillside looming over the town. The veterans were the town's business, and the town was full of people who fed off the veterans. The president and vice-president of the Yountville Improvement Club operated the town's thriving taxi fleet, which carried the resident veterans down the hill to the nearest bar, beginning at six in the morning, when the bars opened. (Back then, serving alcoholic beverages within a mile of the veterans' home was forbidden.) Some of the more enterprising old-timers would actually ride their wheelchairs down the hill, go drinking, and then get the taxi cab to give them a ride back up. The same upright civic boosters from the Improvement Club also managed the cigarette machines, some sleazy rooms, and a card game. But underneath the bad side, the bones of Yountville were beautiful. The town was really ripe for a little shake-up, just waiting to be reawakened when we arrived.

The times were exhilarating. That spring, even though Ronald Reagan had just been inaugurated governor of California, ten thousand people marched in San Francisco against the Vietnam War. Then, just weeks later, the Beatles released their song "All You Need Is Love." And in June, the US Supreme Court decided unanimously in favor of the Lovings in *Loving v. Virginia*, striking down laws forbidding marriage between races. That summer, one hundred thousand young people arrived in San Francisco's Haight-Ashbury.

The hit musical *Hair* opened on Broadway in 1968 (right after we moved to Napa Valley). The musical premiered at San Francisco's Geary Theater in the summer of 1969. One lovely day, we had a visit from the cast of the musical. I remember them all wandering in the garden of the Vintage 1870, picking flowers and stretching out on the grass, enjoying the sunshine. It felt like a perfect expression of the times.

Vintage 1870

What drew us north was the chance to be managing partners of a one-hundred-year-old abandoned brick winery building in Yountville, which was being converted into a shopping arcade called the Vintage 1870. This was in exchange for a roof over our heads, though it was a very ugly one, and a meager $325 monthly salary. There had been talk of demolishing the old buildings, but in 1967, a group of businessmen Don knew in Fresno, where we were living, came to the rescue. Don was working as a bank appraiser, but the group asked him if he was interested in taking on the restoration and management of the old winery.

The building was filled with possibilities, but needed work. When you walked in, there were just a few shops lining either side of the front door. There was nothing in the back, and the whole upstairs was totally vacant, with bats flying above the rotten floors. You really took your life in your hands going upstairs for a look. Don would have to finish cleaning the back of the building, fill the downstairs with tenants, and start restoring the upstairs. Then there was a whole second building in back, which he would turn into office space.

It was a leap for us, but we jumped. Most of the businessmen eventually bowed out, leaving only two: Don, and a retired Napa school teacher and artist, Kenneth Wilkins. It took years of hard work to clean and restore the property and get it ready for its new role. Don decided to keep the rustic charm of the buildings, the uneven brick flooring and unfinished woodwork. He told a news reporter, "We've stayed away from the slick approach and want nothing to mar the original character." No franchises were allowed to lease space in the complex, and by 1970, he had twenty-three shops doing business there. Most of them belonged to first-time business owners. There was a glass blower, a leather worker, an art gallery, an antique dealer, and a Victorian candy store. In the old distillery building, a potter worked and sold his wares. The brick building that once held the stables was used to sell winemaking supplies, an important source for the local vintners, and the café was set up in the old train depot.

Those first years, we fed our hungry hoard with leftovers from the café. It wasn't bad fare in the eyes of our young troupe: day-old bread, hamburgers, and milk shakes—and very good ones at that!

A memory from Bill Hoffman, my son-in-law and Kathy's husband: The year 1968 was such a big time of change and experimentation, everyone trying to do things a bit differently. I was just seventeen and living in Napa. My father, John Hoffman, was the winemaker for Christian Brothers' winery at the monastery at Mont La Salle.

We were, of course, a good Catholic family, and I went to church every Sunday. That is, until the day my father picked me up after mass and said to me, "Son, I think you need a job, and I've got a place in mind." Then, as he drove us up the valley out of Napa, he told me, "There's this big, old building in Yountville, and this group of people working on it. I've been watching them. They've kinda taken it over, and they just look like they need somebody." He parked in front of the old Groezinger winery and said to me, "Go find somebody to talk to." He stayed in the car.

I went in and found Don, and when I finally came back out, my dad asked, "Well?" "He hired me," I said. He asked, "When do you start?" "He kinda wants me to stay and start right now," I said, even though I was dressed in my best black pants, my church-going pants. Still, I went right to work that day.

I was a junior in high school then and I worked weekends and summers, initially sort of as Don's chief gofer. Mornings would be spent cleaning the hallways and outside

Continued…

The old winery building had deep roots going back to 1870, when Gottlieb Groezinger, a San Francisco wine merchant who hailed from Germany, purchased 20 acres [8.1 hectares] in Yountville for $250 in gold coins. In his San Francisco location, he was already producing 100,000 gallons [378,540 liters] of wine per year. This at a time when other Napa Valley vintners were churning out a third that amount, or less. He proceeded to build what was, and still is, the largest complex of brick buildings in Napa Valley, beginning with the 24,000-square-foot [2,230-square-meter], gabled-roof, two-story winery, capable of holding 400,000 gallons [1,514,165 liters] of wine. And behind that, a stable, and a 3,000-square-foot [278-square-meter], two-story distillery to produce brandy. The distillery didn't last long though; a fire and explosion a year after it was built destroyed the equipment, but fortunately, not the building.

The Napa Valley Railroad depot in front of the winery was perfectly located for the barrels of wine he was shipping out, up to 300,000 gallons [1,135,623 liters] by the 1880s, the wine being shipped as far away as Mexico and Central America.

Through the Depression, bad weather, and the vine-destroying pest phylloxera, the winery managed to survive, even though it was reduced to producing concentrated grape juice during the years of Prohibition. It lasted until 1954, and then it sat vacant, derelict.

grounds, where I received my first lessons in how to rake gravel from Don. Later I would sweep all the old, uneven brick floors inside the winery, and clean the bathrooms near the café, which were the only bathrooms at that point.

After Don taught me how to recaulk windows, I did the ones way up in the cupola of the two-story main building. I became interested in gardening when Don had me water and care for the plants in the huge wine barrels, 12 feet [3.66 meters] across, which he had placed by the front door of the winery. I guess I did a good job of it, as he gave me his blessing to marry his oldest daughter.

Don and I handpicked every shop, with the requirement that each would be run by the owner, not by employees. This advertisement ran in the local *Napa Valley Register* and *St. Helena Star*, and showed the range of artistic enterprises we encouraged.

A memory from Cindy Pawlcyn: What was happening in the Yountville area in the 1970s with Don and Sally was the beginning of the Valley as we know it today. People in their twenties felt like the Schmitts were the Mom and Dad of Yountville, always helping others to be successful in business and in life. At the Vintage 1870, the thirty-five-to-fifty-year-old set loved to hang out at Sally's Chutney Kitchen, and the Vintage Cafe was where twenty-somethings gathered. People still talk about the monthly dinners at the Chutney Kitchen, a prix fixe menu served by Sally. The lunches at the restaurant after wine-tasting class on Fridays, with Sally's memorable green enchiladas, were loved by so many of the Napa winery founders. The Schmitt families' May Day parties were also legendary.

More Than
a Hamburger Joint

When Don took on our handful of tenants and the restoration and property management of the run-down old winery building, he suggested I focus on the café. It had been set up by a very savvy man who ran a wildly popular spot in Fresno, so the bones were tried and true. There was no wait staff. You ordered at the counter from a menu on the wall, paid, and were called when your food was ready. We had a real soda fountain, and Napa Valley's first and only espresso machine. This made it very avant-garde in our eyes.

The kitchen had a large gas grill at one end of the small space, and the espresso machine at the other end. The prep counter between them had a butcher-block surface for making the sandwiches, salads, and hamburgers. There was a small refrigerator under the counter, and a space for placing orders and paying bills. During the lunch rush, three people manned the kitchen: one on the grill, one in the middle to make the burgers and salads, and one at the end near the entrance to take orders, handle the checks, and operate the espresso machine. Behind the counter was the soda fountain, where we made milkshakes, sodas, and even egg creams.

There was a pass-through window above the freezer, where we sent the dishes to be washed in the scullery. The scullery also had a prep counter where we made dressings, sliced ham, and patted out the meat for the burgers. The whole area was well planned and we turned out simple food that was top of the line.

Even our regular coffee was good. We didn't use MJB or Folgers; we had freshly roasted and ground beans shipped to us from San Francisco's original artisan coffee roaster, Graffeo, in business in North Beach since 1935. We had three big, hourglass-shaped Chemex glass flasks sitting on countertop burners, where we dripped the coffee. This was in 1967, just a year after Alfred Peet starting roasting and selling his beans in Berkeley, which is considered the starting point of the gourmet coffee movement in America.

The meat and bread had all been sourced from local quality purveyors before we arrived. All I had to do was to learn how to use what was already set up. It should have been easy, but it turned out to be quite a challenge.

Within a very short time, I had to fire the cook, who was steadily eroding the quality of the café. From my first day there, I had watched the whole operation through the dishwashing pass-through window, and had grown increasingly impatient to make some changes. When I suggested that he use romaine lettuce for salads and hamburgers, rather than the soggy and lifeless iceberg lettuce he had been using, he just stood there and glared at me. And

opposite: Lunchtime at the Vintage Cafe, about 1970.

A memory from my daughter Kathy: One day, my Dad just looked at Mom and said, "Sal, We know you can cook a better burger. We know you can make a great salad. You can make an incredible liverwurst sandwich with good mustard and pickles. Look at the menu. That's all stuff you can do. This is where I need you. Just go in there and see if you can whip it into shape."

My mother wasn't planning on a career in cooking. I think she was really hoping to have some sort of shop; an art gallery would have been perfect for her in the old winery building. I don't think she ever planned on staying with the café. She got hooked, despite herself.

A memory from Don Schmitt: We had a philosophy that every bun, every piece of meat, everything, was as freshly made as possible.

when I finally suggested forming the burger patties gently by hand, instead of smashing them with a giant can, he took off his apron and threw it on the floor. So I fired him. His response was, "I can't wait to see you fall on your face, *girly!*"

So we did it my way. We shaped the beef by hand and washed and crisped the romaine for the salad, and I put Don on the grill during the lunch rush. Before too long, we went from serving as few as five people a day to having a line out the door on weekends.

It was a whole-family operation. Our teenage daughters, Kathy and Karen, made milkshakes and manned the espresso machine. I took orders and handled the cash while Jeannie, our first real employee, made sandwiches. She worked in between Don and me to keep me from bossing him around too much! We soon knew we were onto something good.

The Vintage Cafe Hamburger

The gas grill at the Vintage Cafe was our only source of heat for cooking, other than the three burners where we made our drip coffee. We cooked everything on the grill—meat patties, rolls for toasting, and the occasional swordfish steak. Our beef was ground chuck with about 20 percent fat, which I purchased from a local butcher, Hagemann Meats in Santa Rosa. We were fortunate to have found them early on, and I continued dealing with them until we closed the French Laundry. The same salesman came calling on me every week, and he ended up retiring around the same time we left Yountville, twenty-five years later!

We used our hands to shape the patties, which were just firm enough so they didn't fall apart on the grill. There were no gourmet additions, just salt and pepper. The burgers came in two sizes: quarter of a pound and half a pound. The larger one eventually became our French Burger, named for the French roll we served it in.

The buns were an issue at the beginning. When our first source disappeared, we searched for a good replacement. We finally found a roll from Sciambra Bakery in Napa, a nice, chewy French roll that didn't disintegrate when faced with the meat juices. We served the burgers with grilled onions and a healthy amount of romaine lettuce. We added sliced tomatoes when they were in season, and grilled red peppers the rest of the year.

It was all very straightforward, but very, very good.

opposite: The Vintage Cafe was set up in the old red-brick Napa Valley Railroad depot constructed in 1868, two years before the winery was built.

Bill's Buttermilk Vanilla Milkshake

SERVES 2 / TOTAL TIME: 10 MIN

The initial recipe for this milkshake was simple: just vanilla ice cream and buttermilk, thinned with a little milk to counter the tang of the buttermilk and let the vanilla flavor come through. In the chocolate and strawberry versions, it didn't need the milk because the flavors were stronger. It was the tang of the buttermilk that gave them all that cheesecake taste.

If you can wait, let your ice cream soften up a bit. In a large bowl or pitcher, mix with a wooden spoon:

6 to 8 large scoops good vanilla ice cream
⅔ cup [160 ml] buttermilk, or a bit more, depending on how thick you like your milkshake
A scant ¼ cup [60 ml] whole milk (optional)

You can also use a blender on low speed for this, but be careful not to overmix. If it is too thick for your taste, add more buttermilk. Or if you don't want more tang, a little milk is fine too.

Pour, serve, enjoy.

Another memory from Bill Hoffman, my son-in-law: At the café, the buttermilk milkshake was never added to the menu board written on the wall, though you could get it if you were in the know and asked for it. Later, I had my friends at the Diner in Yountville make me one, and it blew them away. "My God, it tastes like cheesecake!" they said. The Diner actually added it to their printed menu and became quite well known for it. Food writers Jane and Michael Stern, visiting the Diner in 1987, called it "liquid cheesecake" and wrote it was "a specialty that we've seen at no other lunch counter." And then one day, Julia Child swept into the Diner to have lunch. She ordered the buttermilk milkshake, loved it, and wrote about it in an article for *Gourmet* magazine. It stayed on the menu at the Diner until it closed in 2001.

Another memory from my daughter Kathy, shown here about 1970, on the deck of the Vintage Café: After my mom kicked the cook out of the Vintage Cafe and took it over, it soon became so busy that my sister and I were working there afternoons after school and every weekend. We did everything, learned every station, with my three other siblings joining the workforce as soon as they were old enough.

Across the street from Vintage 1870, there was a brothel. So when my mother needed to change a $20 bill, she told me to cross the street and knock on the door, with the added admonition "Do not step over the threshold! You stand outside and you wait for them to open the door again and hand you back the change!"

"Better Food" Mayonnaise

I was fortunate to grow up in a household that used nothing but Best Foods mayonnaise (known as Hellmann's east of the Rockies). My mother would occasionally make her own, as I have done over the years, but convenience won out in the end. I don't consider making mayonnaise from scratch difficult, and with the right frame of mind, it is quite pleasurable, especially when done by hand. It is just that it doesn't hold up for some sauces and dressings, and it has to be used the same day.

As much as I like Best Foods, I never use it straight. I always whisk it to smooth out the texture, and then I whisk in olive oil and add some flavor, such as herbs, lemon zest, or pepper, depending on my whim. I always keep a small container of doctored mayo in the fridge for sandwiches and salads.

All of these mayonnaises keep well, covered, in the refrigerator for up to 2 weeks. You can use them as a spread on sandwiches, a garnish, or a base for salad dressings.

Garlic Mayonnaise

MAKES 3 CUPS [720 G] / TOTAL TIME: 15 MIN

At the café, we would slather the wonderful rye bread we had with garlic mayonnaise, sprinkle it with grated Parmesan cheese, and put it on the char broiler to melt the cheese and toast the bread. We served this popular side with all our salads.

In a blender, purée until smooth:

2 or 3 garlic cloves, peeled and sliced
1 cup [240 ml] good olive oil

In a medium bowl, whisk until smooth:

2 cups [480 g] Best Foods/ Hellmann's mayonnaise

Strain the garlic and oil mixture into the mayonnaise and whisk until smooth, discarding the solids in the sieve.

Stir in and whisk again:

Zest and juice of 1 lemon
Fresh ground black pepper

Sorrel Mayonnaise

MAKES 2½ CUPS [600 G] / TOTAL TIME: 15 MIN

This is my favorite sauce for cold poached salmon, topped with slivered sorrel leaves. The sorrel is so lemony that it doesn't need any other seasoning.

In a blender, purée until smooth:

1 generous bunch fresh sorrel leaves, stripped from the stems and slivered
½ cup [120 ml] melted butter, slightly cooled, or olive oil

In a medium bowl, whisk until smooth:

2 cups [480 g] Best Foods/ Hellmann's mayonnaise

Fold the sorrel purée into the mayonnaise.

VARIATIONS: To make my Green Mayonnaise (used for the Basil Eggs on page 119) you can substitute 1 or 2 handfuls of fresh herbs, such as parsley, basil, or chives, or a mixture of these. Really, any fleshy green herb can be substituted. Also, add 1 Tbsp of fresh lemon juice while blending to keep the bright green color.

Red Pepper Mayonnaise

MAKES 2½ CUPS [600 G] / TOTAL TIME: 15 MIN

This is wonderful with cracked crab and as a spread for sandwiches.

Purée in a blender until smooth:

2 or 3 garlic cloves (peeling is optional)
½ cup [120 ml] good olive oil

Strain the oil into a bowl, discarding the solids. Return the oil to the blender and add:

1 large roasted red pepper (see Margin Note), coarsely chopped

Purée until smooth.

In a medium bowl, whisk until smooth:

2 cups [480 g] Best Foods/ Hellman's mayonnaise
¼ cup [60 ml] olive oil

Fold the pepper purée into the mayonnaise mixture.

You can char a red pepper over a gas burner, on a grill, or under a broiler, or toss with a little olive oil and place in a very hot oven. This should take about 5 to 10 minutes, depending on the method you use. Char until the skin blisters and blackens all over. Put the roasted pepper in a bowl and cover with a damp kitchen towel until cool enough to handle. The easiest way to remove the skin is next to a slow stream of running water, with a colander in the sink to catch the peels. You don't want to put the peppers under the water, which will dilute their flavor. Use the water to rinse your hands clean as you rub the charred skin off.

Keeping It Simple

I was greatly influenced by M. F. K. Fisher, who wrote exquisitely about truly simple, wonderful foods, eaten in equally simple but interesting surroundings. Pretensions were never high on her list; she could be quite happy sitting alone, eating oysters out of the shell in the roughest neighborhood of Marseille.

I first knew her through reading her books, but then I met her when she introduced a series of cooking demonstrations for a group of Napa Valley ladies, one of which I gave. When we first arrived in Yountville, M. F. K. lived in St. Helena, just up the Napa Valley. By the time we opened the Chutney Kitchen, she had moved across the Mayacamas Mountains to Glen Ellen, in the Sonoma Valley. My first proposed title for this book, "Simply Delicious," was actually in homage to her.

There was something in her writing that touched me deep inside. It was about the things that bring people together around the dining table: carefully preparing a dish and sharing it with friends, maybe with a fire crackling in the fireplace, and a glass of good wine in hand. This is what I strove to achieve, both in the dining room and the kitchen.

I was never into complexity. When I ate something, I wanted to know what I was tasting. So I liked having just one or two flavors that would stand out in a dish. I tried to balance color and texture with the flavor. In the seventies, people were using every combination of herbs imaginable, usually dried, to flavor everything. And then there were those scourges of the kitchen, seasoning salts.

And during these early years of running my own kitchen, I realized how important timing was and doing things in the right order. We always did the prep work first, and had things ready before we needed them. I liked to keep it calm in the kitchen. There was no throwing pots and pans around or angry chopping at the cutting board. And I learned early on that a glass of wine never hurt the prep.

M. F. K. (Mary Frances Kennedy) Fisher (1908 to 1992), was an American food writer who wrote more about the pleasures of eating a dish than about how to cook it. In the introduction to her 1943 book, *The Gastronomical Me*, she noted that what she actually wrote about was hunger. "It seems to me that our three basic needs, for food and security and love, are so mixed and mingled and entwined that we cannot straightly think of one without the others. So it happens that when I write of hunger, I am really writing about love and the hunger for it . . . and the warmth and richness and fine reality of hunger satisfied . . . and it is all one."

Third: The Chutney Kitchen

The Kitchen I Designed (1970 to 1978)

More Than Chutney

At Vintage 1870, we soon knew that food was a big draw. The café was about hamburgers and milkshakes, done well, the way I wanted. But I wanted to do more.

In a corner downstairs in the old red-brick winery building, there was a large vacant space, which we put a claim on, broken pavement and all. We would need to install a commercial kitchen in order to use it as a restaurant, and to justify the expense, it would have to produce more than just lunch.

While we were pondering that, along came Hal Sands, who asked us if we wanted to purchase his modest chutney business, so that he and his partner could retire to Mexico. The bones were solid: The chutney was delicious, and the recipes and labels had all been legally approved. So despite the fact that chutney was new to me, it answered our problem. We would serve lunch and sell chutney on the side.

Over the months that we spent constructing the new kitchen, one day each week I made the forty-minute drive over the winding road across the Mayacamas Mountains to Hal's lovely house on Sonoma Mountain Road, just outside of Glen Ellen. I was learning the chutney business and building an inventory, so we would have something to fill our shelves with when we opened.

Hal Sands taught me a great deal more than just how to make chutney. His house was far enough removed from traffic of any kind to offer utter peace, which I had really never experienced before. I have always lived close to a major road. The garden was designed by the noted landscape architect Thomas Church and offered a choice of several outdoor areas to relax or dine, depending on where the sun was, or how the breeze might be blowing.

Hal was an accomplished and enthusiastic cook and teacher who, I think, appreciated having an audience. His first rule was: When you enter the kitchen to cook, go straight to the sink and fill a tub with hot soapy water. This is for washing your hands with ease, and washing up as you finish each task. This rule I took to heart and I have lived by it ever since. Then you need a second sink, or a tub within a large sink, so that you can rinse things off without fouling your nice, clean soapy suds. He sharpened my knife skills while running a steady stream of wisdom mixed with a liberal dose of wit. This was good training beyond what my mother and Aunt Polly had taught me.

The best part was when we stopped for lunch! Hal insisted that I lounge on one of his outdoor porches—I think he realized that it was a rare opportunity for me to take a break in my hectic life. He fed me my first tastes of artichoke soup and curried chicken breasts, which have been staples in my kitchen ever since. Those were such lovely days.

previous: I came up with this composition of many of my favorite things to separate the dining room from the kitchen. It allowed a peek in on the action without exposing us completely. I think my inspiration came from our trips to the Nut Tree, a design mecca at the time.

opposite: Here I am at the Chutney Kitchen preparing a roast pig for a gathering organized by Chuck Carpy of Freemark Abbey.

A memory from Robin Daniel Lail, fourth-generation Napa Valley vintner and founder of Lail Vineyards: For locals and visitors alike, Sally's Chutney Kitchen was the happening place, the great "foodie" delight of the '70s. She was brilliant and at the forefront of the farm-to-table movement. I particularly loved her lip-smacking soups—she had a large roster of them, many of them green. Set in the back corner of Vintage 1870, every lunch the restaurant served was fully booked. Among the legion of Sally's followers was an enthusiastic group of men who came every Friday, arriving at noon, and drinking copious amounts of wine, eating and telling stories until the kitchen closed at 5 p.m.

But we had the new kitchen to design and build. The back corner of the old winery building had no windows, and normally I like to look out on a garden. It had the space we needed, though, lots of space for people to work in. So we built the kitchen there, and added an office, storage space, and the dining area. It was thrilling for me to be able to make the design decisions myself, knowing that I would soon be working in the space.

On the red brick wall, we brushed many coats of a clear sealer, so it would pass the health inspection while keeping the beautiful old bricks visible. We built a raised floor above the broken pavement and all the pipes and drains we needed to make the kitchen function. I wanted an open kitchen, rare in those days, where our customers could look in over the Dutch door and see what was happening behind the scenes.

I placed my two new six-burner stoves back-to-back in the middle, with a beautiful, huge chopping block set right beside them. I had found this gem at an auction of kitchen equipment, along with my first big stainless-steel stockpot. (That pot lives at our Apple Farm today and is still my favorite!) We used the chopping block for both prep and chutney making, and later it worked very well when I taught small classes. Around the perimeter of the kitchen, I put deep counters for more prep space along with the sinks and dishwasher.

I added lots of lights to the high ceiling. My old friend Tom Bartlett, who is an interior designer, told me to "put lots of canned lights up and put them all on dimmers," advice I have followed since in all my kitchens. This gave us a range of lighting: bright for food prep and cooking, and soft when we wanted to entertain. All of our kitchens through the years were designed with parties in mind. To finish it all off, I had all the interior walls painted a soft yellow to counter the dark brick of the building. In spite of being a windowless space, it was a delightfully light, airy, and comfortable one to work in. This was very important to me.

We opened for lunch six days a week. My two ovens were used for the daily specials and for the occasional dinner party and catering job. One corner was reserved for the chutney preparation. About twice a week, two big pots of chutney bubbled away on the stove top, and after lunch was over, we would fill jars with the chutney and process them. There was room enough for labeling, which we did by hand. The chutney was then sold at the stand where our guests settled their lunch bills. Even with everything going on, it worked out very smoothly and cheerfully.

The Chutney Kitchen was an immediate hit. Napa Valley was hungry in those days! In the early 1970s people were just starting to realize that good cooking didn't have to be French or include rare ingredients imported in cans from overseas. On our new lunch menu we offered a soup of the day, a daily special entrée, a salad, a couple of sandwiches (open-faced smoked salmon and smoked tongue), and dessert. Of course, I soon ran out of ideas for specials, so I started experimenting with what was available locally. The beauty of a daily special was that if I wasn't pleased with the results, I never had to repeat it. I began catering dinner parties, using tried and true recipes from my past. This fit in perfectly with my schedule, since I was free in the evenings and I had the afternoons available for prep work. The special parties and catering added to our experience and confidence, but our customers wanted to eat dinner out, not just lunch. So we soon started serving dinner, at first once a month, and then, with the growing demand, we upped it to twice monthly.

Salmon with Sorrel Sauce

SERVES 6 TO 8 / TOTAL TIME: 1 HOUR

I only bought salmon when it was in season, from sometime in May through August, and with luck, September. If the fish wasn't available locally, I didn't serve it.

Preheat the oven to 400°F [200°]. Line a baking sheet with parchment paper or aluminum foil.

Prepare and set aside:	**Sorrel Mayonnaise (page 79)**
With a pair of needle-nose pliers or tweezers, remove any small bones from:	**1 large salmon fillet, 2 to 3 lb [910 g to 1.4 kg]**
Lay the fillet, skin-side down, on the prepared baking sheet. Brush the top generously with:	**⅓ cup [80 ml] melted butter**
Sprinkle with:	**Salt**
Cover the surface of the salmon with:	**1 lemon, sliced paper thin** **1 white onion, sliced paper thin**

Cover the fillet with more parchment paper or aluminum foil, and bake until the salmon is firmed up but still a little wobbly in the center and still showing some of its bright color, about 15 minutes.

Pour off the juices and reserve. Set aside the lemon and onion slices.

Let the salmon cool to room temperature, at least 30 minutes, but do not refrigerate. With the salmon juices, thin the sorrel mayonnaise until pourable.

To serve the salmon, use your fingers to gently divide the fillet into portions. The fish will pull apart easily, creating attractive servings. Pool some of the sorrel sauce on each plate and place the salmon on top.

Place a few of the reserved lemon slices and onion rings over each serving and sprinkle with:	**Sorrel leaves, thinly sliced**

The first thing I would do every morning, even before I got out of bed, was to call up Osprey Seafood in Napa and ask, "What's available?" If fish was going to be the main course that night, I needed to nail it down early so I could plan the rest of my menu.

To slice the sorrel leaves, take a few at a time and either stack them or roll them up like a cigar and slice them quite thinly into ribbons. This technique works well with broad-leaved greens or herbs such as sorrel, mint, or basil, but not small-leaved or stalky herbs, such as thyme or rosemary. Make sure your knife is sharp or you'll bruise the leaves.

Green Eggs & Ham

SERVES 6 / TOTAL TIME: 1 HOUR

Years ago, at one of our favorite restaurants, Señor Pico, in San Francisco's Ghirardelli Square, Don and I were served enchiladas with a green sauce that had a cream base. I was surprised by the use of the cream. As soon as we got home, I started experimenting by adding cream to the green sauce I had already developed for our chicken enchiladas. The enchiladas, with their improved sauce, became a favorite daily special at the Chutney Kitchen. We found another great use for this sauce one Easter when I dreamed up a dish I called Green Eggs and Ham, a tribute to Dr. Seuss. Our family has enjoyed it for almost every Easter breakfast since.

To make the green sauce, chop coarsely:	**1 bunch fresh parsley** **1 bunch fresh cilantro, including tender stems** **1 bunch green onions (white and light green parts)**
Transfer to a blender and add:	**2 cups [480 ml] half-and-half** **½ tsp salt**
Purée until smooth. Add to the blender:	**1 green poblano pepper, charred (see Margin Note, page 79), peeled, and chopped** **2 or 3 small jalapeño peppers, depending on how hot you want the sauce**

Purée until smooth.

In a large saucepan over medium heat, melt:	**3 Tbsp butter**
Whisk in:	**2 Tbsp all-purpose flour**

Cook, stirring, until just starting to brown. Pour in the green sauce and cook, stirring, until it comes to a boil and thickens.

If necessary, thin until pourable with:	**2 or 3 Tbsp chicken stock or cream**

Remove from the heat and stir in:	**1 cup [80 g] shredded Monterey Jack cheese**
Taste for seasoning and add:	**More salt, if needed, and freshly ground black pepper**

Set aside, uncovered, until needed. A skin may form, but if you cover it while it's hot, you may lose the beautiful bright green color.

Gently warm in a large skillet over low heat:	**12 thin slices ham**
Toast:	**3 English muffins, halved**
Using a knife, spread on the muffins:	**2 Tbsp butter**
In another large skillet, melt over low heat:	**3 Tbsp butter**
Gently fry, sunny-side up, just until the whites are firm:	**6 eggs**

To assemble the dish, gently reheat the green sauce, whisking smooth if necessary, and ladle a generous amount onto each plate. Top with a buttered English muffin half. Ladle more of the green sauce on the muffin. Place two slices of ham on each muffin half, and then a beautiful egg on top of it all.

Garnish with:	**Sprigs of cilantro** **A sprinkle of sweet red chili powder**

Serve immediately. Although best the first day, the sauce will keep, covered, for 3 to 5 days in the fridge.

The Chutney Kitchen Open-Faced Turkey Sandwich

SERVES 4 / TOTAL TIME: 1 ½ HOURS

This was a favorite daily special we developed at the Chutney Kitchen. It may sound a little fussy, but when you bite into it, all the effort seems worthwhile. Everyone will need a knife and fork.

Preheat the oven to 350°F [180°C]. Butter a 9 by 5 in [23 by 13 cm] loaf pan.

First make the stuffing. Heat or melt in a large sauté pan over medium heat:

¼ cup [55 g] butter or [60 ml] olive oil

Add:

½ onion, diced
½ cup [60 g] finely diced celery
1 Tbsp chopped fresh thyme
1 Tbsp chopped fresh parsley

Cook until the onion is softened, about 10 minutes. Generously season with:

Salt and freshly ground black pepper

Transfer the vegetable mixture to a large bowl and add:

4 cups bite-size pieces of torn sourdough or firm white bread

Moisten with:

½ cup [120 ml] chicken stock

Put the stuffing in the prepared loaf pan. Cover with foil and bake for 30 minutes. Let cool while you prepare the rest of the ingredients for the sandwich.

Make the cheese sauce:

In a medium saucepan over medium heat, melt:

2 Tbsp butter

Stir in:

2 Tbsp all-purpose flour

Cook, stirring, until the mixture starts to brown a little. Then stir in:

1 cup [240 ml] half-and-half
1 cup [240 ml] strong chicken stock

Yes, stuffing goes inside a turkey, but these days the term is used often for a side dish made from the usual bread cubes mixed with cooked onion, celery, and herbs. So yes, I call it stuffing, though it goes on this sandwich. And yes, it's also called dressing, but that's below the Mason-Dixon Line.

This was the 1970s. We didn't use the term *artisan* when we talked about bread, but we got good bread from a local baker, and good bread makes a difference.

Cook, stirring, until the sauce comes to a boil and thickens, about 5 minutes. Season with:

Salt and freshly ground white pepper

Stir in:

1 cup [30 g] grated Parmesan cheese

Remove from the heat, cover, and set aside until needed. If necessary, rewarm when ready to serve, adding a little more cream or water if too thick.

In a small bowl, mix together:

½ cup [150 g] apricot chutney, or, if unavailable, apricot jam
¼ cup [60 g] Dijon mustard

Raise the oven temperature to 400°F [200°C].

To assemble the sandwiches, in a small saucepan melt:

3 Tbsp butter

With the butter, brush:

4 slices rye bread, lightly toasted

Turn over each slice and brush on the second side. Transfer to a baking sheet, and spread with the chutney and mustard mixture.

Top each sandwich with:

2 thick slices turkey

Add a generous mound of the stuffing. Cover with aluminum foil and heat the sandwiches in the oven until they are heated through, about 15 minutes.

Transfer to individual plates, and spoon some of the cheese sauce over each sandwich.

Garnish with:

A handful of assertive greens

Serve immediately.

This deserves a nice glass of Chenin Blanc or Chardonnay.

Curried Chicken Breast

SERVES 6 TO 8 / TOTAL TIME: 1 TO 1½ HOURS

Hal Sands, who taught me how to make chutney, passed on this lovely way of using chicken breasts to show off the chutney we were making at the Chutney Kitchen. It became a standard luncheon offering years later at the Apple Farm, where we continued to make our chutneys. It is easy and very tasty.

Preheat the oven to 325°F [165°C].

Generously salt:	**2½ lb [1.2 kg] boneless, skinless chicken breasts**
Mix together in a large skillet:	**⅓ cup [80 ml] olive oil** **2 Tbsp curry powder**

Heat over very low heat, and gently sauté the chicken breasts, turning once. Don't attempt to cook them; you just want to firm them up a bit and coat them with the oil and curry mixture, about 3 minutes per side.

Transfer to a rimmed baking pan, smooth-side up.

Add to the skillet:	**⅓ cup [80 ml] white wine or chicken stock**

Deglaze the pan off the heat, disolving any good flavors stuck to the bottom of the pan. Return to medium heat and cook until slightly thickened, 3 to 5 minutes. Pour over the chicken and cover lightly with parchment paper or aluminum foil. Bake in the oven until the chicken is barely firm to the touch and the juices run clear when poked at the thickest part, 10 to 15 minutes.

Meanwhile, prepare (see Margin Note):	**1½ to 2 cups [270 to 360 g] couscous**

Transfer the chicken to a platter, and set aside, uncovered, to cool to room temperature.

Add to the skillet:	**Juice of 1 lemon** **Juice of 2 limes**

Deglaze the pan off the heat with a brush.

Return to medium heat, and whisk in:	**1 cup [240 ml] strong chicken stock**

HOW TO MAKE COUSCOUS: Couscous is not a grain, but a pasta made from wheat or barley. To prepare it, use a ratio of 1 cup [240 ml] water or chicken stock for 1 cup [180 g] couscous. A cup of uncooked couscous should be enough for four people, unless they're very hungry. Put the couscous in a heatproof shallow roasting pan. Bring the liquid to a boil in a small saucepan. Remove from the heat, and let sit for a moment. Pour over the couscous, cover, and let sit until the grains have swelled, no more than 5 minutes. Use a fork to fluff it, a little at a time to avoid lumpiness. Covered, it will hold nicely while the chicken is cooking.

Allow pan juices to reduce and thicken for about 5 minutes.

Slice the chicken breasts diagonally.

Make a bed of couscous in the middle of each plate, and fan out the chicken slices on top.

Spoon the juices over the chicken.

If the chicken breasts are very large, you may not need a whole one for a single serving. If so, remove a couple of slices from the middle and save for another use.

Add a large spoonful of any or all of these suggested condiments or garnishes:

1 or 2 chutneys, such as Peach Chutney (page 105)
Plain yogurt
Sprigs of cilantro
Toasted pumpkin seeds or nuts
Cubed Avocado
Toasted Coconut
Currants plumped in wine

Serve at room temperature.

Soup

I have a few unbreakable rules about these cream-based soups. Half as a joke, I mentally label them "cream of green." This is because I can apply this formula to almost any green vegetable.

First, keep it simple and uncomplicated. I like zucchini soup to taste like zucchini, not just a combination of pleasant flavors, so I have often deliberately left out onion, garlic, or other ingredients that might have been added.

Second, even though the quality of the flavor depends on the quality of the ingredients, you can get excellent flavor from less-than-perfect-looking vegetables. I imagine one of the reasons soup was invented was to use up a handful of vegetables or a few bones, or to find another way to cook a food that grew abundantly. I tend to make soup out of whatever is at hand and at the height of its season, thereby making it thrifty as well as delicious.

Third, try to consume a cream-based soup the day you make it. While a good stock seems to improve with reheating, a cream soup tastes tired and loses its fresh flavor by the next day. For the same reason, I have always resisted the temptation to freeze either the soup or the purée. After freezing, it may still be nutritious, but not really delicious.

Fourth, I never use a thickener such as arrowroot or cornstarch, which were very popular in days gone by. The resulting texture is immediately recognizable and rather revolting. Often the vegetable itself will give the soup enough body. If not, just add potatoes. Or, if it's a stock-based soup, a handful of rice, pasta, or barley will do the job.

Finally, when making soup, learn to season by tasting. There is no way anyone could give you the correct amounts of salt and pepper or any other seasoning. A trick I sometimes use is to ladle a little of the soup into a bowl, add a little more salt or a squeeze of lemon, or whatever I think would improve it. After tasting the sample, I correct the pot if I like the results. But sometimes that last-minute inspiration is wrong, and it is better to find out before throwing off the whole batch. Let it sit for a while if you are not sure. Come back to it in a few minutes, or ask for a second opinion. Better too little than too much of a seasoning, but when I am able to get it just right, I still get a little thrill.

opposite: Me, behind my helper Carol at the stove in the Chutney Kitchen.

Until I opened the Chutney Kitchen, I had no real idea of the appeal that soups held for so many people. As it was to be the second lunchroom in our shopping complex, I meant for it to be a complement to the café, which specialized in grilled sandwiches and salads. I envisioned a few comfortable tables, a pot of soup on the stove, and some good desserts. By the time we opened, the number of tables had grown, they were all filled, and our customers were holding out their soup cups and asking for more. I found it hard to keep up a good supply of soup stock, so I became more and more inventive with cream-based soups, which were quicker to produce. I discovered that almost any vegetable, when added to a base of stock and light cream, thickened with potato, and seasoned with an herb or two, became very good soup.

Cold Cucumber Soup with Garlic Chives & Mint

SERVES 6 TO 8 / TOTAL TIME: 1 ½ HOURS

This is a beautiful soup to serve on a hot day. It can be served in shot glasses at a large party, and works well as a bridge between cocktails and seating time. If you don't have garlic chives, you can use regular ones, but plant some garlic chives in your garden for next time. You will love them!

In a small bowl, combine and set aside to develop the flavor:

4 garlic cloves, sliced
2 cups [480 g] yogurt

Cut into chunks:

About 2 lb [910 g] of unwaxed English or Armenian cucumbers, thoroughly chilled

Transfer to a blender and add:

1 cup [240 ml] water
3 Tbsp chopped fresh mint
3 Tbsp chopped garlic chives

Purée until smooth. Transfer to a large bowl and stir in:

4 cups [960 ml] buttermilk

Strain the yogurt and discard the garlic. Add the yogurt to the soup.

Season with:

Salt and black pepper

For a little crunch, stir in:

1 sweet onion, such as a Vidalia, very finely minced and rinsed with 3 Tbsp white vinegar (see Sally's Basics, page 16)

Chill the soup thoroughly, at least 1 hour.

Serve very cold. Sprinkle the soup with:

Garlic chive blossoms or minced chives

If you are lucky enough to have borage growing in your yard or neighborhood, pick off some of those beautiful blue blossoms and float them on the soup.

It will keep in the fridge, covered, for up to 3 days.

Zucchini Soup

SERVES 8 / TOTAL TIME: 1 HOUR

One day at the Chutney Kitchen, while I was trying to decide what kind of soup to make, I spied a box of garden-fresh zucchini. I'd never heard of zucchini soup, but nothing ventured, nothing gained. When I served it, it was a big hit, and we became known for our zucchini soup.

The best zucchini is the pale green Italian variety, which you seldom see in the markets, as it is quite fragile. But it does have a wonderful flavor, without the bitterness of out-of-season zucchini. Look for it at your farmers' market.

Into a large soup pot, put:	**2 lb [910 g] zucchini, sliced**
Sprinkle with:	**1 generous tsp salt**
Pour in:	**4 cups [960 ml] water** **4 cups [960 ml] chicken stock**

The liquid should come just below the level of the zucchini. Cook uncovered at medium-high heat until just tender, but still bright green, 10 to 15 minutes.

Let cool a little, purée in a blender in batches, and return to the soup pot.

Add, depending on your desired thickness:	**1½ to 2 cups [360 to 480 ml] half-and-half**
In a sauté pan over medium heat, melt:	**2 Tbsp olive oil or butter**
Add:	**3 or 4 shallots, thinly sliced** **1 cup [140 g] shredded zucchini**

Sauté just until really hot. Add the shallots and zucchini to the soup pot, give it a stir, check for salt, and bring it up to a steamy hot serving temperature. Boiling may cause it to curdle. Remove from the heat.

Serve, garnished with:	**A sprinkle of chopped fresh flat-leaf parsley or lemon thyme**

VARIATION: Later, when we made this at the Apple Farm, we added a touch of basil and mint to the soup before blending.

Eggplant Soup

SERVES 10 TO 12 / TOTAL TIME: 1 HOUR

I've always loved eggplants, but it's very hard to choose a good one. You find one that looks good on the outside, firm and shiny, but when you cut it in half, it's already past its peak and grayish on the inside. It's best to grow eggplants yourself, or buy them at a farmers' market.

In a small bowl, combine:

1 cup [240 g] yogurt
2 or 3 garlic cloves, sliced

Let sit to develop flavor while the eggplant is cooking.

Put into a medium soup pot:

2 lb [910 g] eggplant, unpeeled, cut into 1 in [2.5 cm] pieces

Add:

Enough chicken stock or water to almost cover the eggplants

Sprinkle generously with:

Salt

Bring to a boil, reduce the heat, and simmer until tender, about 15 to 20 minutes

Cool slightly, and in a blender, purée in batches until smooth. Return the eggplant to the soup pot.

Strain the yogurt and stir into the soup. Discard the garlic.

Add:

2 cups [480 ml] half-and-half

Taste for salt and add more if needed. Season with:

Freshly ground toasted black pepper

Taste again and add more stock or cream if the soup is too thick, rewarming if necessary.

Serve at room temperature in wide bowls and add one or more garnishes to each serving:

A swirl of Red Pepper Sauce (page 173)
A swirl of pesto
Shiitake mushrooms, thinly sliced and sautéed in olive oil
A drizzle of your best olive oil
Fresh basil leaves, finely slivered

Although the soup is not a very attractive color, somewhere between brown and gray, the flavor is wonderful and rather unusual. You can brighten its drab color up by adding garnishes, which actually make it quite attractive.

Use any variety of eggplant, from the large, dark purple globes to the smaller, skinnier Japanese variety. Choose small to medium ones; they tend to be less bitter. I would only make this recipe when I could be sure of having good eggplants.

Sorrel & Potato Soup

SERVES 6 / TOTAL TIME: 1 HOUR

Fresh sorrel is hard to find in markets, but it is a very easy to grow perennial. Plant some in early summer and it will last for years. Just keep it fresh by pulling out the old leaves; they will come out easily and leave the plant nice and tidy. If you have two plants, you can clean them up at alternate times, so you always have fresh growth for a soup or sauce.

To a heavy-bottom soup pot over medium-high heat, add and sauté until crisp, but not too dark:	**2 slices bacon, diced**
Remove and drain the bacon bits on a paper towel, leaving the fat in the pot. Add and sauté until softened:	**1 small onion, minced**
To the pot, add:	**1 large russet potato, peeled, or 2 smaller Yukon gold potatoes, unpeeled, cut into chunks** **6 cups [1.4 L] chicken stock or salted water, or enough to cover potatoes**

Bring to a boil, lower the heat, and simmer, uncovered, until the potatoes are very tender, 15 to 20 minutes. Let cool a little. Transfer the mixture to a blender and purée until smooth. Return to the soup pot.

In a blender or food processor, purée, adding a handful of leaves at a time:	**¼ cup [55 g] butter, melted** **3 cups [60 g] packed sorrel leaves, washed and torn**
As you purée the sorrel leaves, thin as needed with:	**2 to 3 Tbsp chicken stock or water**
Add the purée to the soup pot, along with:	**2 cups [480 ml] half-and-half or more stock**

Stir and taste for seasoning. When ready to serve, reheat but do not boil to avoid curdling.

Garnish with:	**Reserved bacon bits**

When heated, sorrel tends to turn an ugly olive green, so I use a trick that I learned by accident: I blend it with melted butter, which helps maintain the fresh green color until you reach the bottom of the pot!

To make this vegetarian, simply leave out the bacon bits; the soup can stand on its own very nicely.

Chilled Tomato & Avocado Soup

SERVES 6 TO 8 / TOTAL TIME: 1½ HOURS

I make this soup in late spring or early summer, when we have warm weather but are still waiting for our local tomatoes to ripen.

In a blender, purée until smooth:

One 16 oz [455 g] can good tomatoes
One 8 oz can [225 g] tomato purée
½ cup [120 g] sour cream

Good canned tomatoes are always better than "Super Market" tomatoes because they have been allowed to ripen before being harvested and canned. I have never seen what I call a real tomato on a supermarket shelf. You have to get them from your garden, a neighbor's garden, or a farmers' market.

In a large bowl, whisk together until smooth:

1 cup [240 ml] half-and-half
2 Tbsp good olive oil
1 Tbsp fresh lemon juice
Salt and freshly ground black pepper

Add your tomato mixture to the bowl and stir in:

2 avocados, cubed
½ sweet white onion, minced and rinsed with 2 Tbsp vinegar (see Sally's Basics, page 16)

Refrigerate the soup until thoroughly chilled, at least 1 hour.

Serve cold and garnish each serving with:

A swirl of your best olive oil
A sprinkle of chopped fresh chives, with their blossoms, if available

This can be made 1 day in advance, as it keeps remarkably well.

Our Chutney

We have been making chutney ever since we first started producing it at the Chutney Kitchen. I learned from Hal Sands (see page 84) that this, I suppose you could call it a relish, is always vegetarian, and is made with herbs, spices, and whole pieces of fruit or vegetables. It can be a cold, fresh cilantro chutney with hot green chiles, or the slow-cooked spiced fruit chutneys we still make at the farm. They are all delicious.

We try to confine our chutneys to the fruits we have on hand here, using them when they are in season and most plentiful. In the off-season, we use dried fruits.

We have found many uses for our chutneys beyond an accompaniment for traditional curries. They add a sweet, acidic, spicy tanginess and complexity that complements turkey or chicken. And they're lovely alongside a roasted duck leg or on a ham sandwich. Lately, our family has been using chutney instead of cranberry sauce at the end-of-the-year holidays.

We prefer not to overcook our chutneys; we like to preserve the fruit's consistency and shape and the freshness of its flavor. For spices, we like a mixture of whole and ground, where appropriate, to add interest. We generally go easy on the spices, as we want to let the flavor of the fruit dominate.

below: Me (left) and my helper Carol filling chutney jars.

Peach Chutney

MAKES ENOUGH TO FILL FIVE OR SIX ½ PINT [240 ML] JARS /
TOTAL TIME: 1½ HOURS

These days, we produce a whole line of chutneys at the Apple Farm.
Although this recipe is made with peaches, you can substitute whatever fruits
you have in abundance. Peach chutney remains one of my favorites, because
it tastes so fresh and light and goes perfectly with a chicken breast.

Have ready:

**12 large peaches, blanched,
peeled, and cut into ½ in
[12 mm] dice, to end up with
8 cups [1.2 kg] of fruit**

To blanch your peaches
for easy peeling, bring a
large pot of water to a boil,
and have a bowl of ice
water ready. Drop several
peaches at a time into the
pot, making sure they are
entirely submerged. After
about 30 seconds, remove
with a slotted spoon and
drop into the ice water.

In a large pot, combine and bring to
a boil, stirring to disolve the sugar:

**1½ cups [300 g] sugar
1 cup [240 ml] cider vinegar**

Lower the heat and stir in:

**1 onion, slivered
1 to 2 hot red chiles, minced
2 garlic cloves, minced
2 Tbsp slivered ginger
2 tsp salt
1½ tsp whole mustard seeds
6 cardamom pods, crushed**

Simmer for about 15 minutes. Drain the peaches and add them to the
pot. Return the chutney to a boil and cook until slightly thickened, about
30 minutes. Boil down reserved juices separately to concentrate, then return
to the pot.

Peaches can be very juicy.
By reducing them separately,
you'll avoid overcooking the
chutney.

    Let cool, and ladle into sterile jars. Cover and refrigerate for up to 3 weeks.
When opened, it does tend to disappear quickly, but discard any that starts to
ferment or grow mold.

Cooking for the Napa Valley

During these early years, I was trying to cook not just the tastes I had grown up with but also dishes that would please the locals—the wine lovers and winemakers walking through our door in search of good food that would go with local wines.

I got my first gig, beyond my daily lunch service, when this hearty, cheerful woman walked in one day and introduced herself as Martha May. She asked if I would be interested in doing a luncheon for her group of Napa Valley ladies. Martha explained that there was no formal structure to her group, that it was just a group of ladies who gathered together once a month for lunch. She asked me to come up with a menu and promised that she or another member of the group would be back to talk about it.

A few days later, Martha came back with a tiny woman, whom she introduced to me as Belle Rhodes. I had heard of her also—a legendary, bottomless source of wine and food lore. Belle marched into the restaurant, very upright and straight-backed, which reflected her service in the Waves during World War II. In her arms, she lugged a pile of cookbooks, including a copy of the massive *Larousse Gastronomique*. To these two legends, I had to present my proposed menu.

I had decided to make *jambon persillé*, the classic French dish of parslied ham, from a recipe in a newspaper. Unbelievably, it was a dish that I had never prepared before, nor ever eaten, had not even heard of, and was foolish enough to try out on this group. But they said, "Fine." So, feeling very brave and foolhardy at the same time, I served it to them.

As it turned out, most of the women in the group were vintners' wives, the who's who of Napa Valley society. When they arrived and filled my dining room, I was really worried. But I realized I had passed the test when they asked me to cater a second lunch, and then another, and still another after that.

From then on, the ladies started coming into the Chutney Kitchen in small groups, sometimes bringing their husbands. They became not just my best customers but also my friends. They would ask me to cater dinner parties and lunches at their homes. Thanks to them, I learned not only the skills it takes to cook for a large group, but also the rhythm of serving a more formal meal than I had experienced before. I learned a lot from being exposed to those ladies. Most of them are gone now, and I miss them very much.

opposite: The Chutney Kitchen lunch crew, ever-changing and always entertaining. Pictured here: Joanne, Laurie, Paul, and me.

I knew who Martha and Belle were: two of Napa Valley's royalty. Martha May was the Martha of the renowned Martha's Vineyard, in Oakville, the first single-vineyard Cabernet Sauvignon produced in Napa Valley. Made by her friend Joe Heitz, of Heitz Wine Cellars, it's considered one of the finest red wines produced in America. Martha and her husband, Tom, had purchased their vineyard from pioneer grape growers Belle and Barney Rhodes, proprietors of Bella Oaks Vineyard. Belle was also known for having one of the largest cookbook collections in the country. I already had my own copy of that formidable culinary reference book, *Larousse Gastronomique* that she carried in with her that first day. Everyone was using French terms in cooking and on restaurant menus in those days, and I relied on its wealth of information.

Chilled Beet Soup Shots

MAKES ENOUGH TO FILL 12 SHOT GLASSES / TOTAL TIME: 1 ½ HOURS

We created this for a large party we catered, at which people were milling around before dinner, talking and sipping wine. We walked around with trays of small shot glasses filled with the beet soup, trading them for the wine glasses and announcing that dinner was about to be served. "So find your places!" Of course you can use red beets here. I just prefer the color of the golden variety.

At the French Laundry, we actually found that small glass votive candle holders worked beautifully to serve the beet soup shots.

Preheat the oven to 400°F [200°C].

Individually wrap tightly in aluminum foil:

4 large golden beets

Roast until a beet pierced with a fork through the foil feels tender all the way through, about 1 hour. Unwrap and set aside until cool enough to handle. Rub off the peel and chop coarsely.

Transfer the beets to a blender and add:

4 cups [960 ml] vegetable or chicken stock

Blend until puréed. Stir into the mixture:

½ sweet white onion, minced and rinsed with 3 Tbsp white vinegar (see Sally's Basics, page 16)

Add:

3 Tbsp chopped fresh dill
Salt

Refrigerate the soup, covered, to let the flavors develop for at least 1 hour and up to 3 days. Serve in small glasses as an appetizer, topped with:

A dab of yogurt

Steak Tartare

SERVES 6 / TOTAL TIME: 30 MIN

This is my simple version of an old classic. I prefer to add a minimum of seasonings to the steak and pile the condiments on the top. My secret whammy is to add a generous amount of melted butter to the meat mixture. It gives an amazing boost of flavor and texture. For small amounts, I like to finely dice the meat rather than grind it, another texture boost.

Grind, or have ground for you, a few hours before using:

1 lb [455 g] top sirloin beef

If the meat is cold, let warm to room temperature, or a little cooler. Transfer to a bowl and add:

¼ cup [60 ml] melted butter
¼ cup [35 g] minced white onion, rinsed with 2 Tbsp [30 ml] white vinegar (see Sally's Basics, page 16)
2 tsp coarsely ground toasted black pepper
1 tsp salt

Toss gently with your hands, being careful not to overhandle. The texture should be rather loose.

Serve with Toast Rounds (page 176) and your choice of these condiments:

1 egg yolk or 2 or 3 quail eggs
Minced fresh chives
Minced fresh parsley
Capers
Mustard butter
Finishing Salt

I like this presented in a mound with the egg in a well on the top of the mound of meat. For individual servings, try to find the quail eggs. They are a delight because of their size. For a large platter, the condiments can be in small dishes around the meat with a basket of toast rounds on the side.

THE TARTARES: For large parties, we always included one of these raw protein offerings. They are wonderful served on toast rounds or presented on slices of raw vegetables.

Instead of grinding, with a very sharp knife, thinly slice the meat, stack up the slices, and cut them crosswise. Repeat until you have tiny cubes of meat.

To make mustard butter, stir together ½ cup [110 g] butter, at room temperature, and ½ cup [120 g] Dijon mustard.

Fresh Salmon Tartare

SERVES 16 TO 20 / TOTAL TIME: 45 MIN

This is something I liked to serve for large parties, especially when I could get a beautiful, big fillet of salmon. A whole fillet tastes so much better than those cut-up pieces you often find in the market.

With needle-nose pliers or tweezers, carefully pull any bones from:

1 very large fresh skinless salmon fillet, at least 2 lb [910 g]

Slice and cut gently into very small dice. If very cold, let sit for 5 minutes to warm up.

Transfer to a bowl and add:

½ cup [120 ml] melted butter
½ cup [70 g] finely diced white onion, rinsed with 3 Tbsp rice vinegar (see Sally's Basics, page 16)
Coarse sea salt and coarsely ground toasted black pepper

Toss gently with your hands.

Serve on:

Toast Rounds (page 176)

Sprinkle each serving with:

Maldon salt, if needed
Minced fresh chives
Minced fresh dill
Minced garden cress

Tuna Tartare

SERVES 8 TO 10 / TOTAL TIME: 45 MIN

Good quality ahi tuna is a special treat, but it is a good alternative when salmon is out of season. It has a bit more assertive flavor than salmon, so can be seasoned more generously.

Slice and cut gently into very small dice, avoiding the connective tissue:

1 lb [455 g] of the very best ahi (yellowfin) tuna you can find

Transfer to a bowl and add:

2 Tbsp toasted sesame oil
1 Tbsp finely chopped jalapeño pepper
1 Tbsp finely chopped fresh ginger
1 Tbsp finely chopped green onions (white and light green parts)
Sea salt and freshly ground toasted black pepper

Using your fingers or a fork, toss gently until combined.

Serve on:

Toast Rounds (page 176) or very crisp cucumber slices (cut on a slight diagonal)

Garnish each serving with:

1 little sprig cilantro
Maldon salt

Lamb en Croûte

SERVES 6 TO 8 / PREP: 2 HOURS / COOK: 1 HOUR

In a spin on a beef Wellington, I substitute a boned-and-tied leg of lamb for the traditional beef tenderloin. I usually reserve this for small parties of six to eight; it's a little ambitious for a larger group.

Preheat the oven to 350°F [180°C].

Bring to room temperature, 1 hour or more:

One 4 to 6 lb [1.8 to 2.7 kg] boned-and-tied leg of lamb

If browning the lamb on the grill, build a hot fire.

Put the lamb on the grill and cook just until it has a nice brown crust, about 5 minutes per side. (Don't attempt to cook it all the way through.)

Alternatively, heat 2 to 3 Tbsp olive oil in a large cast-iron skillet over high heat and brown the lamb. You want to cook it until it develops a little char on all sides.

Transfer to the oven and roast to your preferred doneness: for rare, until a meat thermometer registers 120°F [50°C], about 50 minutes; and for medium-rare, until it registers 135°F [60°C], about 60 minutes.

While the lamb is roasting, make the pastry using the piecrust recipe on page 38.

Alternatively, you can use frozen puff pastry.

While the ball of dough is resting, prepare your duxelles. Finely chop and mix together, or pulse until fine in a food processor:

¾ cup [45 g] shiitake mushrooms
¾ cup [45 g] cremini mushrooms
2 shallots
Leaves of 2 sprigs thyme

In a large sauté pan over medium heat, melt and heat:

2 Tbsp butter
2 Tbsp good olive oil

Transfer the mushroom mixture to the pan and season with:

Salt and freshly ground black pepper

Cook the mushrooms, stirring occasionally, until they are really dry, 15 to 20 minutes. You want to avoid moisture as best you can to keep the bottom crust crispy.

Remove the roasted lamb from the pan and let rest on a rack. This, too, will help preserve the bottom crust.

With a pastry brush, stir into the pan juices:

2 Tbsp butter

Set aside until serving time. Raise the oven temperature to 400°F [200°C].

Roll out the pastry to a rectangle that is about 4 in [10 cm] longer than the length of the leg of lamb, and wide enough to wrap around the leg, with 1 or 2 in [2.5 or 5 cm] to spare.

Spread your duxelles mixture evenly over the pastry, leaving a 2 in [5 cm] border uncovered.

Untie the lamb. It should keep its shape at this point. Place, top-side down, in the middle of the pastry.

Carefully roll the pastry around the lamb. Fold under the ends as neatly as possible, and use the tines of a fork to press them in. Roll out any scraps of dough and cut out leaves. Gently press them onto the top of the pastry for decoration.

| Make an egg wash by whisking together: | 1 egg |
| | 2 Tbsp water |

Brush the pastry sparingly with the egg wash. Place the lamb on a baking sheet and bake until the crust turns golden, 30 minutes.

Let the lamb rest in the pan, raising one side so it won't rest in any juices. If not serving right away, the lamb can be reheated later at 300° [150°C] for about 20 minutes to warm the crust. Avoid leaving the lamb in the oven too long, or it will be overcooked.

After presenting the roast to the table, bring it back to the kitchen to carve. Mark off each slice to make sure you'll have enough for everyone. Starting from the middle, to get the prettiest pieces, make the slices as thick as possible. You want to give everyone a big, beautiful slice. The crust will probably fall apart in places. It's remarkably easy to make it look whole again on the plate with a little push and shove.

Pour the reserved mixture of lamb juices and butter into a small saucepan and heat until warm. Paint the meaty part of each portion with the juices before serving.

The most important piece of advice I have is this: Do it ahead of time! I finally learned the importance of this after a near disaster. I was preparing the lamb en croûte for a ladies lunch in a residence way up a mountainside, too far from the restaurant to be able to return if I'd forgotten something. I hadn't inspected the kitchen ahead of time, and it was only when I was ready to roll out the pastry dough that I realized that the available counter space was a 2 foot [61 cm] square, barely big enough. And to make matters worse, I had neglected to bring flour with me for rolling the pastry, and there was no flour in the house, not even a box of Bisquick. Fortunately, I survived, and the lamb en croûte survived. Despite my trepidation, it was not a disaster, but it was close.

The ends are wonderful for nibbling the next day or after your guests go home.

Cooking for the Vintners

We were the middle of the Napa Valley, and even in those early days, the heady scent of crushed grapes filled the air in the fall. When we moved to Yountville, there were only about twenty wineries producing premium wine. Today I believe there are over seventeen hundred registered wineries, and over five hundred of them having tasting rooms.

I don't remember just when or who first asked me to consider catering the monthly luncheons for the Napa Valley Vintners Association. The association had been formed in 1944 by seven winemakers, including Robert Mondavi and Louis M. Martini, who both became friends and patrons. This was just a few years before the so-called Judgment of Paris, the 1976 blind wine tasting competition in Paris between French and California wines. Napa Valley wineries took the top honors, much to the astonishment of not just the French but the whole world.

Since its beginning the Napa Valley Vintners Association had been meeting at the century-old Miramonte Hotel in St. Helena. But then, sadly, the hotel closed, and they came to me. At first they gathered in the little private room we had at the Chutney Kitchen, but we could only seat a dozen or so. When their numbers outgrew that space, they moved their luncheons to the old Lodi Farm Center, in St. Helena, a century-old former schoolhouse. So once a month I would pack up the food, bring along our signature tablecloths (rough linen with a pattern of leaves on), and head north with one helper.

Jim Beard, a letterpress printer, was secretary of the association and soon became one of my favorite people. He would call to provide a head count for me, and always arrived at the farm center early to make sure the heat was turned on. (He sometimes had to lie on the floor to light the pilot for the old water heater.) It was rather primitive, but I loved the whole scene. Most of the men came in through the kitchen door to greet me and sniff out what was for lunch. They always brought their own wines and glasses, but never a corkscrew! It became a standard joke that they always had to borrow mine.

The president of the vintners for a time was Chuck Carpy, the founder of Freemark Abbey, who had started us on good wines at the Chutney Kitchen (see page 83). He was absolutely bigger than life, having grown up in St. Helena, where he was the star of the football team. He was tall, and in later years, a very large man, but light on his feet and a good dancer. Aside from his fame as a vintner, he was known as a true gourmand, as opposed to a gourmet, meaning there seemed to be no end to his appetite for good food.

I remember we went on several picnics with him and a group of his friends, out along the Napa River. They called it "splendor in the vetch," as they would set up a volleyball net so we could all play volleyball in knee-high vetch. And of course, we drank of lot of wine. I have a vivid memory of Chuck walking away from me, a bottle of Cabernet Sauvignon in the back pocket of his Levis. He did make very good Cabernet Sauvignon, which was one of his favorites and ours.

I learned the most valuable lesson from cooking for these vintners. Simple food, without fancy frills, was what pleased them the most. And from that, I gained much confidence. I figured if I could please their palates, I didn't have to worry much about anyone else's. It was liberating because, in reality, I was just cooking what I had always made with a few upgrades for my own amusement and to keep up with the world.

In time, the group grew too large to fit into the farm center; they outnumbered the stacks of plates and silverware there. And so they moved on to their new space at Meadowood Country Club. Several of them have told me in recent years that they remember those lunches very fondly and have never eaten so well since. I couldn't ask for higher praise!

below: This bottle of Heitz was presented to us on our departure from the Vintage 1870 and the Chutney Kitchen by Martha and Tom May. The inscription reads "With love and thanks to Sally and Don for all the marvelous years of eating, Martha and Tom."

Basil Eggs

SERVES AS MANY AS YOU LIKE / TOTAL TIME: 15 MIN

I can't believe I once made this for a vintners' lunch, which meant I had to get fifty of these eggs just right! I learned that a sprig of basil, properly placed, will cover up a rough edge, if the eggs don't peel perfectly. This is a rich and lush way to present a simple egg, which of course is perfection all by itself. It looks beautiful on a plain white plate. Save the leftover basil mayonnaise to use on sandwiches.

For the basil mayonnaise, make: **Green Mayonnaise (page 79), using basil and melted butter**

I usually cook 1 egg per person, boiling them in their shells just until the whites are set, but the yolks are still runny. Use the very finest extra-large, farm-fresh, free-range eggs you can find, the ones that have those lovely orange yolks with the very best flavor.

Peel very carefully (see Margin Note).

To serve, put a dollop of the basil mayonnaise on a small plate and place an egg on top.

Garnish with: **1 or 2 sprigs green or purple basil (or 1 of each)**

There are many tricks to boiling eggs so that they peel nicely. Here are some of mine:

• Prick the eggs first at the end with a pushpin.

• Have the eggs at room temperature before boiling.

• Bring the cooking water to a boil, add the eggs, and simmer for 5 to 6 minutes.

• Don't crowd the pan.

• Try one first to check the timing. When you break into the egg with a fork, the yolk should begin to run. Then you'll know you have achieved perfection.

• If you use a steamer, cook for the same amount of time.

• Once cooked, plunge the eggs into a bowl of cold water. After they have cooled, crack the shells all over, very gently, and let them rest for a few minutes in the water. This will allow some water to loosen the shells for easier peeling.

• When peeling, use the pad of your thumb to gently push up on the cracked shells to try to get under the membrane.

• Hold the eggs in cold water until serving time. This will help keep them from splitting open.

Chicken & Oysters in Lemon Cream with Frozen Cranberry Mousse

SERVES 6 GENEROUSLY / TOTAL TIME: 1 ½ HOURS EXCLUDING CHILL TIME

In December, when the holidays were all around us, I would serve this for the Napa Valley Vintners Association's lunch, as it's delicate, very tasty, and rather festive. A glass of sparkling wine was the perfect accompaniment.

One day ahead of time make the Frozen Cranberry Orange Mousse (recipe following).

Make the Basic White Sauce (page 30) and stir in:	**Zest and juice of 1 lemon**
Set aside, covered.	
Prepare and set aside:	**12 to 18 Toast Rounds (page 176)**
In a large skillet that will accommodate the chicken breasts, melt:	**2 Tbsp butter**
Add to the skillet:	**2½ lb [1.2 kg] boneless, skinless chicken breasts**
And sprinkle generously with:	**Salt**

We often make this to accompany our holiday turkey. To make it easier to serve, freeze portioned scoops of the mousse, ready to bring out when the dinner is hot. But don't forget them in the freezer. Out of sight is out of mind, and on several occasions we've left them in the freezer, much to our regret.

A perfectly cooked chicken breast should be delicate and juicy. Practice makes perfect.

Fit the chicken breasts in a single layer in the skillet, breast-side down, and cook just until they feel firm to a light touch, 5 to 10 minutes. Remove from the heat, cover the skillet, and set it at the back of the stove to continue cooking from the retained heat. Test them again in about 10 minutes; they're done when they've lost their pink color.

If the chicken breasts cannot fit in your largest skillet in one layer, preheat the oven to 300°F [150°C]. Put the chicken on a baking sheet, cover, and bake just until they begin to firm up, 10 to 15 minutes. Remove from the oven and cover loosely to finish off the cooking.

Trim the edges to neaten:	**12 to 18 fresh oysters, shelled or jarred, drained**
In a sauté pan, melt over low heat:	**2 Tbsp butter**

Trimming is a little trick I learned from Chef Thomas Keller. They look so nice when perfectly round.

Add the oysters and warm in the butter. Remove from the heat.

Before serving, rewarm the lemon cream sauce and thin, if necessary, with:	**2 to 3 Tbsp chicken stock**

The sauce should be pourable, but thick enough to nap the oysters and chicken on the plates.

To serve, warm six of your prettiest plates. Place a chicken breast on each plate and nestle 2 to 3 toast rounds beside it. Place an oyster on each round.

Nap both the oysters and chicken with the lemon cream sauce and sprinkle with:	**Zest of 1 lemon** **Chopped fresh parsley or fresh lemon thyme leaves**
Serve with:	**Roasted broccolini or sautéed greens, cooked until just tender, but still retaining their bright green color**

To make this offering even more festive, finish off each serving with a scoop of the frozen cranberry mousse.

FROZEN CRANBERRY MOUSSE

Combine in a food processor until very finely chopped:	**2 cups [260 g] fresh cranberries** **1 orange, unpeeled, cut into chunks**
Transfer the orange-cranberry mixture to a medium bowl and add:	**1 cup [200 g] sugar** **1 cup [240 g] sour cream**

Stir to combine. If you plan to serve the mousse in individual portions, freeze for 2 hours and use an ice-cream scoop to form into balls. Arrange on a baking sheet so they're not touching, cover with aluminum foil, and freeze for at least 1 hour more.

Or you can put the fruit through a meat grinder. I use my mother's old hand-crank meat grinder for this, but the ones that come as attachments for stand mixers will work as well. If you don't have a meat grinder or food processor, you can use a very sharp knife to chop the orange and cranberries very fine.

Braised Lamb with Green Garlic & Mint

SERVES 6 TO 8 / PREP TIME: 30 MIN / COOK TIME: 2 HOURS

When Don was in the Air Force, I discovered lamb neck with a price I could afford, nineteen cents, and I couldn't resist the challenge of trying to cook with it. The only drawback was that lamb necks have a lot of fat, which has to be skimmed. But that's why they taste so good—the fat is where the flavor is. Here, though, I am using lamb shoulder, which also takes well to long, slow cooking and has great taste.

Cut into 2 in [5 cm] chunks:	**3 to 4 lb [1.4 to 1.8 kg] lamb shoulder**
Season the lamb with:	**Salt and freshly ground black pepper**
In a large Dutch oven over medium-high heat, warm:	**2 Tbsp olive oil**

Add a third of the meat in a single layer; do not crowd your pan. Brown for about 3 minutes, turn, and brown the second side for 3 minutes, adjusting the heat as necessary to avoid burning.

Transfer the lamb to a plate and set aside. Repeat with the remaining lamb, adding a little more olive oil if necessary.

When you have browned all the lamb and set aside, if you don't have 3 Tbsp of fat in the pot, add more:

Olive oil

Place the pot over medium heat and add:

3 medium sweet onions, such as Vidalias, slivered, from stem to root, into eighths, 8 to 10 stems green garlic, cut into 2 in [5 cm] lengths, or 4 to 6 garlic cloves, sliced lengthwise (for a milder flavor)

The recipe calls for a lot of green garlic, or garlic scapes, the thin, curly, bright green stalks that sprout from garlic plants as the cloves form. Their season is very short, but you can substitute garlic cloves. I have also made this recipe with shallots, to replace both the onion and green garlic.

Sprinkle the vegetables with:

Salt (a generous amount) and freshly ground black pepper

Toss the vegetables and cook until the onions wilt, 10 minutes.

Return the meat to the pot and stir in:

1½ cups [360 ml] chicken stock
1½ cups [360 ml] white wine

On top of the meat, layer:

1 lemon, thinly sliced
6 to 8 sprigs mint

The mint will fall off the stems, which will make the stems easy to remove.

Bring to a boil and cover. Lower the heat, and simmer gently until the meat is very tender, about 1½ hours.

Pour off the juices into a large heatproof measuring cup and skim off the fat, which will float to the top. Now is your chance to taste the juices and add more salt and black pepper if needed.

You can also put the pot in a preheated 325°F [165°C] oven for about the same amount of time, covered with a parchment lid, crinkled into a round to fit over the surface of the meat.

Return the juices to the pot. If you like, serve the lamb and juices over:

A bed of mashed potatoes or a delicate pasta, such as orzo

Sprinkle each serving with:

Fresh mint leaves, finely slivered, or chopped fresh chives

Real California Cooking

It's odd how, when people talk about California cuisine, they assume it had its start in the 1970s in Yountville and Berkeley, and later spread to Los Angeles. But real California cuisine was the cooking that was here before we were: the cuisine of Native America and Spanish-Mexican America, before the gold miners, the train tracks, and the rest of us.

My father would bring home tamales made by the wife of one of his employees. But aside from those, California-Mexican food was not part of my early years, despite the small roadside Mexican cafés of the 1930s and '40s. During the Depression, we didn't eat out in restaurants. For us "eating out" meant we had been invited to a neighbor's home for supper, or were going to a church dinner.

If you had asked me back then, not knowing any better, I'm sure I would have told you loud and clear that I didn't like Mexican cuisine. Spicy food wasn't part of my upbringing, but I fell in love with it as an adult. A touch of chile pepper can bring something alive. And there are times I crave a really hot salsa or a fiery hot stew awash in chiles. Sometimes I will throw in a whole jalapeño when I get a pot of stock going on the back of the stove, just to add a little zip.

I learned about Mexican food from *Sunset* magazine in the 1950s. After reading an article on tostadas, I decided to try making them for a family gathering. I made them again and again. It became almost a game for the family to see who could pile the tostada the highest with the beans, meat, lettuce, cheese, and salsas, and then eat it without spilling it all over themselves. My love of this early California cuisine grew from there.

Shortly after we moved to Yountville, we had a favorite Mexican restaurant just south of town that we adored. But then the owners, Frances Solis and her family, sold it. Our family and friends all mourned its closing, missing their spicy, colorful food.

I don't remember how the idea was born, but we ended up offering to let Frances and a couple of her family members present her much-loved food at the Chutney Kitchen every Friday and Saturday night. It worked out well, because the restaurant was underused. We were only serving lunch, doing some catering, and making the chutney there. And we had little experience with dinner service at that time.

We provided the waitstaff. I ordered whatever Frances needed and stayed in the kitchen during service to do the expediting. It was a wonderful learning experience for me, even though there were several ingredients that Frances needed that were a stretch for us, such as the two kinds of tortillas she wanted from two different places, the special type of black bean, and

I learned about more than Mexican cuisine from Frances. She soon introduced us to *sangrita*, or literally, "little blood." This is a chaser, meant to follow a shot of good tequila with its traditional salt and lime routine. The wonderful taste of the sangrita lingers on the tongue. To make 2 shots, simply mix together the juices of 1 orange and 1 lime with 1 finely diced jalapeño pepper.

I took a series of classes in Oaxaca, Mexico, from that great authority on Mexican cuisine, Diana Kennedy, who explained that *tostada* simply means "toasted"—in this case, the tortilla.

the pungent Mexican herb epazote, which, thankfully, we could pick from her garden.

Every weekend for as long as it lasted, which wasn't long, we would put together a bunch of people, recipes, and new cooking techniques, and it would end up being a party. It was a lot of work for us, but it was so much fun.

Unfortunately, those Friday and Saturday nights soon came to a screeching halt. Frances had signed an agreement to refrain from competing with the new owners of her old restaurant, and they called her on it. On the positive side, we had learned from Frances how to make some of our favorite foods. And she brought into my kitchen not just cilantro and lime juice but the whole range of chiles, from poblanos and anchos to jalapeños and serranos. Her food was very hot and exciting to us in the early seventies. Most importantly, she brought authentic California cooking into my repertoire, for which I will be forever grateful to her. I miss her; she delighted everyone who came in contact with her.

below: Frances (pictured on the sign) still reigns in Yountville. The Solis family manages to retain an authentic taste of what Napa Valley was like in the old days at their bar, Pancha's, in Yountville.

Tomatillo Tortilla Soup

SERVES 4 TO 6 / TOTAL TIME: 45 MIN

I love tomatillos—"little tomatoes" that are native to Mexico. Their flavor is brighter and less sweet than red tomatoes (to which they are not related). Tomatillos work so well in this soup. Don always liked me to make a big pot of it, since we enjoyed the leftovers so much the next day.

In a medium soup pot over medium heat, warm:

3 Tbsp olive oil

Add and sauté until wilted and starting to brown, about 5 minutes:

2 onions, thinly sliced

Then add and cook another 5 minutes, while stirring:

Three 6 in [15 cm] corn tortillas, cut into ½ in [12 mm] strips
3 or 4 garlic cloves, thinly sliced
1 Tbsp toasted cumin seeds
½ tsp minced jalapeño pepper

You never know how hot a jalapeño pepper is until you cut it open and taste a little bit. But be careful—they can be quite hot!

Add:

3 to 4 cups [395 to 525 g] tomatillos, husked and cut into wedges
Zest and juice of 1 orange
4 cups [960 ml] chicken stock
Salt and freshly ground black pepper

Bring to a simmer and continue simmering, uncovered, until the tomatillos are tender, at least 30 minutes.

Garnish with:

Roasted red peppers (see Margin Note, page 79)
A spoonful of sour cream
A generous sprinkle of chopped fresh oregano
A sprinkle of toasted pumpkin seeds or crispy fried tortilla strips

Steak à la Chicana

SERVES 4 TO 6 / TOTAL TIME: 30 MIN TO 1 HOUR

This was another one of Don's favorite Mexican dinners. It filled all the squares for him. Good red meat, garden tomatoes, and some spice. Frances always insisted on good top sirloin, the best we could find. This dish comes together very quickly and is extremely satisfying. Perfect for one of those summer evenings when you haven't planned ahead and don't want to turn on the oven.

Heat in a large heavy skillet over high heat:	**3 Tbsp lard**
In batches, without crowding the pan, brown:	**1 lb [455 g] top sirloin, sliced against the grain into thin strips and sprinkled with salt**
Set the meat aside and in the same pan, over medium heat, sauté:	**1 bunch green onions (white and green parts), sliced** **2 to 4 jalapeño peppers, seeded (unless you like it hot) and finely chopped (or sliced)**
When soft and tender, add:	**4 medium tomatoes, diced (peeling is optional)**

Return the meat to the pan and simmer over low heat until tender, at least 10 minutes. I've let it simmer for as long as 30 minutes, but if you do that, watch the liquid level, and add a little stock or water if necessary.

Season with:	**Salt**
Garnish with:	**A generous dollop of sour cream** **Sprigs of fresh cilantro** **Roasted pumpkin seeds (optional)**
Serve with:	**Black beans or Soft Polenta (page 162), or both** **Warm tortillas to scoop up the juices**

Good unadulterated lard is worth searching out at your local butcher. Beware of the packaged lard in supermarkets, which is hydrogenated, often bleached, and filled with additives to make it smell better and allow it to sit on the shelf, unrefrigerated. Better yet, make your own by melting pork fat over low heat so that it separates from any connective tissue, a process that is called rendering. You will need either the soft fat (leaf lard) from around the kidneys, or the hard fat (fatback) from the back of the pig. Ask your butcher for either one. Cut the fat into small chunks, transfer to a pot, and melt it down over low heat, as low as your burner will go. Avoid browning the fat. A slow cooker works well, too. When the fat is completely melted, strain it through a triple layer of cheesecloth. Pour into clean sterile half-pint jars. They will keep unopened for up to 3 months in your pantry. Your lard will have none of the unhealthy trans fats. In Mexico, home cooks use a caramel-colored lard that is rendered at a higher temperature and has a fuller, richer, more porky flavor.

Pozole Verde

SERVES 6 / TOTAL TIME: 1 HOUR IF USING CANNED HOMINY

I learned to make pozole verde from the vivacious Diana Kennedy when I took a series of classes from her in Oaxaca. The heart of this robust Mexican stew is the hominy. It is made from field corn, which, in the United States, is usually dried on the stalk and fed to the livestock. In a technique that dates back to pre-Columbian times, field corn intended for hominy is cooked and then soaked in an alkaline solution. The solution softens the kernels and loosens the skins, which are then rubbed and washed away. This process is called nixtamalization, from *nixtamal*, a modern version of the Aztec word for this processed corn. It really has a history!

You can find dried hominy, which is just corn that went through this process and was then dried. It's also available already cooked in cans. If you use the dried hominy, you'll need to cook it, but it does have a bit more flavor. The canned version can work in a pinch.

Rinse:

1 ½ cups [260 g] dried hominy

Transfer to a medium saucepan with a lid and cover by at least 2 in [5 cm] of water. Soak overnight. In the morning, drain the water, replace with fresh water, and season with:

Salt

Bring to a boil, lower the heat, and simmer until almost tender, about 1½ hours. Set aside.

Meanwhile, in a small dry skillet, toast, but do not brown:

¾ cup [105 g] raw hulled pumpkin seeds

Cool and grind in a mortar and pestle, but not too fine. You may also use a blender or food processor. Set aside.

In a medium saucepan, combine:

¾ cup [180 ml] water
3 cups [500 g] husked and quartered tomatillos
¾ cup [105 g] chopped white onion
3 garlic cloves, coarsely chopped

Cook over medium heat until the tomatillos are tender and the liquid is almost gone, about 10 minutes.

Cool for a few minutes. Transfer to a blender and add:

2 small serrano peppers, chopped
1½ cups [360 ml] water
Salt
18 sorrel leaves (optional)

Purée until smooth and, if you like, strain to remove the seeds.

In a sauté pan over high heat, melt or warm:

2 Tbsp lard or olive oil

All you have to do to turn this into a vegan or vegetarian dish is to substitute olive oil for the lard.

Add the blended mixture to the pan and cook, stirring, about 5 minutes.

Add the ground pumpkin seeds and continue to cook, stirring and scraping from the bottom of the pan, until thickened, about 5 minutes longer.

Drain and add the cooked hominy. Or drain, rinse, and add to the pan:

Two 15 oz [600 g] cans hominy

Bring to a simmer and cook for another 5 to 10 minutes for the flavors to meld. Taste for salt and add more if needed. Thin with a little water if the pozole seems too thick.

Serve in soup bowls, topping each portion with any or all of the following:

¼ cup [40 g] cubed avocado
¼ cup [15 g] finely slivered cabbage
2 lime quarters
A spoonful of finely chopped white onion, tossed with a squeeze of lime juice
A pinch of dried Mexican oregano or chopped fresh oregano
A dollop of sour cream

Any remaining toppings can be put on the table in small bowls to be added as desired.

Poblanos Stuffed with Polenta & Cheese

SERVES 6 / PREP TIME: 1 HOUR / COOK TIME: 15 MIN

We started making these at the Chutney Kitchen, and now at the Apple Farm, we often serve them for Sunday brunch. It is a perfect recipe if you have willing helpers, as it takes much hands-on preparation. We like to serve the stuffed poblanos in wide soup bowls filled with Pozole Verde (page 130), placing a stuffed poblano on each bed of pozole, and sprinkling it with a little finely shredded red cabbage and a dollop of sour cream. I often finish it with a sprinkle of toasted pumpkin seeds.

Preheat the oven to 350°F [180°C].

Char, steam, cool, and peel (see Margin Note, page 79):

6 poblano peppers

Make a 2 to 3 inch [5 to 7.5 cm] slit lengthwise in each one, and remove the seedy core, if it's very large. Set aside.

Next, prepare the polenta filling. In a large pot with a lid, bring to a boil:

4 cups [960 ml] chicken stock or water
1 scant tsp salt

Stir in:

1 cup [140 g] polenta

Return to a boil, whisking constantly. Set the heat to low, cover, and cook until the polenta thickens, 10 to 15 minutes.

Stir into the polenta:

¼ cup [30 g] crumbled fresh goat cheese
¼ cup [20 g] grated Monterey Jack cheese
2 small hot red chile peppers or jalapeño peppers, minced
2 Tbsp grated white onion
3 Tbsp olive oil or butter
Salt and freshly ground black pepper

Taste for seasoning. It should be both nippy and rich. Set aside until cool enough to handle. Divide the stuffing into six portions and spoon one into each poblano. Using your hands, gently reshape the peppers into their original forms. The polenta will be firming up, which will help.

Place on a baking sheet and rub their surfaces with:

1 or 2 Tbsp olive oil

Bake the peppers until bubbling hot, 10 to 5 minutes.

Serve with:

Pozole Verde (page 130) or a good salsa

Southwest Pork

SERVES 8 TO 10 / PREP TIME: 45 MIN / COOK TIME: 1½ TO 2 HOURS

I loved Frances Solis's chile verde. But since it was spicy, it was not so wonderful when served with wine. Since I wanted our foods to be good companions to our wines, I developed this recipe, softening Frances's fire a bit.

Preheat the oven to 325°F [165 °C].

Char, cool, and peel (see Margin Note, page 79):

2 to 3 red peppers

Cut into wide strips and set aside.

In a large skillet over medium heat, melt or warm:

2 Tbsp lard or olive oil

In batches, without crowding the pan, add:

2½ to 3 lb [1.2 to 1.4 kg] pork shoulder with enough fat to make a good stew, cut into 1½ in [4 cm] cubes

Brown the pork on both sides, about 10 to 15 minutes, and transfer to a Dutch oven. Set aside.

Lower the heat under the skillet to medium. If needed, melt another:

2 Tbsp lard

Add to the skillet:

**1 lb [455 g] tomatillos, husked
2 medium onions, each cut lengthwise into 8 wedges
1 to 3 jalapeño peppers, seeded and sliced into half-rounds
6 to 8 sun-dried tomatoes, slivered
12 garlic cloves
Salt and freshly ground black pepper**

The Solis family would become our neighbors when we opened the French Laundry. Their house was across Creek Street from the restaurant, and they put up a "no parking" sign in front, which our guests would occasionally ignore. One memorable night, Frances's daughter, Rose, charged into the dining room during service wearing only her bathrobe with her hair all done up in orange cans, which she used for rollers. She stood there screaming at Don about people parking on their side of the street. But it was, and is, a small town, so we are all still good friends.

You'll need to decide the number of jalapeño peppers, since they vary in heat. Include the seeds if you want the stew hotter.

Cook the vegetables, stirring, until wilted, 5 or 10 minutes, then add the charred red pepper strips.

Pour into the skillet: **2 cups [480 ml] chicken stock**

Bring to a boil, remove from the heat, and transfer to the Dutch oven, smothering the pork with the vegetables. Do not stir. Cover loosely with parchment paper to avoid building up steam, and place in oven.

Cook for 1½ hours and test for tenderness. The meat should be a little springy. Add more stock or water if needed, keeping the level almost to the top of the meat. When done, let rest for at least 30 minutes.

Pour off the juices into a heatproof measuring cup, check seasoning, skim, and return to the pot.

Serve the pork and vegetables over: **Soft Polenta (page 162)**

Garnish each serving with: **A dollop of sour cream**
                                                Sprigs of cilantro

Just in case the pork isn't hot enough,   **Jalapeño peppers,**
on the table place a small bowl of: **finely chopped**

And next time, use more!

April Dinner
AT THE
Chutney Kitchen

Steak Tartare

Rabbit in Mustard Cream
WITH
Stuffed Mushrooms
and Green Beans

Green Salad

Chocolate Chinchilla

Coffee

Friday Night Dinners

After the Mexican dinners ended, the Chutney Kitchen had a dark kitchen most nights. We were looking for someone to open a dinner operation upstairs, over our corner of the main building at the Vintage 1870, but we searched in vain. No one satisfied us, or we them. We wanted simple, good food, without pretensions. So we decided to throw a party, one Friday night a month, and charge for it. (That may have been the first pop-up venue!) This truly was the training ground for what was to become the French Laundry. And we stepped into it slowly, but steadily.

We planned for it to be only one seating, and one menu, at one price. We would serve Don's choice of wines. It really was like throwing a big party at our home. We set a date for the first dinner, and we intended to send out flyers to our mailing list. But before we got them printed, word got around and the dinner sold out.

We started by serving forty guests. After five years, the guest list had grown to over seventy. Step by step, we learned how to cope, buying more dishes and expanding our seating beyond the original dining area.

We never did send out those flyers. Our customers would simply call Don's secretary, Mimi, ask the date and menu for the next dinner, and reserve a table for two to eight people. We almost always had a waiting list. One loyal couple always came by themselves and never missed one of our dinners. By the end, we were doing two a month.

Most of our menus were repeated yearly, maybe with a few changes here and there. It was a five-course, prix fixe meal with accompanying Napa Valley wines. I wanted the main course to reflect the season. For example, in January, I liked to serve braised oxtails. At Easter, I would serve rabbit (which someone pointed out to me maybe wasn't the best idea).

Those Friday nights at the Chutney Kitchen gave me the chance to plan and cook dinners for a large number of people, using fresh, local, in-season ingredients. And so without any forethought, we had our blueprint for the French Laundry! We had a vision for what it could be, plus menus, my recipes, even a staff. And there was our lovely old French Laundry building, which we had purchased by then, just waiting for us to start a new chapter in our lives!

opposite: Our monthly Friday Night Dinners were designed to reflect the season. My daughter, Kathy, hand-lettered and illustrated menus for each of the twelve tables we served. I had one menu each month to perfect, but no room for error.

Date, Onion & Avocado Salad with Peanuts

SERVES 6 / TOTAL TIME: 30 MIN

The inspiration for this salad was a recipe in the *African Cooking* volume of that amazing series of cookbooks, *Foods of the World*, which Time Life began publishing in the late 1960s. I added the sliced avocados, and placed the dates and onions on a bed of aggressive greens, but the sprinkle of peanuts came with the original recipe. It is such a lovely contrast in texture and flavor.

Combine in a medium bowl:

8 oz [225 g] Medjool or other good-quality dates, quartered lengthwise
½ large white onion, thinly slivered lengthwise

In a small bowl, whisk together:

2 Tbsp fresh lime juice
2 Tbsp balsamic vinegar
A pinch of salt
A pinch of sugar

Add the dressing to the salad and toss well until completely coated. The dates will probably soak up any excess dressing. Let sit for at least 15 minutes to allow the flavors to meld.

At serving time, on each of six plates, arrange a small bed of:

Greens, preferably arugula or garden cress

Slice lengthwise:

2 avocados

Fan out some of the avocado slices over the greens on each plate. Spoon the date and onion mixture between the avocado slices.

Sprinkle generously with:

Chopped roasted peanuts

Zanzibar Duck with Rice & Papaya

SERVES 6 / PREP: 1 HOUR / COOK TIME: 2 HOURS

I love cooking and serving duck, so, inspired by a recipe I saw in the *African Cooking* volume of the Time Life series, I developed my own version of Zanzibar duck for our monthly dinners at the Chutney Kitchen. The zesty citrus flavors work well at taming the richness of the duck.

The dish became so popular that our local baseball team adopted the name the Zanzibar Ducks! The team included our sons and several of our employees, so we cheered them on at their rather dorky games. I once promised to treat the team to a French Laundry dinner of Zanzibar duck if they won the championship. To my amazement, they won! And so our dining room was filled with the players and their significant others for a very festive night.

When we served the duck, we would finish the meal with a dessert that Don loved. It was a delicate custard flavored with ginger and orange, molded into a layer of ladyfingers, which were brushed with a tangerine liquor. It was delicious and beautiful, but unfortunately, I lost the source of those wonderful ladyfingers and no longer make it.

The duck needs plenty of time to prepare, so start early. It will benefit from an hour or so in a low oven after cooking.

Preheat the oven to 400°F [200°C].

| On a rimmed baking sheet: | **6 whole duck legs** |

| Arrange them skin-side up and season with: | **Salt and freshly ground black pepper** |

Roast in the oven until they are very brown, but not dried out, about 45 minutes.

| While the duck legs are cooking, prepare and set aside: | **2 green or red bell peppers, charred, peeled, and torn into strips (see Margin Note, page 79)** | Unless they have really thick flesh, bell peppers will tear beautifully into nice strips. If they are too thick, go ahead and use your knife. |

| In a medium saucepan, combine and bring to a simmer: | **2 cups [480 ml] chicken stock**
12 whole cloves
2 jalapeño peppers, halved |

Drain the fat from the duck legs and lower the oven temperature to 300°F [150 °C].

Do reserve the flavorful duck fat for another use, such as fried potatoes.

Pour the prepared stock over the duck legs and cover the pan with parchment. Return to the oven and steam until tender, 45 minutes to 1 hour more.

Discard the cloves and jalapeños.

| Carefully pour off the cooking juices into a large saucepan. Add: | **4 cups [960 ml] chicken stock**
1 cup [240 ml] fresh orange juice
⅔ cup [160 ml] fresh lime juice | I have a little trick here. When you want to scrape up those precious bits on the baking sheet, add a little stock and use a pastry brush to gradually dissolve them into the stock. It takes a while, but it's really worth it, as it turns the stock a beautiful brown color. |

Return the duck to the 300°F [150 °C] oven, uncovered, for at least 30 minutes to let the skin crisp up again. At this point it can sit in a very low oven up to 30 minutes more until you are ready to serve.

Bring the stock and juices to a gentle simmer, and keep it simmering until it reduces down to about 3 cups [720 ml]. After the stock is reduced, taste for salt and add more if needed.

Meanwhile, in a medium saucepan over low heat, melt:	¼ cup [55 g] butter
Peel, seed, cut into cubes, and add to the pan:	2 fresh papayas
Gently warm and sprinkle with:	¼ tsp freshly grated nutmeg Salt

When ready to serve, place a generous spoonful of rice on each plate. Add a duck leg and scatter the reserved pepper strips over the leg.

Place a serving of the warmed papaya on the side and spoon the reduced stock over all. Be very generous. There should be enough liquid to really soak into the rice.

Garnish with:	Lime and orange zest

A bowl of oranges studded with cloves, which we like to do at holiday time, would be a fragrant addition to the table when serving this duck.

Roast Leg of Lamb

SERVES 6 TO 8 / PREP TIME: 1 HOUR / COOK TIME: 1 HOUR

When I served this at the restaurant, I used boned-and-tied legs because they could be sliced into nice, thick, evenly proportioned pieces. After marinating them, I would often hand them over to Don to take outside and cook over the open flames of the grill to brown the outside and get a nice rich color before finishing them in the oven. We preferred our lamb quite rare, which sometimes raised eyebrows with our customers.

Preheat the oven to 350°F [180°C].

When you buy this at the butcher shop, they often charge you for the entire bone-in lamb roast, but will graciously bone it for you. You want to end up with 4 to 6 lb [1.8 to 2.7 kg] of boned meat.

If you want your lamb well done, you're on your own.

Prepare the marinade, which should give you enough for at least 1 large whole leg. Combine in a blender:

½ **onion, chopped**
½ **cup [20 g] fresh mint leaves**
½ **head garlic, sliced and peeled**
¼ **cup [60 ml] fresh lemon juice**
¼ **cup [60 ml] white wine**
¼ **cup [60 ml] olive oil**
1 **Tbsp salt**
1 **Tbsp freshly ground black pepper**

Don't bother to peel the garlic if you're browning the lamb on a grill. The peel will burn off.

Whirl the ingredients just until smooth. Rub the marinade into:

One 4 to 6 lb [1.8 to 2.7 kg] boned-and-tied leg of lamb

Let rest at room temperature for at least 1 hour.

If browning the lamb on the grill, build a medium-hot fire. Put the lamb on the grill and cook until nicely browned, about 5 minutes per side. (Don't attempt to cook it all the way through.)

Alternatively, heat a large cast-iron skillet over high heat and brown the lamb. You don't need any oil, as any retained marinade will have enough oil in it to keep the lamb from sticking.

Transfer to the oven and roast to your preferred doneness: for rare, until a meat thermometer registers 120°F [50°C], about 45 minutes; and for medium-rare, until it registers 135°F [60°C], about 60 minutes.

Remove the roast from the pan and let rest for at least 30 minutes. It will still be warm when you slice it, but you can always pop it back in the oven briefly to reheat the outside.

While the meat is resting, pour out any fat and add to the pan:

1 **cup [240 ml] stock**
¼ **cup wine, red or white, depending on what you have on hand**
¼ **cup [55 g] butter**

Use a pastry brush to dissolve all those browned bits in the liquid. It will take a while, but stay with it; it all dissolves eventually. When you have finished, reduce the juices and stock over medium heat for a few minutes, and it will come together into a delicious sauce.

Before you start cutting into the meat, mark off where you want to slice to make sure you have enough for everyone; but try to make the slices as thick as possible. Cut straight slices, starting from the middle and working out to the ends.

To serve, paint each slice with some of the sauce in the pan.

Fourth: The French Laundry

Just up the Street (1978 to 1994)

Finding the French Laundry

When Don and I first moved to Yountville in 1967, one of the locals gave us a tour of the town. There were four or five interesting old buildings that he showed us. One of them, built of fieldstone, was squeezed onto a corner, almost in the street. He explained to us that everyone called it the French Laundry because, in fact, it had housed a laundry in the old days. It had seen many uses since then, and was now occupied by an elderly couple. The building looked rather unloved, but we felt a pull toward it.

Several years later, our friend Lorraine Jones, who was checking in for a lunch shift at the Chutney Kitchen, sidled up to me and whispered in my ear, "Guess what? The French Laundry is for sale!" I picked up the phone right away and made an appointment to see the building that afternoon.

After the lunch service was over, we were met by a cousin of the people who had inherited the building. Rather apologetically, he led us through the old structure. While Don talked to him, Lorraine and I followed behind, trying to conceal our glee at what we saw. The poor man exclaimed, when we entered one room upstairs, "At least there is one square room!" He was obviously out of his element and didn't understand what we were seeing.

The three of us retreated to our house to strategize. We decided to pool our resources and made an offer the next morning for the asking price, with no contingencies. We waived all the normal inspections because we knew the building was a mess. But underneath all the overgrown blackberries, the kicked-in lath and plaster upstairs, the curvy walls, and the warren of tiny rooms, there lay something very special, at least to our eyes.

We really had no plans at the time. We simply knew we wanted that wonderful old building. So we cleaned it up as best we could, and Lorraine moved into the downstairs, where there was a living room, a little bedroom, and a small kitchen. The upstairs was pretty much uninhabitable, except for the bathroom with a claw-foot tub. It certainly wasn't lovely.

For several years, we didn't do anything major to it. The building had been vacant for quite some time, and Lorraine puttered around in the garden, uncovering a rosebush that had been neglected and the remains of an old chicken coop, covered with blackberries.

previous: Posing in my kitchen at the French Laundry, photographed for the cover of *Napa Valley Magazine*, 1979.

The day we decided to do a restaurant at the French Laundry was the day we left Vintage 1870. This was the summer of 1977, and we had been abruptly told there was no place for us anymore as partners at the Vintage. The new owners did want us to continue as employees, but the news was a blow. Hours later, we drove over to Sonoma and had dinner at our favorite Mexican restaurant on the square. Over a bottle of wine, we talked it over and decided the thing to do was to open our own restaurant in the building we already owned. So the whole decision was made in just a few hours. Lorraine backed out gracefully, leaving renovation to us. To get to our new venture, all we would have to do was travel a couple of blocks north, to the corner of Washington and Creek Streets.

AN OLD STONE BUILDING

We have always taken a simple, straightforward approach to our projects, and we dove into this new challenge in the same way. There would be no attempt at grandeur. We didn't want to gussy it up.

The interior spaces were small because, on the ground floor, the walls were made of heavy fieldstone—wider at the base and tapering as they rose. The result, in addition to small rooms, were wonderfully deep window sills. We reversed the stairway, moving it over 6 in [15 cm], to provide a wider space for my kitchen.

How I loved that little kitchen! Unlike the one at the Chutney Kitchen, it had two casement windows, which cranked open, and two six-paned glass doors, one of which opened out directly onto what eventually became my herb garden. We bought a big, two-door refrigerator and freezer for one end,

below: When we started to work on the structure in 1977, it became all too clear that this was a simple building, built around 1900 by unprofessional people, using the materials that were on hand. I'm sure the original builders didn't own a plumb bob or even a level. But we loved that and decided that whatever improvements we made would be done in the same spirit. And since our budget was very limited, this approach suited us well.

and designed an island with a butcher-block surface and prep sink for the other end. We installed a dumbwaiter to service the upstairs dining room. That kitchen was the most efficient workspace I have ever had. There was not an inch of wasted space, and yet it felt open and airy.

We resisted the urge to hang doors leading into the dining area, leaving the doorways open instead. Many diners would poke their heads into the kitchen to say hello before ascending the staircase. In fact, we had diners popping in and out of the kitchen all night, and I loved it. I found it unsatisfying to cook for people I never saw, but I didn't like walking the floor. I preferred to receive compliments that were unsolicited and appreciated those who came into the kitchen to say good night, to comment on the meal on their way out.

We turned the original small kitchen into the entryway. It was where Don presided over the seating arrangements, delivered and opened the wines, poured water into our Chemex coffeepots, and took in the cash. We never accepted credit cards, partly because there simply wasn't enough room behind his counter for the equipment. We operated out of a metal cash box in the drawer of his counter. There were several regular customers who had standing accounts with us, so they could bring guests to eat there without the awkwardness of being presented with a bill. We usually billed the regulars at the end of the month.

Upstairs was that room the real estate salesman had liked, the only one in the building that was actually squared off. In our minds, it was the one room without character. We turned it into a pantry, with the water heater curtained off in a corner. We also had a counter with a small sink in it; the dumbwaiter stopped there with plates filled with food from the kitchen.

We had a little private dining room at the head of the stairs, with a round table that was reserved for parties of six to eight. It was highly sought after, and requests for the private dining room were made well in advance.

The rooms upstairs opened out onto a balcony. Though it was unusual for that era, we were a nonsmoking place, but we did allow it on the balcony and in the garden. With all those rules and limitations, it's a wonder we survived.

Our experience at the Chutney Kitchen provided us with a plan to follow, with very few changes. We simply moved our act up the street and operated in much the same way as we had with our Friday night dinner series. But there was a little more to it, of course. Instead of one menu per month, I had to dream up a new one every night for the five nights per week we were open. But I didn't have to worry about the lunch service, or making chutney; I could devote myself entirely to our restaurant. It was heaven. At first, I wavered on the one-menu, prix fixe plan, and thought maybe I should offer steak to guests who weren't happy with our offerings that night. My daughter Karen spoke to me most emphatically, saying "Mom, stick to your guns!" So, I did. I settled on a five-course menu with a choice of three different starters, followed by the soup of the night, a single entrée, a simple green salad with cheeses, and a choice of three desserts. In a pinch, I could always expand one of the starters into a main plate. For dessert, I offered a choice between something chocolate, something baked, and a simple fruit, which I thought would keep everyone happy.

OUR BLUEPRINT

The way we set up the restaurant had a lot to do with the design of the building, plus the fact that we wanted to do everything possible by ourselves. I wanted to run the kitchen, and Don wanted to watch over the front of the house and take care of the wines. I did the day-to-day bookkeeping in the mornings at home while sipping my first cup of coffee, while Don oversaw the larger financial picture.

I thought of our plan as a balancing act. We had enough tables and chairs to seat fifty people, pots and pans large enough to cook food for fifty, and enough white porcelain plates and glassware to serve fifty meals. For dessert dishes, I had several small stacks of colorful plates I could mix or match to play around with for presentation. Many of these I had inherited from my mother or were ones my Aunt Saidie had passed along to me. I was always searching antique stores and Cost Plus for more to add to the collection.

I liked to think everything was in balance, including our own energies. We decided to have only a small staff, which varied between two and five employees. Each morning, by the time I arrived at the restaurant, the first of our staff would already be there cleaning the dining rooms and gathering the tablecloths to be laundered. They brought the laundry to the washing machine and dryer at our place, just across the parking lot from the restaurant. Then they would work in the kitchen, helping me with the prep work for that night's dinner. We all took turns answering the phone.

After the morning's work, we all sat down to lunch in the garden, and then we'd take an afternoon break. Some of the staff might head back to their homes for a rest. Others might get some shopping done, or just relax in the garden. When they came back, they'd put fresh aprons on and set the tables in the dining room before waiting tables for the night.

The system worked largely because it didn't leave any room for that competition and conflict that so often builds up between the front and back of the house, between the people preparing and the people serving the food. Also, our employees split the 15 percent service charge, which we had in place of tipping. This included the kitchen workers and the dishwasher. Since everyone contributed to the experience of dining with us, we felt they should share equally in the benefits. Of course, if a party was really pleased with the service, they tipped beyond the service charge, and the waitstaff could keep that for themselves.

We provided minimal service, hoping our guests would have a leisurely dinner with time to stroll in the garden (or have a smoke) between courses. There were no busboys; the server who took orders also served the plates and took them away. We didn't top off wineglasses; we encouraged diners to pour their own wine at their own pace.

We had the occasional customer who thought the pace was too slow, and we tried to honor his or her wishes, but never at the expense of our more leisurely diners. Sometimes, a group in the private dining room, being unaware they were the only ones left in the restaurant, lingered way beyond closing. On a rare occasion, Don even went so far as to ask them to lock the door when they left and to turn out the lights! We never liked to break into a good conversation.

*A memory from Lissa
Doumani, who with her
husband, Hiro Sone, oper-
ated the Michelin-starred
restaurant Terra, in St.
Helena, until 2019:* When
Hiro and I were married
after he moved here from
Japan, the French Laundry
was the first place my parents took the whole family
to dinner. My father had
reserved the upstairs private
dining room, a good idea for
our motley crew, as we can
eat and drink most people
under the table. Hiro didn't
speak much English yet, and
I noticed at one point during
the meal that he had left
the table. When he hadn't
returned after a while, I went
looking for him. I finally
found him in the kitchen,
standing there watching
everything.

   Sally's kitchen was very
different from what he was
used to in Japan, even the
"Western-style kitchen"
where he had worked. It was
quiet, almost peaceful, and
everyone was working hard.
But they also seemed to be
having the best time. I'm
sure every day wasn't like
that, but this was the way
Sally ran her kitchen.

Opening Night at the French Laundry

SALLY REMEMBERS: On Tuesday evening, February 7, 1978, at just about seven o'clock, we welcomed our first customers into the French Laundry. It had been raining hard for several weeks, right up to the day we opened. And just a day or two before, there was a sea of mud outside the front door, with leftover lumber and remnants of our renovation project stacked in the restaurant garden. And everything, inside and out, was muddy from the workmen coming and going. But on that last day, we moved the lumber, dumping it right next door at our house, and called in a load of gravel to spread over the mud. And voilà! We were ready for service.

KATHY, SALLY'S ELDEST DAUGHTER, REMEMBERS: That day we opened was wild. We were washing and buffing plates and silverware, and unwrapping glasses in the middle of what still had the look of a construction site, with table saws in the middle of the dining room. We were stashing the clean stuff anywhere we could. We didn't have a lot of space in the kitchen. Once we filled up the windowsills, we put things in the little waiter's station on the second floor, next to the private dining room. And at some point, my mom just had to yell, "Out, you guys! Enough, enough! We've got to roll the tables in and get this place set for dinner!"

TERRY, SALLY'S YOUNGEST DAUGHTER, REMEMBERS: We all helped. I was only twelve, but I remember working on the floors in the dining room, pulling up all the old linoleum. And then we had to get up this black adhesive that was underneath. We tried using lots of boiling water, and then heat guns, trying to scrape it all off. It seemed to take forever until we could finally sand and then stain the Douglas fir floors, but they came out beautiful.

SALLY REMEMBERS: Don was comfortable swinging a hammer and understood structure. He also had a very good eye for details. We had one carpenter, Roy Lyon, and his son, Randy, who were full-time, but the rest of the work was done by family and friends. Our kids helped when they could, but the older ones all had jobs. My sister and her husband came out for a short visit, and we put them to work helping tear down one of the sheds. We had an architect friend, Ray Rector, who helped us with the plans. A bricklayer, Fritz Dilsaver, who had done work for us at the Vintage, did all of our tuck-pointing on the nooks and crannies, and repaired the brickwork around the windows. He was delightful, and did all the work for free, as a friend, since he had hung out so much with us at the Vintage. After we opened, we invited him to come to dinner whenever he could manage it, and when he did, there was never a bill.

I had already designed a kitchen for the Chutney Kitchen, so I had a little bit of experience with a commercial kitchen—plus I knew what I wanted, so I charged ahead. We put the kitchen in where Lorraine's bedroom used to be, quite a small space, limited by the old fieldstone walls, which were impossible to alter. The whole kitchen was put together, including appliances, dishes, and silverware, for less than you'd pay for a stove today.

In the dining room, we used artwork that we already owned and very few new things. We used secondhand bentwood chairs, which I managed to find at a really good price. So we scrounged and put together an eclectic collection of furnishings and equipment that didn't cost much of anything, but all together made a warm and inviting atmosphere.

KATHY REMEMBERS: Two or three days before opening, just after we had refinished the wood floor, a whole group of people tromped in over the barely dried floor carrying a very large package. It was a painting Mom had fallen in love with at a local art show, a landscape by a Carmel artist named Keith Lindberg. Friends of my parents and loyal customers heard about it and someone said, "You know, they have no budget for art. They're stretching it just trying to get the place open. Sally loves that painting. Let's buy it for them!" They all put in money, and then the group of them carried the painting into the dining room, tore off the brown paper wrapping, and presented it to them. It hung in the dining room for the next seventeen years. The painting was very special to them, to all of us.

KAREN, ONE OF SALLY'S DAUGHTERS, REMEMBERS: After helping with the demolition of the building, my future husband, Tim Bates, and I went to work on the garden. The herb garden was a major project for us. With Sally, we laid out the plan, and then the two of us put the bricks down and did the planting. We wanted to have at least the bones of a nice garden in place when the restaurant opened.

And then, when it came time for the finish work of the restaurant, we moved back inside and did everything we could to help get it ready for opening. I remember working with my mom and my older sister, Kathy, on the kitchen walls above the old wooden wainscoting, plastering it with Sheetrock mud. We laughed about how it wasn't all that different from putting the finish frosting on a cake. I think we did a pretty good job of it, as it lasted it the entire time we had the restaurant.

opposite: The upstairs dining room was very simple, with its beautiful wool carpet and an Ira Yeager goose painting presiding over it all. Our collection of paintings followed us to the Apple Farm and are still very special to us.

SALLY REMEMBERS: I had had almost no time before the opening to get used to the kitchen. At three or four that afternoon, I had to kick out the carpenter, Roy, who was fussing over a shelf above the sinks in the scullery. Of course, I had planned to be in there a couple of weeks before to get to know the kitchen and play around in it and get my prep work done. But that didn't happen.

Fortunately, even though the space was new to me, on opening night I was going to cook the same food that I had been making for the weekend dinners at the Chutney Kitchen. I had purposely designed a menu that I would be comfortable executing. So I put on my apron and went to work on dinner.

I was in the kitchen when Don opened the doors about seven and the first customers walked in. And, as I remember, there were no disasters. We had a full house and we knew everyone in the dining room, all of them past customers and old friends. I prepared only one appetizer that night, a pasta with clam sauce, and the entrée was a blanquette de veau, served with fresh asparagus, and rice. This was followed by a simple green salad and cheese, and for dessert, I made a rhubarb mousse (recipe page 220), perfect for the season. It was a very, very happy time.

The pasta with clam sauce I cooked for that first night brought Bob Mondavi charging back into the kitchen nearly shouting, "Where did you ever learn to make real clam spaghetti like this? You're not Italian. This is just like my mother used to make!" That put the ultimate seal of approval on our project, leaving us to concentrate on simply doing a good job.

The blanquette de veau I fixed for the main course was a rather delicate preparation of braised veal and mushrooms, finished off with cream. To get good veal, though, I had to drive all the way down to Jacobi Meats, on Grant Avenue in North Beach. He was an Italian butcher who was also the oldest kosher butcher in San Francisco.

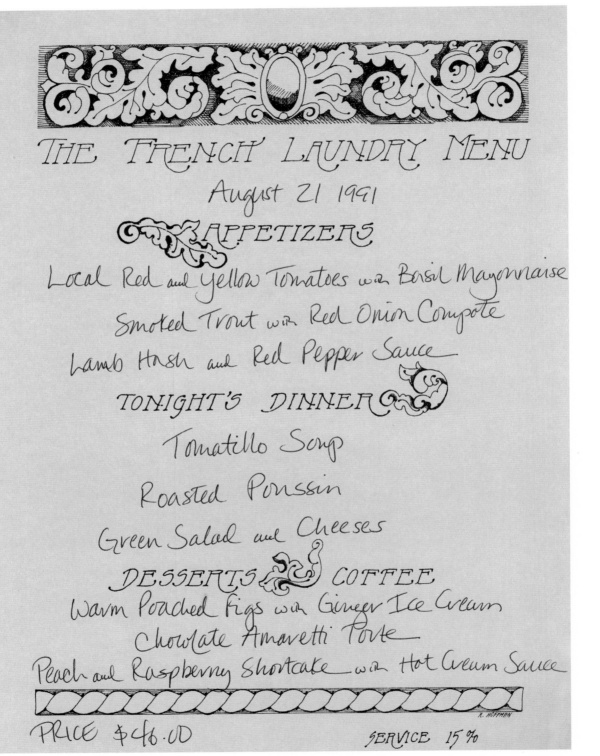

THE FRENCH LAUNDRY MENU
August 21 1991

APPETIZERS

Local Red and Yellow Tomatoes with Basil Mayonnaise

Smoked Trout with Red Onion Compote

Lamb Hash and Red Pepper Sauce

TONIGHT'S DINNER

Tomatillo Soup

Roasted Poussin

Green Salad and Cheeses

DESSERTS COFFEE

Warm Poached Figs with Ginger Ice Cream

Chocolate Amaretti Torte

Peach and Raspberry Shortcake with Hot Cream Sauce

PRICE $46.00   SERVICE 15%

Every Day a New Menu

When the tables were all set and I was putting the finishing touches on the food, our waitstaff—all two of them—would sit down at the kitchen table to write out the menus by hand. It was one of my favorite times of the day. We got to chat, talk about the food, and when there was something new, I could tell them about it and give them a taste. This helped them become familiar with the fare, since it changed often. We did this at the last minute, because it gave me the option to rethink the details and make any changes I wanted on that night's menu.

I planned the menus at the beginning of each week and discussed them with Don in the morning, while he was sitting at home having his coffee. I would say, "Oh, how about lamb shanks this week?" Or, he would say to me, "How about doing your roast veal this Friday?" He was a wonderful support and kept feeding me ideas that were a real help to me. So by the time I got to the restaurant kitchen, I would have the evening's menu mostly planned, save for the final garnishes, swirls, or dollops.

A big issue about serving a set menu is to make sure you have a contrast of color, texture, and flavor. I love serving a simple soup between a more complex appetizer and a hearty main course, which I might follow with a very simple salad and cheese. Although the items on the menu varied, the format remained the same throughout our sixteen years. Each menu, handwritten and dated, offered a choice of three appetizers, a soup, the main course, salad and cheeses, and a selection of desserts.

opposite: My daughter Kathy designed the template for the nightly menu. The illustration depicts the carved wood fireplace mantel in the dining room.

First Courses

I think this was my favorite course to prepare at the French Laundry. My feeling was that it should set the tone for the whole evening, yet give me room in the kitchen to experiment, to try new things out, rather than sticking with my tried-and-true standbys.

Serving only one main course each evening to the fifty or sixty people who came to dine was teetering on a fine edge, so I didn't dare take chances on producing anything I wasn't absolutely sure of. But with the first course, I had room to experiment. And when it worked out well, I could add it to my repertoire of entrées. I have always been very concerned with balancing not only flavors, but textures and colors. The first course often could be more complex because it was always followed by a simple soup course.

Fish was always one of the three appetizers that we offered, so that I could substitute it, in a larger portion, for a guest who could not, or would not, eat the main course. And for the same reason, I would have a vegetarian appetizer that I could expand into a main course. The third appetizer was a product of my imagination and what was fresh at the market or leftover in the pantry.

Asparagus with Sesame Mayonnaise

SERVES 4 AS AN APPETIZER / TOTAL TIME: 30 MIN

Spring is the time for asparagus, when something green is most welcome. There was a time when the thinnest spears were popular, but I have always thought the fatter, the better. I never peel them because I don't think it improves the flavor much, and I love to see the pattern of the scale leaves on the skins of unpeeled spears.

Bring a large pot of salted water to a boil.

Break or cut the tough ends off: **1 bunch asparagus**

This is the way I cooked asparagus for years. An alternative method I do these days is to simply brush them with olive oil, sprinkle them with salt, and grill them over a hot fire, or briefly roast them in a hot oven until they're tender, but still crisp. Any of these methods work well.

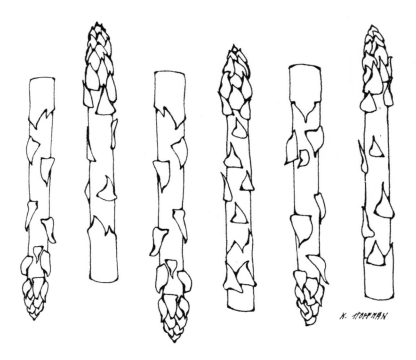

When the water comes to a full boil, drop in a batch of the asparagus and cook until crisp-tender, 2 or 3 minutes (depending on their thickness). Take one out and bite into it near the bottom of the stalk to test for doneness.

When they are ready, drain and plunge the spears into a bowl of ice water. Remove after about 1 minute and spread out on a kitchen towel to cool completely.

Repeat with the rest of the asparagus.

SESAME MAYONNAISE

To make the sesame mayonnaise, in a small bowl, whisk until smooth:

1 cup Best Foods/Hellman's mayonnaise

Stir in:

1 Tbsp toasted sesame oil

To serve, divide the asparagus among four plates. Top with a spoonful of the mayonnaise and sprinkle each serving generously with toasted sesame seeds.

Crispy Quail on Soft Polenta

SERVES 4 AS APPETIZER OR 2 AS AN ENTRÉE / TOTAL TIME: 1 HOUR

I was only able to serve quail for a short time at the French Laundry. My source for them was a man who was an hour's drive east of us, in the small town of Dixon. His mother had come to one of my cooking classes and told me about his raising quail, and she gave me his phone number. This started a series of forgotten orders and missed deliveries, but when they finally arrived, they were very good.

I remember standing at my stove, pondering how to prepare them for that night's menu, when my son-in-law Bill Hoffman, who had dropped by, made a suggestion. "You know, what my grandma always did with quail was throw them in a pot of olive oil. She'd take them out when they were brown, really brown, and they were always perfect." That evening I tried cooking them like Bill's grandmother, and they were wonderful. Unfortunately I couldn't rely on the quail man, so sadly, we could only serve them occasionally.

Cook the:

Soft Polenta (recipe follows)

Meanwhile, in a deep medium saucepan over medium heat, heat:

2 cups [480 ml] olive oil
4 shallots, halved lengthwise if large
2 sprigs fresh rosemary

To test whether the olive oil is hot enough, throw in a little piece of bread. If it browns quickly, the oil is ready.

While the olive oil is heating, pat dry:

4 whole bone-in quail

Sprinkle lightly inside and out with:

Salt and freshly ground toasted black pepper

When the shallots are browned, in about 5 minutes, remove them from the pan. Discard the crisped rosemary.

When the shallots are cool enough to handle, stuff each quail with a shallot and:

A fresh sprig of rosemary

Add the quails to the pan and cook until deep brown on both sides, turning a few times, for a total of 10 to 15 minutes. You may have to turn the heat down to keep the oil from burning.

If you're careful not to burn your oil, you can use it for something else. It will have a nice, lingering hint of rosemary.

Recipe continues…

Serve the quail in shallow soup bowls on a bed of soft polenta, one quail as a first course, two for a main dish. Garnish with:

Sprigs of rosemary

If you're not ready to serve the quail, keep them warm in a low oven.

SOFT POLENTA

In a medium pot, bring to a boil:

5 cups [1.2 L] water
1 Tbsp salt

While whisking, gradually pour in:

1 cup [140 g] polenta

Lower the heat to medium and cook, whisking, until thick and creamy, about 5 minutes.

Adjust the heat so it's very low, cover the pot, and cook for another 15 minutes to develop the flavor, whisking occasionally to even out the texture.

Even longer cooking develops the corn flavor and texture of the polenta. Don't be afraid to continue cooking, adding water to keep the consistency loose. To keep it from stiffening up when it's finished, keep the lid on tight.

When it is done, stir in:

¼ cup [8 g] grated Parmesan cheese
3 Tbsp butter

Taste for salt; it always seems to need a little more.

Bay Shrimp & Celery with Avocado

SERVES 4 TO 6 / TOTAL TIME: 30 MIN

I would often serve this as an appetizer around the holiday season, because it made a crispy, cool, and refreshing contrast with the rich food that followed.

In a large bowl, toss together:

1 lb [455 g] cooked small bay shrimp
1½ cups [180 g] thinly sliced celery
1 large onion, finely diced and rinsed with ¼ cup white vinegar (see Sally's Basics, page 16)
1 cup [40 g] coarsely chopped fresh parsley

I like to cut celery on a sharp diagonal. It's prettier, and I know I won't need to string it.

In a small bowl, whisk together:

Zest and juice of 2 lemons (about ½ cup [120 ml])
½ cup [120 ml] your best olive oil
Salt and coarsely ground black pepper

Add the vinaigrette to the shrimp and toss. If not serving immediately, refrigerate the salad for up to 24 hours.

To serve, on each plate make a bed of:

Red mustard greens, arugula, or large butter lettuce leaves

Serve in or on:

½ avocado, peeled (or peeled, sliced, and fanned)

Spoon the shrimp mixture into the cavity of the avocado half or onto the slices. Don would always remind me to top this with a dollop of:

Green Mayonnaise (page 79), made with fresh parsley or dill

Garnish with:

Sprigs of parsley

I used to buy little bay shrimp from my seafood vendor in Napa. In the old days, these shrimp were so plentiful in the San Francisco Bay, but sad to say, no longer. Now, when I go shopping I ask for them frozen so I can keep them in the freezer and use them whenever I want. They come shelled and cooked. But remember, those lovely shrimp that you see spread out in the fish display have often been frozen and then thawed. So if you purchase those, use them right away.

Butter Lettuce Salad with Cumin, Oregano & Orange

SERVES 4 TO 6 / TOTAL TIME: 30 MIN EXCLUDING WASHING THE LETTUCE

This is a lovely salad to serve as a first course or a light lunch. Make it only when you can get really good butter lettuce. (The two main types are Bibb and Boston.)

Ahead of time, wash and crisp the prettiest leaves of:

1 or 2 heads butter lettuce

I like to keep the smaller leaves whole, and tear the larger ones into big pieces.

When you are ready to make your salad, transfer the lettuce to a large bowl.

In a small bowl, whisk together:

⅔ cup [160 ml] good olive oil
3 Tbsp cider vinegar
Zest of 1 orange
1 Tbsp chopped fresh oregano
½ tsp cumin seeds, toasted and crushed (page 16)
Salt and freshly ground black pepper

Add enough dressing to the lettuce to coat the leaves and toss well. Taste for salt and add more if needed.

To serve, plate the lettuce, making sure, as you remove the leaves from the bowl, that they're not overdressed. It's easy to overdress butter lettuce; after you remove all the leaves, there should be a pool of dressing left in the bowl.

Remove the peel and pith of:

1 or 2 oranges, so that you have four to six segments per serving

Separate into segments and divide evenly among the salads.

Sprinkle each salad generously with:

Toasted pumpkin seeds
Big crumbles of fresh goat cheese

opposite: Me next to my favorite big salad bowl that we kept in the refrigerator filled with lettuce ready for evening service.

If the lettuce is at its prime, you may only need 1 head. If not, grab 2 so that you can pick out the most beautiful leaves.

I don't use a lettuce spinner. I like to cut and core my heads of lettuce, letting them soak a few minutes in cold water. I then shake the leaves, drain them, wrap them in a kitchen towel, and put them in a large plastic bag. This is best done several hours in advance of your meal, but the leaves will keep beautifully for several days.

We were fortunate to have Laura Chenel in Sebastopol, not too far from Yountville. She had learned the craft of cheesemaking in France, and about a year after we opened the French Laundry, she started producing a French-style chèvre that we loved to use. These days, though, we raise our own goats at the Apple Farm, and therefore we have goat cheese, which we call farmhouse cheese instead of chèvre.

Scallops in Tequila Lime Cream with Cilantro Gremolata

SERVES 4 TO 6 / TOTAL TIME: 40 MIN

In a lovely restaurant in Oaxaca, Mexico, Don and I enjoyed fish fillets napped with a cream sauce flavored with tequila and lime. I was smitten, and when we came home, I adapted the combination for a first course at the French Laundry. We used scallops instead of the fish fillet, and served them in large shells on a bed of cilantro.

First, make the gremolata (recipe in margin) and set aside.

Heat a large heavy skillet or a nonstick skillet over medium-high heat and add:

3 Tbsp olive oil or clarified butter

When the oil is very hot but not smoking, quickly cook in batches, to avoid crowding the pan:

1 ½ to 2 lb [680 to 910 g] medium scallops, depending on their size

Brown the scallops on one side, 10 seconds. Turn just once, and brown the second side, another 10 seconds. It is important not to overcook the scallops; they should be just barely firmed up. Remove from the pan, transfer to a plate, and cover loosely with foil to keep warm.

Turn down the heat to low and add to the pan:

2 Tbsp butter
2 Tbsp minced shallot

Cook the shallots in the butter until softened then add:

1 cup [240 ml] heavy cream

Let the sauce come to a boil, lower the heat, and simmer until it thickens, about 3 to 5 minutes, then add:

¼ cup [60 ml] fresh lime juice
¼ cup [60 ml] tequila
A sprinkle of salt

Taste for seasoning. There should be a rather delicate balance of flavors. Simmer until slightly thickened, about 3 minutes.

Divide the scallops among large shells or small plates and nap with the sauce. Sprinkle with the gremolata, and serve with a lime wedge.

Large scallop shells are inexpensive and very handy. We use them not just for this dish but also to pass around small servings of ceviche and other finger foods that need a little place to rest.

To make the gremolata, toss together:
3 Tbsp chopped fresh cilantro
2 garlic cloves, minced
Zest of 2 limes

It is nice to have 3 to 4 scallops per person. Very large ones can be cut down to size if necessary.

VARIATIONS: Of course, this could be a main dish. And instead of scallops, you could substitute a fillet of rockfish, black cod, or sole, and serve it with some tiny new potatoes and a few greens on the side.

When we were working on renovating the French Laundry, a local townsman presented us with this beautiful carved lintel from a historic Napa Valley home that had been torn down—we used it for our mantel in the downstairs dining room. The carved design on the mantel was adapted by our daughter Kathy for the menu (see page 156). Kathy also was in charge of filling the restaurant with flower arrangements, all gathered from our own garden. Beyond the dining room is the wine counter where Don greeted customers.

Warm Salad of Sweetbreads & Mushrooms

SERVES 6 / TOTAL TIME: 1 HOUR

Sweetbreads are one of the few organ meats I use. Years ago, while traveling in France, Don and I stopped to enjoy a meal at a Michelin-starred restaurant that had been highly recommended by our friend Chuck Carpy, of Freemark Abbey Winery. It was a lovely restaurant in the countryside, along the Rhône River, and it was a wonderful meal (even though there was only one bottle of wine on their list under a hundred dollars). At the table next to ours, I couldn't help but notice a delectable looking sweetbread salad being served, and I wished I had ordered it myself. So I came home determined to create a version of what I had seen, but hadn't tasted. I used lemon to counter the blandness of the sweetbreads and added bacon to provide richness.

Preheat the oven to 350°F [180°C].

Have a large bowl of ice water ready.

Bring a large pot of water to a boil and add:

1 lb [455 g] sweetbreads

Cook them in the boiling water for about 10 minutes, then plunge them into the ice water to cool. Pat dry and, using your fingers, or the tip of a paring knife, if necessary, remove the connecting tissue. You will end up with small nuggets, called lobes. If the lobes are large, cut them into bite-size pieces. Refrigerate if you're not ready to continue cooking them.

In a large skillet over low heat, cook until crispy:

3 slices bacon, thinly sliced crosswise

Remove the bacon and set aside. Pour off the bacon fat and set aside.

In the same pan, over medium heat, melt:

2 Tbsp butter

Add:

6 green onions (white and light green parts), cut lengthwise into shreds, then crosswise into 2 in [5 cm] lengths

Sauté for 1 or 2 minutes, remove from the pan, and transfer to a large bowl. Set aside. Return the reserved bacon fat to the pan, heat over medium heat, and add the sweetbreads. Sauté until lightly browned, about 5 minutes.

Transfer to the bowl with the sautéed green onions.

Add and toss:	**Zest and juice of 1 lemon** **¼ cup [10 g] chopped fresh parsley** **¼ cup [10 g] chopped fresh thyme**
Add, taste, and toss again with:	**Freshly ground black pepper** **Salt**
With a small, dry brush, clean:	**6 large cremini mushroom caps, stems removed**
Brush with:	**3 Tbsp melted butter or olive oil**

Transfer to a baking sheet and roast in the oven just until the juices start running, 5 to 10 minutes.

To serve, on each plate make a bed of:	**Arugula, watercress, or another green with an aggressive flavor**

Place a mushroom cap on the greens, and then spoon the sweetbread mixture into the mushroom cap.

Top with the reserved crispy bacon pieces and:	**Lemon zest**

Lamb Hash with Red Pepper Sauce

SERVES 4 TO 6 / TOTAL TIME: 1 HOUR

This was one of my favorite starters at the French Laundry. With an egg on top, a generous dollop of sour cream, and red pepper sauce, it can also make a very satisfying brunch or easy supper at home, especially with a green salad on the side.

Prepare and set aside:

Red Pepper Sauce (recipe follows)

In a large, heavy-bottomed skillet, preferably cast iron, over medium heat, warm:

3 Tbsp olive oil, bacon fat, duck fat, or lard

Sauté:

2 large onions, minced

When the onions are softened, add:

2 large potatoes, peeled and finely chopped (any kind will work)
Salt and coarsely ground black pepper

Sauté until the potatoes are partially cooked, about 15 minutes. Add:

2 cups [300 g] cooked lamb, finely chopped

Stir to distribute evenly, adjust the heat to low, and cook, without stirring, so a crust forms on the bottom of the pan, about 5 to 10 minutes. Remove from the heat, cover the pan, and let stand for 10 to 15 minutes to soften the crust on the bottom of the pan. Stir the crust into the hash, return to the heat, and repeat the process once more.

To serve, spoon 2 or 3 Tbsp of the red pepper sauce onto each plate, making a circle. Place a generous serving of hot hash in the middle of the plate and top with:

A spoonful of sour cream

On top of it all, place:

1 softly fried or poached egg

Use the trimmings and any leftover slices from a leg or shoulder roast. At the French Laundry, I always had the well-done end pieces left over from when we offered Roast Leg of Lamb (page 142). Since I preferred to serve the lamb rare, I would start carving the leg from the middle, working my way toward the well-done ends, until I ran out of perfect slices. So I always had end pieces left over, perfect for this lamb hash.

You can also cook the egg in a pool of sauce right in the pan with the hash (see page 174).

RED PEPPER SAUCE

Char until blackened all over: 6 red bell peppers

Remove the skins and seeds (see Margin Note, page 79), coarsely chop the
peppers, and transfer to a large bowl.

In a small bowl, mix together: 2 Tbsp fresh lemon juice; or
2 Tbsp chopped preserved
lemons, homemade (page 251)
or store bought; or very thin
slices lemon with the rind left on
2 Tbsp olive oil
Salt and coarsely ground
black pepper

Add the dressing to the peppers, toss, and set aside at room temperature
until you're ready to make the sauce. The peppers will keep, covered, in the
refrigerator for 1 week.

In a sauté pan over medium   1 Tbsp olive oil
heat, warm:

Sauté until soft: 1 small onion, slivered
2 garlic cloves, chopped

Drain the prepared red bell   1 cup [240 ml] chicken stock
peppers and add along with: 1 small dried hot red pepper,
minced
Salt and coarsely ground
black pepper

Stir together and simmer for 5 to 10 minutes. Let cool a little, transfer to a
blender or food processor, and in batches if necessary, purée until smooth.

If needed, thin with: A little more stock

Once we discovered this
lovely sauce, we called it
"gourmet ketchup." It had
such flavor and color, I loved
to use it on everything from
the lamb hash to swirling it in
Eggplant Soup (page 101).

The dressed roasted peppers
can be used:

- On a salad

- As a side dish alongside a
  meaty main course, such
  as a Roast Leg of Lamb
  (page 142)

- To top off a bowl of soup

- To add to an omelet or
  serve alongside a fried egg

- To make a stunning splash
  of color and flavor, with a
  dollop with sour cream

Taste for seasoning. It should
have a little zing. The sauce
will keep, covered, in the
refrigerator for 1 week.

It was Don who one day suggested adding the lamb hash to our starter list. When I first tried it out, I was nervous, thinking that it would be too heavy and only men with hearty appetites would go for it. But Don was out in the dining room, opening wine and talking with the guests. He soon realized it wasn't just the men ordering the lamb hash—dainty little ladies were ordering it and finishing every last bite. It was the one appetizer we would often run out of before the evening was over.

Toast Rounds

MAKES ABOUT 24 TOAST ROUNDS / PREP: 15 MIN / COOK: 20 TO 25 MIN

We didn't offer bread and butter at the French Laundry. Since we were serving a five-course meal, I figured, from my own experience, that if a basket of bread was brought to the table, and our guests were hungry, they would happily fill up on it. I wanted people to be hungry for each course.

Still, we had a daily delivery of baguettes into our kitchen. We'd stash them in a basket in the corner, and just let them sit. The next day, they'd slice easily, and we'd cut them quite thin, brush them with a little salted butter, and toast two big trays of them for dinner. These were our toast rounds. They were the basis for many of the appetizers we served, including Chicken and Oysters in Lemon Cream (page 120) and Sautéed Chanterelles (page 178). And we put a basket of them alongside the cheese we served with our salad course.

Each morning, Carl Sciambra from the Sciambra-Passini French Bakery, in Napa, would deliver our order of baguettes. We adored him. He was very cute, and he'd come bustling in through our kitchen door to fill our big basket in the corner with the baguettes. A short, square man, he arrived with sweat dripping from his brow, since he delivered the bread himself after staying up all night baking and loading his van. He made the most wonderful baguettes. Carl confided to me once that he only got about three hours of sleep a night, and that was all he needed. In later years, sadly, he became allergic to flour and had to get out of the bakery.

It's a good idea to make a large batch of these because they complement so many dishes. Use them as a base for cheeses, pâté, and other spreadables.

Preheat the oven to 300°F [150°C].

| Thinly slice: | **1 day-old baguette** |

| Spread out in a single layer on a baking sheet and brush very lightly with: | **¼ cup [60 ml] melted butter or olive oil** |

Bake in the oven until crisp and golden brown, and start checking after 15 minutes. When they start to brown, they go fast.

The rounds will keep for up to 1 week, tightly sealed, in a cool, dry location.

opposite: Seen through the blue kitchen door, my grandchild Sophia standing on a stool in order to paint the toast rounds with melted butter. She is wearing a mini version of the white embroidered bib apron our waitresses wore for evening service.

It's strange, but true, that something as simple as toast rounds played a big role in my cooking career. I didn't discover them until I was at the Chutney Kitchen, planning menus and working with what I could find locally. I didn't use them much initially, but gradually their allure grew. By the time I was behind the stove at the French Laundry, they were an absolute staple.

Sautéed Chanterelles

SERVES 6 TO 8 / TOTAL TIME: 40 MIN

When I'm lucky enough to get some really good fresh (and fragrant) chanterelles, I like to enjoy them as simply as possible and let these gems shine. I usually don't mix them with other mushrooms, as each one has a distinct flavor.

With a small, dry brush, clean: **1 lb [455 g] chanterelles**

Pull the chanterelles apart lengthwise, starting from the top or base, whichever is thicker. They're like a fabric and tear beautifully into shreds, which look more natural than when cut with a knife.

Heat a large skillet over low heat with: **3 Tbsp butter or ¼ cup [60 ml] olive oil**

Add: **1 large shallot, minced**

Sauté until tender. Add the chanterelles and sauté until they begin to give off juices and are lightly browned, about 15 to 20 minutes. If they were harvested during a rain, which happens, they may have a lot of liquid to cook down.

Stir in:
1 cup [240 ml] chardonnay
2 Tbsp chopped fresh thyme
2 Tbsp chopped fresh parsley

Season generously with: **Salt and freshly ground toasted black pepper**

Cook down at a simmer, stirring or shaking the pan until the liquid has somewhat reduced and thickened, but not dried out, about 5 minutes.

Taste for seasoning, and add more salt and pepper, if needed. To sharpen the flavor, add: **A squeeze of lemon juice**

To serve, on each plate, put:
A small handful of greens
2 to 3 toast rounds (page 176)

Spoon the chanterelles over it all.

If there is still debris stuck to the chanterelles, it won't hurt if you give them a quick rinse of running water and pat dry. But don't do this ahead of time. Trim the stems a little if necessary.

Uncork a good bottle and sip what's left.

Red Pepper Tapenade

MAKES ABOUT 2 CUPS [480 ML] / TOTAL TIME: 40 MIN

This should be quite powerful, but not too salty. Play around with it to come up with your own version. Classic recipes usually contain anchovies, but I love it without. Serve the tapenade as an appetizer on toast rounds, or alongside a main course of roasted lamb or chicken.

Char until blackened all over and remove skins and seeds (see Margin Note, page 79):

2 large red bell peppers

Cut into strips, and set aside.

In a medium skillet over low heat, warm:

1 Tbsp olive oil

Sauté until soft:

2 garlic cloves, minced

Add the peppers and cook for 1 minute more. Add:

1 tomato, peeled, seeded, and chopped
6 olives, preferably the large green Italian ones called Cerignolas, pitted and chopped
2 Tbsp capers, rinsed and left whole
1 Tbsp minced fresh thyme, oregano, or rosemary

Cook until blended and the flavors meld together, about 5 minutes. Taste and season with:

Salt and a generous amount of coarsely ground black pepper

Let cool. The tapenade will keep, covered, in the refrigerator for a few days. Eat on toast rounds or spoon alongside roast beef or as part of a cheese board.

Duck Liver Pâté with Rosemary & Orange

SERVES A PARTY OF 8 TO 12 / TOTAL TIME: 1 HOUR EXCLUDING CHILLING TIME

At first, I made pâté with chicken livers, garden herbs, and brown mushrooms. But when duck livers became available through Jim Reichardt's Liberty Ducks (see page 201), I used those instead. And I added rosemary, orange, and shiitake mushrooms for a twist on more traditional duck liver pâté. But the real trick, I found, was to use lots of butter. It adds a richness to the pâté and softens the strong liver flavor. Smeared on crispy Toast Rounds (page 176), it is delightfully rich, creamy, and unctuous.

For large groups, and later for parties at the Apple Farm, this would last the whole length of the party, with guests coming back to help themselves until the very end. I have always felt it was the backbone of our large parties.

In a large sauté pan over medium heat, melt:	½ cup [110 g] butter
Sauté:	¼ cup [40 g] shallots, minced ¼ cup [15 g] fresh shiitake mushrooms, minced
When the shallots are softened and the mushrooms have wilted, about 5 minutes, add:	1 lb [455 g] duck livers, cut into 1 in [2.5 cm] pieces, with the connecting tissue and the little bits of blood removed

Sauté the livers, shaking the pan, until they are cooked through but still a little pink, about 5 minutes. To check, cut into one of the larger pieces. It should be firmed up but a little pink in the center. If still too raw, cook another 2 to 5 minutes. Be careful not to overcook. The flavor will be so much better.

Add:	¼ cup [60 ml] Madeira or sherry A generous sprinkle of coarsely ground black pepper

Remove from the heat and stir in:

1 cup [220 g] butter, at room temperature, cut into pieces
¼ cup [10 g] minced fresh parsley
Zest of 1 orange, minced
2 Tbsp finely chopped fresh rosemary

Let cool a little without stirring. You want the butter softened, but not melted. Process the mixture in a blender or food processer in small batches to get the pâté really smooth. You may have to repeat in order to get a velvety texture.

Check for salt and stir in if necessary.

Line a terrine with a large sheet of plastic wrap so you have long ends overhanging the terrine, and pour in the pâté. Fold the ends over the top of the dish to cover, and chill in the fridge to firm up, at least 4 hours or overnight.

When ready to serve, unfold the excess wrap and use it to help lift the pâté out of the pan. You may have to bang it a little to loosen it. Gently shape it into a log.

In a small bowl, toss together:

½ cup [20 g] minced fresh parsley
2 Tbsp finely chopped fresh rosemary
Zest of 1 orange

Scatter the mixture on a work surface and roll the pâté log in it, coating the outside.

I like to drape ribbons of orange zest over the top and place the log on a bed of rosemary. Serve it with the toast rounds.

For a simpler preparation, the pâté can always be spooned into ramekins with a sprinkle of the parsley, rosemary, and orange zest mixture on top.

One Nightly Entrée

Serving a single entrée each evening was both a challenge and a juggling act. By the time we opened the French Laundry, I had gained experience from our Friday night dinners at the Chutney Kitchen and had developed what I considered a tried-and-true repertoire. I wanted to satisfy the diverse crowd that kept us busy—our locals as well as the visitors. But planning the nightly menu depended a great deal on what was possible in my very small kitchen and, of course, on what was in season and available from local farmers.

During salmon season, we served fresh salmon. When I found a source for local rabbit, we served rabbit. We had a wonderful source for local chickens, and I could always fall back on those. Midwinter called for hearty stews and braises. We have dealt with the same butchers from the time we took over the café in 1967 to our present-day Apple Farm.

The one important requirement for main courses was that they complement our Napa Valley wines. So I avoided highly spiced dishes or ones with exotic flavors. It wasn't just that we had vintners and wine lovers coming in to dine. We felt that since we were in Napa Valley, we should be serving food to complement the wine of the region.

opposite: When a customer made a reservation, the table was theirs for the entire evening. Here, shown in the late afternoon sun, is a table ready to be set for service. For each table, our daughter Kathy made a bouquet from our garden.

Chicken Tarragon

SERVES 8 / TOTAL TIME: 1 HOUR

This beautiful chicken breast, with a white sour cream glaze and a tarragon sprig pressed into it, was always a crowd-pleaser. Among its fans were the members of the Napa Valley Wine Library Association. For several years, the association sponsored a series of lectures, field trips, and tastings (M. F. K. Fisher helped organize the lectures). The series was directed by my good friend, the letterpress printer Jim Beard, and was offered over the course of three weeks each summer. To keep the attendees from wandering off during lunch time, it was brought in for them. And I was the lucky one they chose to provide the meal.

It was a great experience to feed fifty wine lovers lunch on Saturday and Sunday, three weeks in a row. With the help of one assistant, I was able to pack everything up and make the trip up to the old schoolhouse in St. Helena. We served a cold soup in mugs, a buffet of chicken tarragon, and a green salad or sliced tomatoes, followed by fruit and cookies.

Preheat the oven to 300°F [150°C].

In a large skillet over low heat, warm:	**2 Tbsp olive oil** **2 Tbsp butter**
In batches, lightly sauté for 2 to 3 minutes per side, just so they firm up:	**8 boneless, skinless chicken breasts, about 2½ lb [1.2 kg]**
Transfer to a shallow roasting pan, smooth side up, and sprinkle with:	**1 Tbsp finely chopped fresh tarragon**
Pour into the skillet:	**½ cup [120 ml] white wine** **½ cup [120 ml] chicken stock**

Deglaze the pan off the heat, using a pastry brush to dissolve the bits and pieces on the bottom of the pan in the liquid. Return to low heat and stir until slightly thickened, about 5 minutes. Pour the pan juices around the chicken breasts.

Cover the chicken loosely with aluminum foil and bake until just barely firm to the touch, checking after 15 minutes by touching lightly. They should be firm, but not too hard. Pour off and strain the juices and set aside. Let the chicken breasts cool.

A memory from Dr. Joe Pramuk: For a June anniversary dinner date at the French Laundry, I arranged with Don if he would be complicit in a surprise gift plan. The anniversary gift was an Italian "Della Robbia" ceramic plaque, in the style favored by my bride (now of forty-seven years). Don was all over the idea and we hung it on a fence near a bench in the garden. At dinner that night, between courses I maneuvered us out to the garden to sit on the bench for a glass of bubbly. My wife, Julie, predictably commented on the "Della Robbia" hanging on the fence over my shoulder. "Exquisite, isn't it?" she observed. "Isn't it though," I replied, and as she watched, somewhat horrified, I stepped through the flower bed and took it down from the fence. I turned it over to reveal her name on the back of it. Marriage can sometimes be a lot of fouled pitches, but that one, for once, went out of the park. We were the last ones out of the restaurant that evening, and were walking through the otherwise empty parking lot to our car when we heard somewhat urgent footsteps on the gravel behind us. We turned, and it was Don. With a mock worried expression he said: " I hope you enjoyed dinner, but—this is somewhat awkward—one of our garden decorations seems to be missing." The charade, of course, didn't last but a moment, and we laughed as he put his arm around us and wished us a happy anniversary.

Pour into a 4 cup [960 ml] heatproof measuring cup:

¼ cup [60 ml] cold water

Sprinkle with:

2 Tbsp gelatin

Place the measuring cup in a pan of hot water to liquify further. Wait until it turns clear, 5 to 10 minutes. You may need to turn the heat on under the pan if it cools too much. Set aside. It can be reheated if it cools and starts to gel before you are ready for it.

Add enough of the reserved juices from the chicken to the gelatin mixture to make 1 cup [240 ml] of liquid. Then stir in:

2 cups [480 g] sour cream

Whisk the mixture until smooth. If it is too thick to pour well, thin it a little with a little water. Using a spoon, coat the tops of the chicken breasts generously with this mixture.

On each chicken breast, press in:

1 sprig tarragon

Refrigerate for 15 minutes to firm up the glaze, but not too long, as the texture and the flavor are better if not too cold.

Serve at room temperature, along with:

Sliced tomatoes from your summer garden

Roast Loin of Pork with Mustard Caper Sauce

SERVES 6 TO 8 / TOTAL TIME: 1½ HOURS

This is a way to add a little zip to a slice of pork loin. I make it all year round, because it isn't too heavy or too light. It's wonderful with braised bitter greens or a mound of arugula.

Preheat the oven to 325°F [165°C].

In a roasting pan, put:	**One 2 to 3 lb [910 g to 1.4 kg] boneless pork loin, tied**
Coat the loin with:	**2 to 3 Tbsp Dijon mustard** **Salt**

Ask your butcher to tie up the loin, or do it yourself. It firms up while cooking and makes pretty slices for serving.

Let sit at room temperature for about 1 hour. Roast until just done—a little pink in the middle is good—and a meat thermometer registers 140°F [60°C], 1 to 1½ hours depending on its size.

Let rest for at least 30 minutes. Remove roast to a clean tray. Drain off and strain all the juices from the roasting pan and set aside.

While the roast is resting, pour into the pan:	**1 cup [240 ml] chicken stock or wine**

Deglaze the pan, using a pastry brush to dissolve the bits and pieces on the bottom of the pan in the liquid. Add to the reserved juices and set aside.

In a medium saucepan over medium heat, melt:	**2 Tbsp butter**
Whisk in and cook, stirring, until lightly browned:	**2 Tbsp all-purpose flour**
Whisk until smooth and add:	**1 cup [240 ml] chicken stock** **1 cup [240 ml] half-and-half**
Whisk in the juices from the roasting pan, along with:	**¼ cup [30 g] capers, rinsed** **1 Tbsp Dijon mustard** **1 tsp freshly ground white pepper** **½ tsp of salt**

If not serving right away, cover and set aside. At serving time, reheat the sauce. Thin, if necessary, with stock or water, so it flows as you spoon it over the slices of pork.

To serve, remove the strings from the roast and slice medium-thin. The slices need not be perfect or whole. On each plate, overlap a few slices of pork, then spoon the sauce over the slices, but don't cover them completely.

Sprinkle with:

Mustard seeds or crisped capers

To crisp capers, warm a small sauté pan over low heat with 2 Tbsp butter or olive oil. Then add 3 Tbsp capers, drained and patted dry. Cook for a few minutes, just until they have expanded and opened up. Remove with a slotted spoon and allow to cool and drain on paper towels.

If you like, serve alongside each portion of pork:

**A spoonful of rice or couscous
A cooked green, such as broccoli rabe**

Braised Lamb on Saffron Couscous with Tomato Concassé

SERVES 6 / PREP TIME: 1 HOUR / COOK TIME: 2 HOURS

This recipe is a favorite of mine. I also enjoy it immensely made with eggplant (see page 192), which is slightly more complicated. Concassé is a French cooking term that means "crushed" or "ground," with tomato concassé being a good example.

Preheat the oven to 350°F [180°C].

In a large skillet over medium heat, warm:	**2 Tbsp olive oil**
Add:	**3 large lamb shanks**

Brown well, about 5 minutes per side.

Season with:	**Salt and coarsely ground black pepper**

Transfer the lamb to a Dutch oven.

Add to the skillet:	**1 large onion, thinly sliced** **6 garlic cloves, peeled but left whole** **1 cup [240 ml] chicken stock** **1 cup [240 ml] white wine** **1 lemon (rind included), diced** **2 Tbsp coarsely chopped fresh thyme** **A handful of thyme sprigs**
Season generously with:	**Salt and coarsely ground black pepper**

Bring to a boil, lower the heat, and simmer for about 5 minutes. Pour over the lamb.

Cover and braise the lamb in the oven for 1½ to 2 hours, until the lamb is tender and starts to pull away from the bone. Let rest for at least 15 minutes.

Pour off the juices into a large heatproof measuring cup and skim off the fat. Taste for seasoning, and add more salt and pepper, if needed.

When the lamb is cool enough to handle, tear it into large chunks. Transfer to a heatproof bowl, add the meat juices, and keep warm.

While the lamb is cooking, make the tomato concassé.

Have ready:	**A large bowl of ice water**
Bring a large potful of water to a boil. Add:	**6 large vine-ripened tomatoes**

Blanch for 30 seconds and transfer to the bowl of ice water. Leave for 2 or 3 minutes and remove. Peel off the skins, and halve the tomatoes through the equator. Place a strainer over a bowl and squeeze out the tomato seeds, reserving the juice for another use, such as a Bloody Mary.

Dice the tomatoes coarsely and season generously with:	**Salt and coarsely ground black pepper**

Set aside in a warm place until serving time to enhance their flavor.

For the couscous, in a small flat roasting pan, put:	**2 cups [280 g] couscous** **1 tsp salt**
In a small saucepan, bring to a boil:	**A large pinch of saffron threads** **2 Tbsp chopped orange zest** **3 Tbsp olive oil or butter** **1 cup [240 ml] water** **1 cup [240 ml] chicken stock**

Pour over the couscous, cover, and let stand for a maximum of 5 minutes. Fluff with a fork, scraping layer by layer to avoid clumps, and cover to keep warm until serving time. Fluff again if necessary.

To serve, spoon some couscous onto the center of each large dinner plate. Add several chunks of the lamb, and spoon the meat juices over it all. Top with a generous spoonful of the tomatoes.

Sprinkle generously with:	**Sprigs of fresh thyme leaves** **Coarsely chopped fresh parsley**

Braised Lamb & Eggplant on Saffron Couscous with Tomato Concassé

SERVES 6 TO 8 / PREP TIME: 1 HOUR / TOTAL TIME: 2 HOURS

This was one of Don's favorite dishes. He loved the complexity of the fancier preparation.

Prepare: **1 recipe Braised Lamb on Saffron Couscous with Tomato Concassé (page 190)**

While the lamb is cooking, cut 2 to 3 large eggplants lengthwise into 16 slices.

Brush the eggplant with: **About ⅓ cup [80 ml] olive oil**

Place on a large baking sheet in a single layer and sprinkle lightly with salt. Place in the oven to cook alongside the lamb. Check after 15 minutes. They are done if they are softened and beginning to brown. Make sure the slices are all completely cooked, as the flavor of the eggplant will be a little bitter if they are undercooked.

To serve, spoon some couscous onto each plate, and top with an eggplant slice. Spoon some of the lamb pieces over the eggplant.

Spoon a generous amount of the tomato concassé over all.

To gild the lily, add: **A dollop of sour cream**

Garnish with: **Fresh thyme leaves**
Coarsely chopped fresh parsley

This needs no side dish. It can hold its own and looks as wonderful as it tastes.

Roasted Rib Eye of Veal

SERVES 6 TO 8 / PREP TIME: 30 MIN / COOK TIME: 2 HOURS

Good veal is getting harder to find. It's not that I'm looking for milk-fed; it is the color, and especially the flavor, that I appreciate.

Preheat the oven to 350°F [180°C].

Place on a work surface:	**One 3 lb [1.4 kg] rib eye of veal, boned and tied**
Using a suribachi or mortar and pestle, crush:	**1 Tbsp toasted cumin seeds** **1 Tbsp toasted fennel seeds**
Add and pound to a paste:	**3 or 4 garlic cloves, finely diced**
Then add and work to emulsify:	**¼ cup [60 ml] olive oil** **2 Tbsp balsamic vinegar**

Rub the paste all over and under the veal roast. Let rest for 1 hour to bring it up to room temperature.

Place the meat in a roasting pan and roast until it is browned and registers 120° to 130°F [50° to 55°C], about 45 minutes to 1 hour.

Remove from the pan and let rest for at least 30 minutes.

Pour into the pan:	**¼ cup [60 ml] wine, red or white** **¼ cup [60 ml] chicken stock**

Using a pastry brush, dissolve the bits and pieces on the bottom of the pan in the liquid, then turn the heat to low and simmer until slightly thickened, about 5 minutes.

Remove the strings and slice the roast into nice thick slices. Place one slice on each dinner plate, and spoon some of the pan juices over the meat.

Serve with any or all of the following:	**Roasted red peppers (see Margin Note, page 79)** **Stuffed Mushrooms (page 47)** **Mashed potatoes**
Garnish with:	**Something green, such as cooked little green beans**

Veal is elusive in my mind. Culinary experts debate what real veal is—milk-fed or the veal used for scallopini, which you find on every traditional Italian restaurant menu? In the early years, to get the veal I wanted, I needed to drive from Yountville down to San Francisco's North Beach. In those days, North Beach was still steeped in its Italian heritage, and there was an old butcher shop that stocked excellent veal for the Italians in the neighborhood.

In later years, our Hagemann Meats sales-man introduced us to a boned-and-tied rib eye of veal. It was a very lovely piece of meat, which we roasted on the rare side. We presented one rather thick slice of it, drizzled with pan juices, and proudly served it on special occasions.

The trick is to get a hold of one. There are no standards set for veal. Baby calves are milk-fed, and then introduced to grain as they grow older. The veal I got through Hagemann, I called teenage veal, as it was in between; the flesh was finer than beef, and somewhat paler. But the difference was subtle.

Steak with Three Peppercorns

SERVES 4 TO 6 / TOTAL TIME: 1 HOUR

This is my variation of the French classic steak au poivre. I use three different peppercorns in it, which makes the flavor more complex and the sauce finger-licking good. Tom, our dishwasher at the French Laundry, was so fond of the dish that I often sent him home with some of the leftover sauce. The nights I cooked it, he almost didn't have to wash the pan when he was through sopping up every last bit of sauce. Choose the best top sirloin steak you can find for this dish.

Preheat the oven to 350°F [180°C].

In a small dish, make a paste from:	**¼ cup [50 g] green peppercorns, crushed with a fork (if using dried green peppercorns, soak in warm water for about 30 minutes first)** **1 cup [220 g] butter, at room temperature**
Set the paste aside. On a work surface, put:	**One 3 to 4 lb [1.4 to 1.8 kg] top sirloin steak, 1½ to 2 in [4 to 5 cm] thick**
Rub on both sides:	**Coarse salt and a generous sprinkle of coarsely ground toasted black pepper**

Heat a large heavy skillet over high heat until just short of smoking.

Add:	**2 Tbsp olive oil**

Do not use a nonstick pan for this recipe, because the browned bits that stick to the pan are very important to the flavor.

Sear the steak on both sides, just until nicely browned.

Transfer to a rimmed baking sheet and roast in the oven until just firmed up, checking after 10 minutes. A meat thermometer should register 120°F to 130°F [50°C to 55°C] for very rare (our preference) to just rare.

Spread the peppercorn paste generously on both sides of the steak and set aside to rest in a shallow dish to catch the juices.

Pour off any remaining fat from the skillet you used to sear the steak, leaving the browned bits.

Turn the heat to medium, and add a hearty splash of brandy, maybe a ¼ cup [60 ml]. Tilt the pan a little to ignite the brandy with the flame of the burner, or use a long match. Be careful: It really does flare up dramatically!

When the flames subside, add: **½ cup [120 ml] heavy cream**

Bring to a simmer and, using a pastry brush, scrape up all the browned goodies from the bottom of the pan. Cook until the sauce thickens a little, in 3 to 5 minutes.

When ready to serve, pour all the juices that have accumulated from under the steak into the sauce. Reheat and taste for salt. Strain if you want to; I usually don't. Slice diagonally and overlap the slices on each plate. Drizzle with a spoonful of sauce.

Sprinkle each serving with: **A pinch of pink peppercorns, crushed with your fingers**

Serve with: **A zippy green salad or sautéed spinach**

In through the Kitchen Door

I had many of our food sources nailed down before we opened the doors to the French Laundry, some of them a little unusual. Early on, in the summertime, this wonderful, vivacious Italian woman, Elly Fracchia, would drive up to the restaurant in her black sedan and open up the trunk, and there would be the most beautiful tomatoes, zucchini, and red onions. To this day I don't believe I've ever seen such gorgeous produce, either at the local farmers' markets or from the abundance of lovely things we grew in our own garden. She was an attractive woman—I won't say middle-aged, because that doesn't mean much to me anymore. I was just turning forty then, and she had a few years on me.

I don't recall the tomato variety she grew, but they were very large, deep-red globes with a deep flavor to match. Elly claimed the secret was to wait until the plants had fruit on them, and then stop the water. Her zucchini was equally good; it was the pale green, delicate, medium-sized variety. It doesn't travel well but has such great flavor. And her red onions were huge. They were so big that one slice would fill a salad plate. Other growers claimed their onions were very sweet, but hers really were! I'm not sure if her success came from her amazing soil or her amazing self, but I think it was a little of both.

I once had a wonderful source for poussin livers, which I would sauté with a little bacon and pan juices and serve with toast rounds. I can't include the recipe here, because the source doesn't exist anymore. We bought those glorious poussins and poussin livers from a local farmer. I don't know what he fed his chickens, but we hadn't seen livers like those before and haven't since. He went out of business, and nobody has ever reached those standards again.

I was lucky to get chanterelles from Karen Rector, who at one time worked as a waitress for me at the Chutney Kitchen. She lived up in St. Helena and walked a lot in the mornings. For two or three years, she would come across chanterelles in such abundance that she could hardly take a step without stomping on one. So she gathered baskets of them and came around to ask if we could use them. We jumped on them. The next year, the mushrooms were just as abundant. But after that, the supply dwindled.

Mostly, I just sautéed the chanterelles in a generous amount of butter, then splashed them with a little good chardonnay and maybe a little stock. I'd serve them over my crispy Toast Rounds (page 176), or polenta, with a smattering of herbs on top. It was very simple and straightforward, so that you really got the flavor of the chanterelles.

We were a few years into the French Laundry before I had a regular source for local produce. The farmers' market was held on Fridays in St. Helena, only a fifteen-minute drive away then, not the two hours it can take now with traffic congestion. It was just starting up, so there weren't all that many farmers selling, but it was exciting to be able to reach out and get those fruits and vegetables from the people who actually grew them. It was lovely, but I had to get there early, as the market lasted only until noon.

But then, in 1982, Frank Messmer, working with Forni-Brown-Welsh Gardens in Calistoga, started up Frank's Fresh Foods. He specialized in delivering local produce, picking it up where it was grown. He or his wife would do the delivery. He was great fun, a real character, and he used to hang out at one of the local bars when he was finished with his rounds. I learned a lot from him through the years. Eventually, as more and more restaurants turned to him, it got so his van wouldn't hold all the daily produce he had to deliver. Since he didn't want to get a bigger truck, he started cutting back on his offerings and specialized in smaller items, like foie gras.

When Karen walked in with her baskets filled with chanterelles, the smell was absolutely wonderful. I'd never smelled chanterelles with such a lovely, strong scent before. To this day, when I run across what look like chanterelles, the first thing I do is sniff them. If they don't smell like chanterelles, I pass them up.

Though I didn't serve it often as a main course, good seafood was really important to me. If I wanted to serve it, I nailed it down early in the day. I would call Osprey Seafood, in Napa, before I even got out of bed to find out what the morning's catch had brought in. If I was lucky and they had fresh bay shrimp or rock shrimp, I would do something special with them for an appetizer. The main course for each evening I planned ahead of time, but the appetizers I could play around with, depending on what turned up or walked in through the kitchen door.

This view of the herb garden and back of the restaurant was hand drawn by our daughter Kathy. We had it printed, and each table received their handwritten bill on this lovely card.

My Love Affair with Duck

Duck is my favorite meat. I started cooking it at the Chutney Kitchen, and in those early years, I could only get frozen duck from somewhere in the Midwest. I would have to take them out the night before to thaw them so I could bone them in the morning. And since I usually cooked legs rather than breasts, I would end up with a bunch of leftover breasts in the freezer. Bruce LeFavour, that extraordinary chef who ran Rose et LeFavour, over in St. Helena, preferred the breasts. So we would trade my leftover duck breasts for his legs.

Then I heard about Liberty Ducks, which Jim Reichardt was starting up in the Sonoma Valley. Even though it was a new business, Jim was a fourth-generation duck grower. His family ran, and still runs, the Reichardt Duck Farm in Petaluma, where they raise Pekin ducks.

But Jim wanted to strike out on his own, thus the name Liberty. He chose to raise a leaner and meatier strain of Pekin duck, which came out of Denmark. In addition, he refused to use antibiotics or hormones and he didn't cage his ducks. He let them roam freely outdoors, feeding them corn and other grains. It made a difference. Their meat had a better texture, was more tender, and was definitely tastier.

And Jim was willing to sell pieces and parts. Hallelujah! I could buy great legs, breasts, livers, and duck fat in separate packages. Oh joy, because I could cook my legs several different ways on different nights. I had only one way that I liked to present the breasts, which was to panfry them and fan out the rare slices over bitter greens or cabbage, with something a little sweet to add contrast, such as sautéed apples (see pages 204 and 290).

The livers we made into my favorite presentation for big parties, Duck Liver Pâté with Rosemary & Orange (page 180). In later years, I learned to make a confit, gently poaching the legs in large quantities of duck fat. But I gave that up because I decided that cooking the legs my way was just as good and quicker, and much less extravagant than using all that duck fat.

When it was just Don and me and I was cooking mostly for two, I was buying whole ducks again, still from Jim at my beloved Liberty Ducks. I enjoyed boning out just one duck, as opposed to the fifteen to twenty I used to do for the restaurant. I'd cook a duck leg for dinner one night, or two legs so I'd have enough left over to garnish a salad the next day or use for tacos. The breast I'd put in the freezer and save for a special occasion. The trimmings produced a little jar of duck fat and enough cracklings to garnish a salad or soup. The bonus, which I value most highly, was the large pot of stock I could make from the bones.

opposite: Portuguese Duck and Sausage in Rice (page 202)

HOW TO BONE A DUCK: Boning a duck is just as easy as boning a chicken, and you do it almost the same way. The plan is to end up with two whole bone-in leg-and-thigh pieces, and two boneless breast halves, all with skins attached. I use the tip of my santoku knife, which is always sharp, but a boning knife works just as well.

1. With the breast side up, remove the wings and save them for the stockpot.

2. Carefully find the joint between the thigh and the carcass and cut around it, breaking it loose as you go. Don't separate the legs from the thighs. Do not skin.

3. Still with the breast side up, locate the tip of the breast bone, and with the tip of your knife, remove one breast as cleanly as possible.

4. Repeat with the other breast piece. Do not skin, but trim some of the excess fat. Save all the remnants, bones, fat, and trimmings for the stockpot.

Portuguese Duck and Sausage in Rice

SERVES 6 / TOTAL TIME: 2½ HOURS

There's nothing about the ingredients here that are Portuguese, but the idea for this recipe came from the Portuguese *arroz de pato*, a traditional dish of duck and rice from southern Portugal cooked in a clay pot with chouriço, the Portuguese version of chorizo. The clay pot not only looks great but contributes to the flavor of the food you're cooking. Paula Wolfert, whose collection of unglazed earthenware numbers in the hundreds, has said that if she only had one dish to cook in, it would be a clay pot.

In Oaxaca, I was touched by the heartfelt openness of the wonderful chef Abigail Mendoza, who lived in a simple adobe hut with a roll-up metal door. She prepares her native Zapotec food at Tlamanalli, her restaurant in Teotitlán del Valle. In her home, I watched her put a really big cazuela (a Mexican earthenware cooking dish) right on the open gas fire. I was terrified it would break. Later, when I looked at the beautiful cazuelas in the Oaxaca marketplace, they were so plentiful and inexpensive, I realized that if it did break, she could afford to replace it easily. Since then, I've been adding to my own collection. They are as lovely as they are useful.

Preheat the oven to 400°F [200°C].

In a medium saucepan, bring to a boil:	**6 cups [1.4 L] chicken stock**
Lower the heat and keep the stock hot. On a work surface, place:	**6 duck legs, with thighs attached, trimmed of any excess skin and fat, at room temperature**
Season with:	**Salt and freshly ground black pepper**

Transfer to a roasting pan and cook the ducks in the oven until deeply browned, about 45 minutes. Turn off the oven.

Pour off the excess fat, setting aside 3 Tbsp for this dish, and saving the rest to make the cracklings (see Margin Note). Return the duck legs to the oven to rest while you proceed with the recipe.

In a large skillet over medium heat, warm the 3 Tbsp of reserved duck fat.

Add:	**2 large onions, sliced lengthwise** **3 garlic cloves, sliced**

Good chicken or duck stock is really important for flavor in this recipe.

TO MAKE CRACKLINGS: Cut the reserved trimmings of skin and fat into ½ in [12 mm] dice. Warm reserved duck fat in a small saucepan over medium heat. Add the trimmings, turn the heat to low, and cook the diced trimmings until they render their fat and are nicely browned. It will probably take about 10 minutes. Remove with a slotted spoon and salt immediately. Keep warm or rewarm in oven when ready to use. These also make a delicious snack for a hungry cook or helper.

| Sauté until softened and season well with: | **Salt and freshly ground black pepper** |

Transfer the onion and garlic mixture to another large roasting pan, a casserole dish, or, best choice, an earthenware cazuela.

| In the skillet, gently sauté until browned: | **2 andouille sausages, sliced into coins** |

Discard the fat, and transfer the sausage to the roasting pan with the onions.

Add a little of the hot chicken stock to the skillet, heat turned off, and use a pastry brush to dissolve the bits and pieces on the bottom in the liquid. Turn the heat to low and cook, stirring, until slightly thickened, about 5 minutes. Pour into the roasting pan with the onions and sausage.

Remove the duck from the oven and reheat the oven to 350°F [180°C].

| In a clean skillet over medium heat, warm or melt: | **3 Tbsp butter or olive oil** |

| Add: | **2 cups [400 g] rice** |

| Cook, stirring constantly, until the rice is hot and just showing a little color, about 5 minutes. Transfer to the roasting pan along with: | **1 cup [60 g] sun-dried tomatoes, cut into bite-size pieces** |

Arrange the duck on top. Pour over 4 cups [960 ml] of the reserved hot chicken stock. Cover the pan loosely with foil and bake until the rice is cooked, at least 30 minutes.

Uncover to let the duck crisp up again, about 10 more minutes.

The dish will hold, loosely covered in a 300°F [150°C] oven, for at least 1 hour. The extra time in the oven actually improves the flavor and texture. I like the crisp, brown edges around the pan.

To serve, spoon some of the rice on each plate and place a duck leg on top.

| Sprinkle with: | **Cracklings from the reserved rendered duck fat (see Margin Note, page 202) Coarsely chopped fresh parsley** |

Spoon a little of the remaining chicken stock over each serving.

Seared Duck Breasts with Kumquat Mustard Glaze

SERVES 4 TO 6 / TOTAL TIME: 45 MIN

Under the skin of a duck breast, beneath that thick layer of fat, lies a lovely piece of red meat. It is perfect for a quick sear in a cast-iron pan, though the layers of fat need to be rendered a bit. To speed this along, you will make a few diagonal slashes through the skin and fat.

For the sauce, blanch in a small saucepan of boiling water for 2 minutes:

10 to 12 kumquats, thickly sliced

Drain and set aside the slices, but discard the seeds.

In the same saucepan, bring to a boil:

½ cup [100 g] sugar
½ cup [120 ml] water

Add the kumquats, lower the heat, and simmer until tender with a syrupy sauce, 8 to 10 minutes. Remove from the heat and set aside.

On a work surface, place:

4 boneless duck breasts, skin on

With your sharpest knife, make a few diagonal slices through the skin and fat, but don't cut into the meat.

Rub into both sides of the meat:

Salt

Heat a large skillet, preferably cast iron, over medium-high heat. Add the duck breasts, skin-side down, and cook, without turning, while the fat renders and the skin becomes nicely browned, 5 to 10 minutes. Check to make sure the breasts are not getting too dark. Lower the heat a bit, if they're getting too dark. Turn and cook for another 2 to 3 minutes. A medium-rare duck breast will not be soft to the touch. It should be just firmed up.

Pour off all but 2 Tbsp of the duck fat, reserving the excess for another use.

Remove from the heat, partially cover the skillet, and let rest for 5 to 10 minutes. Transfer the duck to a platter and cover loosely with foil.

Try eggs or potatoes fried in duck fat for something special.

Add to the skillet:

¼ cup [60 ml] red wine
2 tsp coarsely ground toasted black pepper

With the heat off, use a pastry brush to deglaze the pan.

Then with the heat on medium, add:

2 medium shallots, thinly sliced
1 jalapeño pepper, thinly sliced
1 Tbsp Dijon mustard
1 tsp mustard seeds

Stir to blend, and add the kumquats and their syrup. Taste for salt and add more if needed.

To serve, on each plate make a bed of:

Arugula, watercress, or another green with an assertive flavor

Slice each duck breast on the diagonal into rather thin slices and fan out over the greens.

Spoon the reserved kumquat mustard glaze over the duck. Add to each plate:

3 to 5 fresh kumquat slices

below: We not only cooked ducks, we collected them. This grouping was found in an antique store in San Francisco and kept in the entry of the French Laundry. One night, one of the ducks was stolen, only to be returned the following morning, left by our front door. We never found out who took it, or who so kindly allowed it to return to its home.

Curry Glazed Duck Legs with Fresh Pineapple Salsa

SERVES 6 / TOTAL TIME: 2½ TO 3 HOURS

This preparation of duck legs is one of my favorites. It's best not to rush the process, so start early!

Prepare:

Fresh Pineapple Salsa (recipe follows)

Preheat the oven to 400°F [200°C].

Massage and smooth the skin to fully cover the meat of:

6 duck legs, with thighs attached

In a blender or food processor, whirl:

2 to 3 Tbsp olive oil
2 or 3 garlic cloves
1 or 2 jalapeño peppers, minced
Zest of 1 orange
2 Tbsp minced fresh ginger
2 Tbsp curry powder
2 tsp salt
Freshly ground black pepper

Blend into a loose paste. Rub into the duck legs and arrange on a rimmed baking sheet. Spreading out the fatty skin on the pan will help it render fully. Roast to render the fat and crisp the skins, about 45 minutes. Remove from the oven, pour off the fat and reserve for another use.

Lower the oven temperature to 300°F [150°C].

In a medium bowl, mix together:

1 cup [240 ml] chicken stock
½ cup [120 ml] fresh orange juice
½ cup [120 ml] fresh lime juice

Pour juices over the duck legs, cover the pan with parchment paper, and return to the oven for about 45 minutes.

Transfer the legs to a clean roasting pan. Return to the 300°F [150°C] oven, uncovered, to crisp up the skin, about 30 minutes.

If there are fewer than 1½ cups [360 ml] of juices left in the first pan, add more stock. Use a pastry brush to dissolve the bits and pieces on the bottom of the pan in the liquid. Transfer to a small saucepan, then over low heat, stir until slightly thickened, 2 to 3 minutes. Taste the juices for salt and add more if needed.

When ready to serve, on each plate, make a bed of:

Cooked couscous, rice, or another grain of your choice

Place one duck leg per serving on top and spoon the juices over. Add a generous spoonful of salsa to each plate and garnish with:

Cilantro sprigs

PINEAPPLE SALSA

Start with:

1 ripe pineapple

Cut away the peel. Slice the fruit into thin rounds, and cut the rounds into small slivers.

Place in a large glass bowl.

VARIATION: Having an abundance of Fuyu persimmons recently, I substituted these delicious non-astringent persimmons for the pineapple and it turned out absolutely wonderful.

Add:

1 white onion, finely slivered
Juice of 2 limes
Juice of 1 lemon
¼ cup [60 g] finely slivered ginger
⅓ cup [15 g] chopped fresh cilantro
1 tsp finely chopped fresh or dried small red chiles
¼ cup [50 g] sugar
A generous amount of salt

Mix gently and set aside for 15 minutes at room temperature to develop the flavor. Taste for seasoning and add more salt or chile if needed.

Roast Duck Legs with Green Peppercorn Sauce

SERVES 6 / TOTAL TIME: 2½ TO 3 HOURS

This is one of the first dishes I prepared with duck legs, and it was so good, we served it over and over again. It remains one of my favorites today, and brings back wonderful memories.

Preheat the oven to 400°F [200°C].

Pat dry and allow to come to room temperature:

6 duck legs, with thighs attached

Using a mortar and pestle, or better yet, a suribachi, pound the following into a paste:

2 Tbsp olive oil
3 garlic cloves, minced
2 Tbsp lemon zest
2 Tbsp kosher salt
2 Tbsp freshly ground toasted black pepper
2 Tbsp finely chopped fresh thyme
1 Tbsp finely chopped rosemary

I find this method of cooking duck produces results equal to that of a confit, but it takes less time and uses less duck fat. It's really an easy approach. By giving the duck a long roasting period, then steaming it to return some of its moisture, and browning it at the end, you keep the meat moist on the inside and crispy outside. Start this recipe early, because it does take time, and the time is very important for the duck's ultimate tenderness.

Rub the paste all over the duck legs and arrange in a roasting pan, skin-side up. Roast until nicely browned, 45 minutes to 1 hour.

Lower the heat to 300°F [150°C], remove the duck from the oven, and pour off the fat. Set aside 2 Tbsp for this recipe.

Pour over the duck legs:

1 cup [240 ml] chicken stock, preferably homemade

Add:

3 or 4 sprigs parsley, thyme, or both

Cover the pan with parchment paper and return to the oven for about 45 minutes.

Transfer the legs to a clean roasting pan. Return to the oven, uncovered, to crisp up the skin, about 30 minutes.

Pour into the first roasting pan: **½ cup [120 ml] chicken stock**

Deglaze the pan off the heat using a pastry brush to dissolve the bits and pieces on the bottom of the pan in the liquid. Transfer to a small saucepan, turn the heat to low, and stir until slightly thickened, about 5 minutes. Set aside.

While the duck is doing its final roasting, make the green peppercorn sauce. With a fork, partially smash: **2 Tbsp green peppercorns**

If you are working with dried green peppercorns, be sure to soak them first in hot water for 15 to 20 minutes and pat dry.

You should have a mixture of small and large pieces. In a saucepan over low heat, warm the reserved 2 Tbsp duck fat, and sauté the crushed green peppercorns quickly until fragrant.

Stir in the reserved juices from the roasting pan and add: **¾ cup [180 ml] heavy cream**

While stirring, allow to come to a simmer to thicken a little, about 5 minutes, and then add:
1 tsp lemon zest
2 pinches of salt

To serve, place one duck leg on each plate and spoon the sauce over it, allowing a little of the leg to show.

Garnish with: **A few green peppercorns**

Serve alongside, to soak up the juices: **Rice or couscous**

Our Wines

Winemaking has always been the heartbeat of the Napa Valley, and the local vintners soon discovered us at the Chutney Kitchen. When we opened, though, all we were pouring were inexpensive wines, red and white, decanted from gallon jugs into recycled fifths. I remember how thrilled I was when Chuck Carpy, the founder of Freemark Abbey, started coming in regularly. I had heard stories about him, that he was a born-and-raised, third-generation native of the valley, a larger than life character. One day, after he had finished lunch, he walked into the kitchen and with a smile on his face, asked me, "Have you ever thought about putting more wines on your wine list?"

"We have," I said nervously, "but don't know where to start." And then, thankfully, it occurred to me to ask, "What would you like to see on our wine list?"

He thought a moment, then answered, "I always like a nice Gewürztraminer with my lunch." So a Gewürztraminer was the first addition to our wine list. And then we added a few more wines, always from Napa Valley, and asked our winemaker customers, as they came in, for more suggestions. Often they arrived bringing their own wines. Robert Mondavi, Joe Heitz, Jack Davies of Schramsberg Vineyards, and the dean of American winemakers, Andre Tchelistcheff, all came, ate lunch, and shared their wines with friends. We'd open their bottles, and they'd invite us to have a taste, suggesting we might add the wine to our list. We often did.

Bob Mondavi further encouraged us, making suggestions and dining with us often. Sometimes it was just he and his wife, Margrit, but he would still order two bottles of wine for dinner, his wines, of course, which we had put on the list. And then he would share the wine with the other guests in the dining room, praising the vintage or varietal. When he brought large groups in to dine, which he did often, he would arrange for a number of special bottles to be sent ahead of time, for us to pour that evening. He would always insist that we add the full price of the bottles to the tab, with our usual markup.

Joe Heitz was one of the first people to befriend us, because he found out we came from Fresno, and he had taught at Fresno State. He was known to be a gruff character, but he couldn't have been warmer to us, and he and his wife, Alice, became valued customers and friends.

So our wine list kept growing, and eventually, winemakers were offering Don verticals that weren't available anywhere else. By the time we opened the French Laundry, we had a not too shabby wine list, all from the Napa Valley, and it continued to grow in depth over the years that followed.

opposite: Don, with the original stone walls of the building behind him, would greet each arriving guest and help them with the wine list.

A GOOD MEMORY: One night, Bob and Margrit Mondavi had reservations for dinner, just the two of them, and we saved them the downstairs corner table by the window. As Bob turned the corner onto Creek Street, pulling up in front of the restaurant, a police car pulled in behind him with its red lights flashing. We seated Margrit while Bob stayed behind to deal with the police.

Evidently, he had been driving erratically, which wasn't unusual because he liked to talk with his hands, and he wasn't great about looking where he was going. Soon, other diners, and even the staff, were gathered around the window watching the events outside unfold.

The policeman took Bob through the full field sobriety test, checking his vision, making him stand on one leg, and challenging him to walk a straight line. It wasn't easy for him, as one leg was shorter than the other one. But he succeeded, passing every test.

The police, satisfied, drove off, and Bob finally walked into the restaurant. He looked around at us standing there, laughed, and said "Funny thing— I usually have a full bottle of wine with lunch. Thank God, today I didn't!"

The wine list was Don's department, and it reflected who he was. There was never any pomp and ceremony to the service. It was simple: We were in the middle of the Napa Valley, so we served Napa Valley wines — how could we not honor this magical place? Because we had only a small staff and not much space, and a plain, family-style approach to service, Don would open the wines at his counter near the restaurant entrance, and then the server would pour the first glass. We would then leave the bottle for our guests to proceed at their own pace. We never topped off their glasses or pushed wine sales. Our patrons certainly didn't need any encouragement.

The wine critic Gerald Asher wrote: The evenings I spent at their Yountville restaurant were among my most memorable in California. "The table is yours for the evening," Don would say as one arrived. If the weather was fine, there was every reason to take a walk through Yountville before dessert, or a last glass of wine in the pretty cottage garden while admiring the moon. "I simply cook for the French Laundry's guests as I cook for a dinner party at home," Sally Schmitt once told me.

From *a Vineyard in my Glass* (Berkeley, CA: University of California Press, 2011)

Outside the Kitchen Door

At the French Laundry, my kitchen window looked out on a field across the street. It was part of an old, abandoned vineyard that was waist high in wild mustard every spring. It's where Chef Thomas Keller now has his vegetable garden. It was so beautiful to look at back then, and I would always send someone out, or go myself, to pick the long mustard stems, with their bright yellow blossoms, so I could make a big bouquet to put in a pitcher at the end of my kitchen counter. Then I could snip right from the bouquet when I wanted a garnish.

Sometimes, I would wander a little farther down the street to gather wild onion blossoms, which grew outside a neighbor's fence. In the same neighborhood, a friendly man on Creek Street with two Meyer lemon trees gave us permission to harvest his lemons whenever we needed them, and we often did. We had our own Eureka lemon tree, so this arrangement gave us access to both.

Most important, though, was our own garden, especially our herb garden, right outside our kitchen door. When we were planning the French Laundry, an herb garden was at the top of my list. At the Chutney Kitchen, I had been buying herbs from my produce man, but now I wanted them to be more accessible, and fresher. I wanted them in my own garden.

So the first thing we did when we were making the move from Vintage 1870 to the French Laundry building was to go to work on laying out the herb garden. My daughter Karen and her husband, Tim, worked on it with me. Tim and I crouched down on our knees, laying the brick, and Karen did the planting. (She likes to remind me that she helped with the brickwork, too.) We started with both seeds and cuttings and planted parsley, chives, thyme (one of my favorites), marjoram, sorrel, oregano, cilantro, and pineapple sage, which was tall and made an impressive centerpiece for the brick path. I loved the symmetry of the design we made, which contrasted with all the angles of the building. My father visited regularly, arriving with plants in the trunk of his car—some tomato plants, maybe a rosebush or three, which he'd plant for us.

Later on, after David Alosi came to work for us as a gardener, he added raised beds for the roses and built more beds to grow arugula. One of my regular customers who lived in Yountville, Dawne Dickenson, visited Italy and brought seeds back, which she shared with me. It was the first I had heard of arugula. David planted them, and we immediately put the peppery green to good use.

Another memory from Lissa Doumani, who with her husband, Hiro Sone, ran the Michelin-starred restaurant Terra, in St. Helena, until 2019: One day, Hiro and I stopped by to see Sally at the French Laundry—this was maybe three or four years before they sold the restaurant. When we walked in, Sally was so excited—she had looked out the window of the kitchen before we arrived, and there, across the road in the redwood mulch, had been morels growing! It was incredible. After we left, we walked over to investigate, but we were too late. Sally had got them all, and she made them part of that night's menu. Now that is local foraging!

David was always introducing me to new things, such as the Japanese herb shiso, which is as important to Japanese cuisine as basil is to Italian. We also had a honeysuckle hedge and a bay tree for snipping leaves. There was flowering quince, a dogwood tree, and violets, all of which were fair game for the bouquets Kathy arranged for our tables, the stairway, and the fireplace mantel. The garden was a wonderful mixture of old and new, in keeping with all that we were doing.

Turnip Soup with Fresh Mustard Greens

SERVES 6 / TOTAL TIME: 45 MIN

Every spring, when that wonderful field across from the French Laundry would turn bright yellow with waist-high wild mustard, we would gather armfuls to fill a pitcher for my kitchen center island, and I would be inspired to make this soup.

In a soup pot, combine:

2 medium potatoes, peeled and sliced
4 cups [960 ml] water or weak chicken stock
2 Tbsp butter
½ tsp salt
½ tsp freshly ground white pepper

VARIATION: We were lucky enough to have access to mustard flowers where we were in the wine country; the plant grew everywhere, wild along the roads outside all the wineries. If mustard flowers and greens aren't available, you can substitute chives, arugula, or mizuna.

Bring to a rolling boil, lower the heat, and simmer, uncovered, until the potatoes are partially cooked, about 10 minutes.

Add to the pot:

4 to 6 medium turnips, peeled and sliced

Continue cooking until the turnips and potatoes are tender, another 15 to 20 minutes. You many need to replenish the water during this cooking time.

Recipe continues…

Remove from the heat and let cool for a few minutes. Purée in a blender, in batches, until smooth, adding more liquid as needed.

Return the purée to the pot. You should have at least 6 cups [1.4 L].

Add and taste for seasoning:	**2 cups [480 ml] half-and-half**
In a blender, purée until smooth and set aside:	**1 cup [20 g] chopped mustard greens or turnip greens** **½ cup [120 ml] melted butter, slightly cooled, or olive oil** **Salt**
When you are ready to serve, gently reheat the soup to just below boiling. Ladle it into warm soup bowls and garnish with:	**A few mustard flowers** **A swirl of the puréed greens**

At this point, the soup can just sit until serving time. I prefer not to refrigerate it, as cream-based soups tend to lose their freshness when overly chilled.

Lemon Cloud with Crispy Lemon Zest

SERVES 8 WITH 3 CUPS [690 G] OF LEMON CURD LEFT OVER FOR THE REFRIGERATOR TOTAL TIME: 1 HOUR EXCLUDING CHILLING TIME

We used the Meyer lemons that we gathered from our neighbor's yard to make a lemon curd, which we folded with whipped cream to make this dessert. First make the lemon curd.

LEMON CURD

Use a Microplane to finely zest:	**6 lemons**

Set aside the zest. Juice the lemons, and set aside 1⅓ cups [320 ml] juice.

Whisk together well in a large bowl:	**8 eggs** **1 cup [200 g] sugar**

Add the reserved lemon juice, whisking until smooth.

Transfer to a heavy-bottomed saucepan over low heat or the top of a double boiler over simmering water. Cook, stirring constantly, until it becomes very thick, about 10 to 12 minutes.

Remove from the heat, and stir in: **1 cup [220 g] butter, cut into pieces**

Add the zest to taste; you may not need all of it. Refrigerate the lemon curd in a covered container for at least 2 hours. It will keep for a month (if well hidden from fridge raiders).

We also used the lemon curd in our Frozen Lemon Meringue Torte (page 299). For another simple dessert, try layering the curd with whipped cream and fresh blueberries in a tall stemmed glass for a lovely end to any meal.

CRISPY LEMON ZEST

With a zester, make the longest curls you can from the peel of: **1 firm lemon**

In a small bowl, put: **¼ cup [50 g] sugar**

Add the strips of lemon peel and toss with the sugar to coat. Spread them out on a parchment paper–lined baking sheet. If you have a shelf over your stove, just leave them to dry out. Otherwise, put them in a very low (250°F [120°C]) oven. Check them after 5 minutes, and then every couple of minutes until they firm up but are not browned. They will crisp up as they cool, but they burn very easily.

When ready to serve, in a large bowl, softly whip: **1 cup [240 ml] heavy cream**

If you don't have a good zester, you can use a vegetable peeler to cut strips off the outer layer of the lemon rind, leaving the bitter white pith behind. Then pile them up and cut them lengthwise into very thin strips.

Gently fold in 3 cups [690 g] of your lemon curd into the whipped cream. It's okay to leave streaks. Top with Crispy Lemon Zest.

Some Baked Apples & Sweet Endings

It was a Sunday afternoon in early September 1991, the last working day of a very long, busy week for me at the French Laundry. I needed a third dessert to go with the two I had already planned: raspberry-filled chocolate meringues and a couple of fat, juicy cobblers made with Indian blood peaches. I always had three desserts: something chocolate, something baked, and something fruity. I needed something simple and fruity. And fast. (It was my break time, and I really needed a short nap before facing the dinner crowd that night.)

I had these gorgeous Gravenstein apples. I should have made a pie or a tart. I had a little of our homemade spicy cinnamon ice cream left over, but no, there wasn't enough ice cream. So if I made pies or tarts, people would order them, and the ice cream would run out. Besides, it was too similar to the peach cobbler.

I had gone to the farmers' market in Napa on Tuesday, looking for more of the crispy pickling cucumbers I had scored a few weeks before. But cukes were all gone for the season, and the market was slow. It was a blistering hot day after our long, cool summer. The one exciting thing I found were two boxes of perfect Gravensteins from Sebastopol. The last two of the season, I was told, picked the day before. I started to bag a few, but realized that I'd stumbled upon some extraordinary apples. They had bright red strips on a gold background, were large and crisp, and were fragrant with that incredible ripe Gravenstein perfume. As I grabbed the whole huge box and paid my fifteen dollars, I felt as though I was cheating the seller. *I offered fifteen but would have paid fifty*, I thought, as I enjoyed their scent on the way home. Back at the restaurant, I made a couple of pies that day. When I tasted them, I thought they were my best effort to date, tart and full of flavor.

But on Sunday, there was no time for pies. How about just baking the apples? There would be enough ice cream to stuff a dozen small cavities, with a little left over for my staff, who adored it.

You aren't supposed to bake Gravensteins. I was perfectly aware of that fact—they shatter. But a little voice in the back of my head reminded me that I'd done it before, with good results. I had experimented with carved apples, inspired by the drawings of carved pears in Sara Midda's gorgeous little book, *In and Out of the Garden* (1981).

I have a channel knife, the kind used in a bar to make twists for your martini, one that we use to carve spiral designs into oranges at Christmas and drape the long twist of peel over a bowl of the oranges. Why not apples?

Gravensteins will always hold a special place in my heart. My first memory of this apple goes back to the 1940s, right after World War II, when my Uncle Willie bought a 200-acre [80-hectare] ranch in Annapolis, near the Mendocino coast. All he paid for it were the back taxes. As I remember, he was still in service on Guam when our family made the trip up there to inspect his purchase for him.

I'll never forget my frugal mother almost frolicking through the abandoned Gravenstein orchard. The drops covered the ground, and the unpruned trees were loaded with them, dead ripe and all ours. Mom would approach a tree, pick an apple, take a single bite out of it, and toss it over her shoulder while moving on to the next tree. She was literally drunk with the profusion of apples we had discovered.

I'm afraid all other apples will forever be held up to that yardstick, and few of them measure up. Somehow, my farmers' market box came as close as any to those in Uncle Willy's orchard, almost forty-five years later.

So I did a dozen, all different designs, because how can anyone bear to do them all the same? I used a melon baller to hollow out the core at the top, and put a piece of butter and a teaspoon of brown sugar in the cavity. I drizzled each apple with apple juice, and painted the exposed flesh with melted butter.

And then into the oven at 350°F [180°C]. In 30 minutes, they were perfect. The heady smell got me out of the hammock to poke at them. They did not shatter. I think leaving that much skin on protected them. The decorations did three things: It made them cook better; it made them easier to eat, because that tough skin had been broken up; and lastly, they looked festive.

To serve them that night, I rewarmed them, filled their cavities with cinnamon ice cream, and poured our apple cider syrup (see Margin Note, page 231) over the top. A garnish of cinnamon basil was the finishing touch. How could any dessert be prettier?

The next morning, we ate the leftovers for breakfast. Perfect.

Marinated Citrus Compote

SERVES 6 / TOTAL TIME: 30 MIN EXCLUDING CHILLING TIME

After a hearty winter meal, this refreshing dessert is light, lovely to look at, and very, very satisfying.

On a work surface, place: **3 oranges**

Using a vegetable peeler, remove the zest in strips (without the bitter pith). Stack them up and cut into very fine slivers. Blanch the zest by dropping the slivers in a small saucepan of boiling water. Return to a boil and immediately drain the water and remove the zest.

In a medium saucepan, bring to a simmer:
2 cups [480 ml] white wine
1 cup [200 g] sugar

Add the zest and continue simmering until syrupy, about 5 minutes.

Pour in:
½ cup [120 ml] Grand Marnier or another orange liqueur

Section or slice the oranges you zested after cutting away the pith. Repeat with:
3 more oranges, peeled with a knife to also remove the pith

VARIATIONS: Add or substitute blood oranges. Add kumquat slices. Serve with a small scoop of any citrus sherbet. Add fresh blueberries.

Transfer the oranges to a bowl, and pour the syrup over them. Refrigerate for at least 2 hours. They will keep, covered, in the refrigerator for three days.

Serve in tall stemmed glasses or your prettiest bowls, with:
Simple, crisp cookies

My Rhubarb Mousse

SERVES 6 / TOTAL TIME: 1 HOUR EXCLUDING CHILLING TIME

I always looked forward to the first hothouse rhubarb, which arrived in January or February. Rhubarb is one of the few things that is actually better coming out of a hothouse than from the fields. The hothouse variety isn't as tart, has better color, and is more tender than rhubarb grown in the field. The usual way to cook rhubarb is to stew it, but I prefer to roast the stalks in the oven with a little butter and sugar, so they don't disintegrate.

Preheat the oven to 350°F [180°C].

In a nonreactive baking dish, such as glass or ceramic, spread out in a single layer:	2 lb [910 g] rhubarb, cut into 1 in [2.5 cm] pieces
Distrubute over it:	1 cup [200 g] sugar ¼ cup [60 ml] apple juice or orange juice

Cover loosely with parchment paper and bake until fork-tender without disturbing it, 30 minutes or so.

Meanwhile, pour into a small bowl:	¼ cup [60 ml] water
Sprinkle with:	1 envelope gelatin

When the rhubarb is done, spoon a little of the hot juices into the gelatin mixture to make sure it is dissolved, or very hot water if you don't have enough hot juices.

Set a large stainless-steel bowl in a larger bowl of ice water and put the rhubarb in the metal bowl. Add the gelatin mixture and stir gently, trying not to break up the rhubarb pieces.

Keep stirring until the mixture shows signs of setting up. Remove from the ice water bath.

In a medium bowl, use an electric mixer or whisk to whip until frothy:	3 egg whites
Gradually add:	2 Tbsp sugar

Continue whipping until soft peaks form. Add the beaten egg whites to the rhubarb mixture, but don't stir it in yet.

In the same medium bowl,   **1 cup [240 ml] heavy cream**
softly whip:

Add the whipped cream to the rhubarb mixture, and fold everything together gently until it's combined. Don't worry about a few small streaks or chunks. Refrigerate until ready to serve, at least 1 hour.

   To serve, spoon into tall glasses. This is so beautiful on its own, I don't think it needs any garnishes.

Three Different Cream Cheese Tarts

SERVES 12; MAKES ONE 10 IN [25 CM] TART / TOTAL TIME: 1 HOUR
EXCLUDING CHILLING TIME

These are my takes on a classic cheesecake. The idea of serving cheesecake at the end of a five-course dinner has always seemed like overkill to me, so I lightened up the filling a bit and used a crumb crust, one of my favorites, as a base. We made many variations of this tart, using different fruits, nuts, and chocolates for the topping. Below are three: two with fruit toppings, and one with chocolate.

To make the crumb crust, preheat the oven to 325°F [165°C]. Butter a 10 by 2 in [25 by 5 cm] fluted tart pan with a removable bottom.

In a medium bowl, combine: **1½ cups [210 g] fine dried bread crumbs**
                                     ½ cup [120 g] finely crushed amaretti cookies

I abandoned graham cracker crusts when I learned to make this; it is definitely a step up, and it gets wonderfully crisp as it cools.

Then add: **½ cup [100 g] sugar**
                                     ½ cup [120 ml] melted butter

Mix together until the butter and sugar are evenly distributed.
   Press firmly into the prepared pan, starting with the sides. Bake until light brown, about 15 minutes. Cool completely before filling.

Recipe continues...

To make the cream cheese filling, stir together in a medium heatproof measuring cup:

⅓ cup [80 ml] cold water

1 envelope gelatin

Let sit for 5 minutes to dissolve. Place the measuring cup in a saucepan of very hot water to liquify it further. Let sit until the mixture turns clear, 5 to 10 minutes. Remove. If it starts to gel before you are ready for it, return it to the saucepan of hot water to liquify.

Stir in:

½ cup [100 g] sugar

¼ cup [60 ml] amaretto liqueur

Keep stirring until the sugar is dissolved and the liquid clear. Set aside.

In a stand mixer at low speed, beat until creamy:

10 oz [280 g] natural cream cheese, at room temperature

Add very gradually, at low speed:

1 ½ cups [360 ml] heavy cream (not too cold)

Please don't use those industrially produced versions of cream cheese, which contain additives and stabilizers. If you can't find natural cream cheese in your market, ask for it at the deli counter or at a natural foods store.

Increase the speed to medium and beat until the cream is incorporated. Remove from mixer. Drizzle in the gelatin mixture, and fold together carefully by hand. Spoon into the cooled crust, being careful not to disturb the sides of the crust. Chill until firm, at least 2 hours.

Before removing the sides of the pan, add one of the following toppings:

RED, WHITE, AND BLUEBERRY (OUR FOURTH OF JULY TOPPING)

Gently press into the surface of the tart:

3 cups [420 g] fresh blueberries

In a small saucepan, gently warm and brush over the top of the fruit:

About ½ cup [150 g] pomegranate jelly

VARIATION: If you don't have jam or jelly, you can top the fruit with crushed and sweetened berries.

RASPBERRY OR STRAWBERRY

Gently press into the surface of the tart in a tight, single layer:

3 cups [360 g] fresh raspberries or hulled strawberries, halved or quartered if they are large

In a blender or food processor, whirl until puréed:

¾ cup [225 g] raspberry or strawberry jam

Brush the tops of the fruit with the jam. If you need to loosen the jam a bit, you can warm it slightly first.

CHOCOLATE TOPPING

Cover the surface of the cheesecake with:

1 recipe My Best Chocolate Sauce (page 224)

Sprinkle with:

Toasted almonds

Removing the sides of the tart pan can be tricky. There are tools for it, such as inverted stands and cake lifters, but I've learned to simply hold the bottom carefully and push the center up while the outer ring slides down my arm. An alternative is to place the tart pan on a large can or inverted bowl that will allow the outer ring to drop down, leaving the tart resting on the can or bowl. When serving, to make it easier to cut the cheesecake neatly, dip your knife in warm water and wipe it off between cuts.

Once you've topped your cheesecake with the fruit or chocolate sauce, remove the sides of the pan and serve.

My Best Chocolate Sauce

MAKES ¾ CUP [180 ML] / TOTAL TIME: 15 MIN

When we opened the Chutney Kitchen, I was given a small, heavy, unlined copper pan with a long handle and a round bottom. I had to ask what it was for, and was told that it was a zabaglione pan. Its only intended use was to make that wonderful Italian custard.

If you lack a zabaglione pan, put a small, heavy-bottomed pot over low heat and combine:

1½ oz [40 g] unsweetened chocolate, chopped into pieces if from a solid bar
¼ cup [60 ml] water

When the chocolate has just melted, whisk in:

½ cup [100 g] sugar

Raise the heat and let the mixture come to a full boil. Remove from the heat and add:

3 Tbsp butter
½ tsp vanilla

This sauce can be reheated gently in a hot water bath to reach pouring consistency. Any extra will keep 2 weeks, covered, in a small jar in the refrigerator.

I quickly figured out it was the perfect vehicle for melting chocolate. Given the round bottom, I couldn't set it down directly on a burner, and had to hold it over the heat and keep stirring to prevent the chocolate from scorching. I only used the pan once to make zabaglione, but have used it many, many times since 1970 to melt chocolate. I still marvel at its beauty, and I love to keep it polished.

I have for years used and recommend the chocolate disks that come from the century-and-a-half-old San Francisco chocolatier, Guittard.

Coffee Pots de Crème

MAKES ENOUGH FOR 6 TO 8 RAMEKINS, OR 8 TO 10 OVENPROOF ESPRESSO CUPS / PREP: 15 MIN / COOK TIME: 30 TO 50 MIN

When my children, and then grandchildren, would come through the blue door into the French Laundry kitchen, the first thing they would do is look for the leftovers from the night before. They were always happy to find these French "pots of cream," little baked custards, which ended a meal so well. I made them first with chocolate, but I liked them so much more with coffee.

Preheat the oven to 325°F [165°C].

In a small, heavy-bottomed saucepan, scald, and remove from the heat:

2 cups [480 ml] half-and-half
3 Tbsp instant espresso coffee
1 cinnamon stick

In a medium bowl, beat gently to avoid having too much foam:

½ cup [120 ml] egg yolks (from about 6 eggs)
½ cup [100 g] sugar

Add the hot half-and-half mixture slowly to the bowl in a thin stream, stirring constantly. Strain the mixture into a large heatproof measuring cup. Fill the ramekins or espresso cups and place in a baking or roasting pan.

Pour enough hot tap water into the pan to come about two-thirds up the sides of the ramekins. Bake until the custard is barely set, 30 to 50 minutes depending on how warm the mixture was to start. It should jiggle in the middle.

Don't pour in too much water because the ramekins will be difficult to lift out when they're hot.

Let cool a little, and then lift the ramekins out of the pan, using a jar lifter if they're still too hot. Then cool before serving, or refrigerate.

To serve, top each serving with:

A spoonful of softly whipped cream
Chocolate-covered coffee beans or chocolate curls

I think they're equally good slightly warm or thoroughly chilled. If you don't have grandchildren raiding the refrigerator, these will last a day or two.

Chocolate Chinchilla Topped with Sherry Cream

SERVES 12 / PREP TIME: 25 MIN / COOK TIME: 45 MIN TO 1 HOUR EXCLUDING COOLING TIME

This chocolate dessert became one of my signature offerings after I was inspired by a recipe of the same name, which I found in *Gourmet* magazine in the 1970s. It's light as air, yet delivers a powerful jolt of chocolate. Plus, it holds well. It doesn't need to be refrigerated, and it is just as good the second day—if it lasts that long. I served it at the French Laundry for years and then taught it to my classes at the Apple Farm. John Scharffenberger, the former winemaker and eminent chocolatier, who once helped me teach a class at the Apple Farm, even featured it in the book he coauthored, *The Essence of Chocolate* (2006).

Preheat the oven to 325° [165°C].

Butter an 8 cup [2 L] Bundt pan or mold. Bring a kettle of water to a boil and keep it at a low boil until needed.

Over a large bowl, sift together:

2 cups [240 g] powdered sugar
1¼ cups [100 g] cocoa powder
1 tsp ground cinnamon

With an electric mixer, beat until soft peaks form:

2 cups [480 ml] egg whites (from about 16 eggs)

Fold the egg whites gently into the dry ingredients with a slotted spoon. Be patient. It takes a while to incorporate the egg whites.

Spoon the mixture into the prepared Bundt pan, and place the Bundt pan in a larger heatproof bowl with tall sides. Pour in enough very hot tap water so it comes halfway up the sides of the Bundt pan.

Bake 45 minutes to 1 hour.

When finished, let cool about 1½ hour. Turn out when still barely warm onto a rimless platter or a parchment-covered cutting board. To slice easily, dip your knife into warm water and wipe it between slices.

Serve with each slice:

Sherry cream (see Margin Note)
1 or 2 violets with their leaves
Chocolate curls

opposite: As I make the Chocolate Chinchilla, here's my grandson Brooks, at age three, in charge of quality control in the kitchen of the French Laundry. He now has a wonderful job at UC Santa Cruz cooking, gardening, and working in their new culinary program.

I puzzled over the name of this dessert for years and then discovered a version of chinchilla in an old cookbook, *Summer Cooking* (1955), by that wonderful food writer Elizabeth David. So I've come to assume the name is an example of English humor, used whimsically because of the silky texture of this magical soufflé-like dessert.

It is difficult to judge the doneness, as you can't probe it or judge it by the color, and the timing depends on your oven, but it needs to feel set. If undercooked, it will shrink too much when it cools, and if overcooked it will be too dry.

To make sherry cream, with an electric mixer, beat 1 cup [240 ml] heavy cream just until soft peaks form. Beat in 1 Tbsp cream sherry.

Icy Treats

Don loved ice cream. In his later years, when I made a quart, it was a ritual of Don's to take it out of the freezer just before we sat down for dinner and put it in the fridge. By dessert time, it was perfect, having softened up enough to be easily scooped. This was a trick we learned when we visited our son Johnny when he was in France. We were lunching at Alain Chapel's three-star restaurant in the French countryside. At dessert time, they brought a beautiful cart to the table with four or five choices of ice cream, slightly softened, making them easier to scoop and delightful to eat.

These recipes are meant for one of those smaller 1 qt [960 ml] ice-cream makers that are so easy to use. I keep the insert to my ice-cream maker in the freezer, so I can use it when the mood strikes.

Warm Fruit with Ice Cream

SERVES 4 / TOTAL TIME: 25 MIN

I first learned this from Jeremiah Tower when he was cooking at the Santa Fe Bar and Grill in the old train station in Berkeley. Heating the fruit dramatically heightens its flavor. There isn't a simpler, more delicious dessert than this one.

Have ready:

4 scoops ice cream, plain vanilla or ginger (see Margin Note, page 231)

In a skillet over medium heat, melt:

3 Tbsp butter

Add in any combination:

2 cups [170 g] assorted fresh berries; roughly chopped fresh peaches, nectarines, or plums; or halved cherries
2 Tbsp sugar

The fruit only needs to get hot, not cooked, so avoid stirring. Just shake the skillet a little and gently heat it until the sugar is dissolved and the juices run, about 3 minutes.

Serve the warm fruit in bowls with a scoop of ice cream. Garnish with:

Fresh mint leaves, a citrus leaf, or berries and leaves (see Margin Note)

We grow our own berries, so I like to go out and pick a tiny twig from the bush that still has leaves and berries on it—a perfect garnish for this dessert.

Three Citrus Sherbet

MAKES 1 QT [960 ML] / TOTAL TIME: 1 HOUR EXCLUDING CHILLING TIME

Nobody uses the word *sherbet* anymore. All you hear these days is talk about sorbets, granitas, and the latest flavor of gelato, but I grew up on ice cream and sherbet, so these are what I liked to make. My parents kept our White Mountain ice-cream maker on the porch, right outside our kitchen door, and I kept the tradition going at the French Laundry with the same kind of ice-cream maker right by the back door of the restaurant. The only difference was that this one had an electric motor, making it so much easier than cranking it by hand.

With a Microplane, grate enough citrus to produce:

2 Tbsp lemon zest
2 Tbsp lime zest
2 Tbsp orange zest

Set aside the zest. Combine in a large bowl:

1 cup [200 g] sugar
1 ½ cups [360 ml] half-and-half

Stir the mixture until the sugar is completely dissolved.

Stir in:

½ cup [120 ml] fresh lemon juice
½ cup [120 ml] fresh lime juice
½ cup [120 ml] fresh orange juice

Transfer to an ice-cream maker and freeze as directed.

Remove the ice-cream maker paddle and use a spatula to fold in the reserved citrus zest. Make sure you don't add it earlier, as it will become attached to the paddle, making it difficult to remove. Transfer to a flat tray, cover, and put into your freezer to firm up to a scoopable texture, at least 1 hour.

Top each serving with:

Crispy Lemon Zest (page 215) or a pretty citrus leaf, if you have a tree

VARIATION: My son Johnny created this version, with even more zing to it. Before freezing the sherbet, ladle ¼ cup [60 ml] of the mixture into a blender or food processor and add 1 ripe mango, peeled and pitted, and 2 Tbsp finely chopped fresh mint. Purée until smooth. Pour the blended mango mixture into the sherbet mixture. Freeze the sherbet, stir in the zest, add 1 Tbsp minced jalapeño pepper or fresh hot red pepper, or more to your taste, and serve.

Pomegranate Sherbet or
Coupe de Grenade

MAKES 1 QT [960 ML] / TOTAL TIME: 1 HOUR EXCLUDING CHILLING TIME

A *coupe* is ice cream or sherbet with a fruit topping, but I enjoy calling this Coupe de Grenade, as it really deserves the fancier name. It is wonderful after a rich dinner, such as oxtails or a cassoulet.

In a medium bowl, stir together:

3 cups [720 ml] pomegranate juice
1 cup [240 ml] half-and-half
2 Tbsp fresh lemon juice
1 cup [200 g] sugar

Transfer to an ice-cream maker and freeze as directed.

Serve in tall, wide-stemmed glasses. Spoon over each serving:

Pomegranate jelly, stirred a bit to smooth it out

Sprinkle with:

Pomegranate seeds

You can purchase pomegranate juice if you want, but it's not difficult to make your own. It can be a bit messy, though. What you're looking for is the sweet nectar that surrounds the seeds.

Cut the pomegranate in half and use a citrus press to extract the juice.

Cinnamon Ice Cream

MAKES 1 QT [960 ML] / TOTAL TIME: 1 HOUR EXCLUDING CHILLING TIME

This is our favorite ice cream to serve with any fruit dessert, especially apple pie and cobbler. It also makes a wonderful sundae, with My Best Chocolate Sauce (page 224) or apple cider syrup (see Margin Note) and topped with toasted walnuts or pecans.

In a heavy-bottomed 1 qt [960 ml] saucepan, scald or bring almost to a boil:	**1 ½ cups [360 ml] half-and-half** **2 cinnamon sticks** **1 tsp ground cinnamon**
In a medium bowl, beat together:	**4 egg yolks** **¾ cup [150 g] sugar**

Slowly pour the scalded half-and-half mixture over the egg yolk mixture, whisking constantly.

Return to the saucepan over low heat and cook, stirring, and watching carefully until the mixture has the consistency of a thin custard and coats the back of a wooden spoon. If it boils, it will curdle.

Stir in:	**2 cups [480 ml] very cold** **heavy cream**

Strain the mixture into a container, cover, and refrigerate for a few hours. Chilling makes it easier for the ice-cream maker to do its job and allows the flavors to develop. Transfer to your ice-cream maker and freeze as directed.

Serve alongside apple pie (page 38) or any fruit dessert.

We make our own apple cider syrup at the Apple Farm, and so can you. Although it won't be quite as good as the real thing, it will still provide a zesty contrast to a sweet dessert. To make it, reduce 4 cups [960 ml] of apple juice—or better yet, fresh, sweet cider—over high heat until it measures 1 cup [240 ml] of syrup. The terms *apple cider* and *apple juice* are, unfortunately, often used interchangeably. Though related, they aren't the same thing. Apple cider is unpasteurized and unfiltered. Apple juice is often filtered, thus clearer, and pasteurized for the sake of shelf life. Enjoy apple cider syrup drizzled over ice cream, clafoutis, apple pie, or French toast. Sometimes I also stir a little into sour cream to spoon over apple pie.

VARIATION: To make ginger ice cream, substitute ¼ cup [30 g] slivered ginger for the ground cinnamon and cinnamon sticks. A scoop of it goes well alongside Ginger Apple Upside-Down Cake (page 41), with My Best Chocolate Sauce (page 224), or topped with slightly warmed chutney and toasted nuts.

I was so proud I was able to have this celebration for my parents' 50th wedding anniversary in our upstairs dining room in 1978. My mother is wearing an antique silk dress that had been worn by her aunt to her own wedding and is holding our silver cake server, getting ready to cut into a two-tier version of Angie's Spice Cake (page 278).

Our Staff

Our aim when we opened the French Laundry was to keep it small and do much of the work ourselves. So we kept our staff small, with many part-timers. I insisted on doing most of the cooking myself, as I was tired of overseeing a large staff. And I wanted very much to have a low-key feeling about the whole place.

We ventured into this world of food and service with our own teenagers, Kathy, Karen, and Johnny. They all learned good work ethics in those very early days at the Vintage Cafe, as well as how to deal with the public. They could see how much people appreciate honest food. As time passed, our two youngest children, Eric and Terry, gained enough years to join us at our workplace. They started out running errands and emptying trash cans for our tenants at the Vintage, helping out in the café, and doing any odd jobs that came their way, which often involved a scrub brush or broom. At the French Laundry, they preferred to help me in the kitchen and did their fair share of dishwashing.

We never had to search for employees; they simply came to us. As soon we needed extra help, our kids brought in their friends from school, choosing carefully whom they asked. They didn't want to be working alongside someone who was a goof-off! In fact, they did such a good job, two of these new employees became sons-in-law!

When our children moved on to their own projects, we acquired more full-time staff. Our oldest child, Kathy, stayed with us, though, right to the end. Early on, she had taken over the flower arranging from me, and then started taking flowers from her garden to Napa's farmers' market. Standing there at the market, she began making small bouquets. Soon women began coming to her, vases in hand, asking her to make floral arrangements to grace their dinner party tables. This informal beginning grew into a business doing floral arrangements for big parties and weddings. Still, she kept us in flowers at the French Laundry, and arranged the flowers for Thomas Keller after he bought the restaurant from us, until she finally retired.

When Kathy would arrive in the morning to do the flowers, she often brought her two oldest boys, Byron and Perry, with her. They were just getting past the crawling stage, and when they weren't playing in the garden, I could hand them a day-old baguette to chew, which would keep them busy for hours. When they were finally old enough to demand jobs in the kitchen, we let them wash the vegetables and paint the toast rounds with butter. Perry says his first real kitchen job during those precious years was charring the skins off red peppers over the flame on our big range. He went on to become the youngest chef to ever earn a Michelin star during his time at Étoile, the restaurant at nearby Domaine Chandon Winery. He is now the chef at the Boonville Hotel, where he works with my oldest son, his uncle Johnny.

The term extended family has been overused, but that is what our staff always was. While I was running and cooking in our restaurants, my real family came and went, leaving for school, heading out on travels, taking time off for babies, and eventually going off to form their own businesses. We are really proud of the fact that our true legacy was to provide inspiration and courage to young people, family and extended family alike, to make their own way in the world. Few ex-employees went on to hold down a nine-to-five job in the corporate world, and none of our children did! For more about our staff, see my acknowledgments on page 343.

A memory from Richard Carter, who worked with me in the French Laundry kitchen: Sally was really there for me, like a good friend, like a mother, like a grandmother. The important thing that I learned from Sally was that if it took a half an hour to do something, you allotted 45 minutes. This was so you could do your work without being frantic, and could enjoy doing it. You could do a good job, could take your time, and do it right.

Johnny, when he worked by my side, became expert at making omelets. He then left, omelet pan in hand, as other chefs have done with their knives. He had a wonderful adventure cooking in southern France for owners of a lovely château, and then for some Americans who spent summers there. In 1985 he followed his sister Karen to the Anderson Valley in western Mendocino County, north of San Francisco, to open his own restaurant, the Floodgate Café. He now runs the Boonville Hotel.

Karen had moved with her husband, Tim, to run the Apple Farm that we had purchased with them, but she soon got tired of the long commute to Yountville from Anderson Valley to waitress for us. Eric left us to start his own construction business, though he did get married to Melissa at the French Laundry, and Melissa became a regular on the waitstaff. Our youngest daughter, Terry, became a wood carver, working alongside her partner, Debey Zito, a renowned furniture designer in the Bay Area.

Moonshine, the cat, sat on the scullery windowsill, just behind the big sink. She would sneak a paw over to collect a shrimp tail when our dishwasher, Tom, wasn't looking. When she died, a good friend made a papier-mâché replica of her, which sat on the windowsill to greet customers as they came up the walk.

Our enthusiastic restaurant staff shown raiding the kitchen larder; from left, longtime employee Joanne, son Johnny, daughter Kathy, and future son-in-law Bill.

Fifth: The Apple Farm

Passing It On (1995 to 2008)

previous: One of my favorite corners in the kitchen at the Apple Fam.

left: Peak harvest time at the farm stand, just as you enter the Apple Farm.

From a Farm to a Farm

I think my life has been a fairly straight road leading to the Apple Farm. I started out on a small farm, a homestead, in Northern California, where we had chickens, a cow, occasional pigs, rabbits, and a garden full of vegetables, fruit, and flowers. We ate simply, but very well. I learned early how to use a knife and to find my way around the kitchen. We almost never ate out, except for the church suppers. (We didn't go to church often, but we never missed the suppers!) My mother often officiated in the church kitchen, roasting turkeys and mashing potatoes for an annual fundraiser. Or we brought our contributions to large potlucks in the local park. Our big thrill was when my father would treat us to a milkshake at the creamery across from the movie theatre on a rare night in town.

In my decades between farms, I was off to college, then married and at home raising five children. I cooked up a storm during that time, waiting eagerly each month for the next *Sunset* magazine to arrive with the mail. I think of those years as the *Sunset* years. The magazine had good information about food, and I still use their recipes. Our love of Mexican food began with a great article on tostadas, which was our family party dish for years.

The habit of gathering a variety of fruit and vegetables from a family garden, which I did as a child, became a faint memory, though I never did give up the practice of using local ingredients. When we had visitors from afar, they were always treated to artichokes, and something with crab, and Sonoma Bakery sourdough. I had neither the interest nor the money for what I considered exotics like caviar and lobster. We always did have some sort of garden, though, and at the very least, we grew tomatoes. Where we lived in Fresno's Fig Garden district, an area of lovely old houses, each home had at least one or two old fig trees. You couldn't share the figs with your neighbors, because we all had too many. How I wish we had that problem now. Oranges we got from the Central Valley, and peaches, from nearby orchards.

When we started renovating the French Laundry, in Yountville, planting the herb garden was our first step toward the physical transformation of the property. And after we opened the restaurant, people started bringing us vegetables, mushrooms, and uncommon seeds to plant. We discovered someone raising poussin who had no customers for the livers; I still remember those gorgeous blond livers, which I gently sautéed with bacon and served on toast rounds. But they were so beautiful I would also simply sauté them on their own and serve with arugula from our garden.

"We are here and here is everywhere we want to be."

—from the Apple Farm guest book, by a grateful visitor

Then came the Apple Farm. Back in the summer of 1984, Don and I were looking for a small getaway spot, when we found this old, run-down, 30-plus-acre [12-plus-hectare] farm in the Anderson Valley, near the one-street town of Philo and not far from the Mendocino coastline. But we needed our daughter Karen and her husband, Tim, to make it feasible. Since they had always wanted to move farther north, their answer to our question was an immediate "Yes!"

Over the next thirty-five years, beginning with a derelict apple orchard, an old farmhouse in sad shape, a few old buildings, and boundless energy and hope, Karen and Tim revived the farm. They grafted heirloom varietals onto rows of existing trees and expanded the range of their products: not just apples but also apple juice, hard cider, boiled cider syrup, and cider vinegar aged in wine barrels, all crafted on the farm. In the original farmhouse, they made applesauce, jams, jellies, and chutneys, all available at their farm stand.

Originally there were twelve varieties of apples in the orchard, including an abundance of Golden Delicious, Red Delicious, Rhode Island Greening, Jonathan, Fall Pippin, Winter Banana, and the amazing Sierra Beauty. Over the years we have added to our collection of trees, which now include eighty varieties, all considered to be heirloom apples.

Teaching Others

When we left the French Laundry behind in 1993 and moved to the Apple Farm, joining Karen and Tim, I felt it was time to stop cooking for others. Instead, I wanted to try to pass on the techniques, habits, knowledge, and recipes I'd acquired through the years. So we took the old farmhouse and added a big kitchen and pantry suitable for a group. We also added an upstairs guest bedroom, three cottages, and a greenhouse, so that we could have our herbs and vegetable seedlings close at hand. Visitors came from all over, not only to stay and learn the craft of cooking, but to have the full farm-to-fork experience.

My mother was a teacher, and of course a major influence on me. So it had been preordained for me, when I headed off to college, that I was going to be a teacher. But back then I had found the curriculum excruciating, and I gave it up. When I could work with students on my own terms, though, I found, very much to my surprise, that I liked teaching.

I had taught some classes before we came to the Apple Farm, while I was still cooking at the French Laundry. Some of them were demonstrations for groups or fundraisers. I also participated in a series of classes on the basics of cooking for the Napa Valley College. I loved those classes because they were full of people who really needed them—a couple of recently divorced winemakers, a bride-to-be, some young mothers—all of them wanted to know where to start. And then, Mary Risley, who ran the Tante Marie cooking school on Telegraph Hill in San Francisco, would bring groups of students to take lessons from me, first at the restaurant, and later at the farm, which she had fallen in love with. She said she wanted the students to learn about lifestyle rather than just recipes.

At the Apple Farm, I didn't want to teach just recipes, though I did use mine to teach from. What I wanted students to take home with them were skills and attitudes: not just how to hold a knife, but the importance of washing and wiping it after each use, as well as wiping the counter constantly. I always emphasized tidiness and order.

We gave our first class in the early summer of 1995. It was full of our old friends and customers from our Yountville days and was a joyful occasion, with a lot of laughter and good food. We had a peach tree right outside our new kitchen, and the peaches were at their full, luscious ripeness. The ladies descended on the tree in full force. I still can picture Barbara Eisele, a regular customer at the French Laundry, with peach juice running down her face.

This first group of twelve Napa Valley ladies came back repeatedly with their husbands and friends, so the word spread, and our calendar was full from the very beginning.

opposite: Here I am with my daughter Karen, poaching eggs for a class. We are proud to have worked as a team for so many years.

Mary Risley is someone I admired greatly. She was one of the early women to take a leadership role in the food world, and she was self-taught, like me. Mary had gumption and energy. When she looked around her and saw how much food was being wasted, she actually did something about it. While running her cooking school (from 1979 to 2014), she started the organization Food Runners, which gathered surplus food from restaurants, grocery stores, and caterers and delivered it to shelters and food programs. Initially run from her home, the program has grown large enough to serve over 20,000 meals weekly in San Francisco.

When we built the three cottages, we were able to host four couples. The Apple Farm became a weekend destination for cooking, eating, and much carousing.

We gave weekday lunch classes for up to twenty people—a demonstration, with lunch included. The weekend classes were based on hands-on participation, eight people at a time, so I could work with them individually.

Don would be in charge of wine, and loved answering questions about what we served with the food. My son-in-law Tim would lead tours of the apple orchards, which he tended, and give advice on growing them. My daughter Karen stepped in as my assistant. Don poured wine, and Tim would take a break from the apples and join us for meals. It was all wonderful, and I didn't take my apron off for fifteen years.

Vodka-Spiked Cherry Tomatoes

SERVES 4 TO 6 / TOTAL TIME: 30 MIN

We introduced this recipe at the Apple Farm cooking weekends. Our students all gasped when they were asked to peel tiny cherry tomatoes, but it's actually quite easy to slip those skins off after a quick dip in boiling water. And this is the time to say yes to the proverbial question, "Can I help?"

In a small bowl, mix together:

½ cup [120 ml] vodka
2 Tbsp balsamic vinegar
1 tsp lemon zest
½ tsp salt

Bring a small pot of water to a boil.

Near the pot, place:

1½ pt [480 g] cherry tomatoes

For the cherry tomatoes, Sungold and Sweet 100 are our choice, for their wonderful flavor.

Fill a small strainer with a handful of the tomatoes and dip it into the boiling water for 2 to 3 seconds. Don't let go! Cool immediately in a bowl of ice water, and test one to see if the skin slips off easily. If the flesh is at all mushy, they have been in the boiling water too long. Repeat with the remaining tomatoes.

Slip the skins off the tomatoes, put the tomatoes in a bowl, and pour the vodka mixture over them. It should cover them nicely, but if it doesn't, add a little more vodka. Refrigerate, uncovered, until needed, but don't prepare them too far in advance. They don't keep well in the refrigerator for long.

We served these in tall martini glasses as a first course at the table or passed them around with sturdy toothpicks at cocktail time. The secret is that the alcohol enhances the flavors and therefore pushes the tomato essence up a notch.

Fennel, Apple & Potato Soup

SERVES 8 / TOTAL TIME: 1 HOUR

At the farm, we were always looking for new ways to show off our apples. I love this trio of ingredients. Fennel has such a fresh aroma and taste.

Scrub and cut into chunks:	**4 small red or Yukon gold potatoes, or 1 large russet**
Put in a soup pot and add:	**2 apples, peeled and quartered** **3 cups [720 ml] weak chicken stock** **Salt**

Bring to a simmer and cook until the potatoes test done, about 20 minutes. The apples will be tender by this time as well.

Remove and set aside the fronds from:	**2 fennel bulbs**

Keep the prettiest of the fronds whole for the garnish, and finely chop the rest. Slice the fennel bulbs.

In a skillet over medium heat, melt:	**3 Tbsp butter**
Add the fennel and:	**1 onion, diced**

Sauté for 5 minutes, and then add 2 cups [480 ml] water. Bring to a simmer, and cook until almost tender. Transfer to the soup pot with the potatoes and apples and cook 5 minutes more. Cool briefly and transfer to a blender. Purée until smooth, and return to the pot.

Thin the soup in the pot with:	**1 to 2 cups [240 to 480 ml] half-and-half**
Taste for salt and add more if needed, along with:	**1 tsp freshly ground white pepper**

Add 3 to 4 Tbsp of the chopped fennel fronds to the soup. Over medium heat, warm up the soup, but avoid reaching a boil, as the added light cream can curdle.

To serve, garnish each bowl of soup with a whole fennel frond.

Use apples such as Philo Gold, Jonathan, or Spitzenberg. End-of-season apples seem to have a more intense flavor, so this is best made in the fall, at the end of the apple season. You can even use flavorful apples you have around that have mellowed and lost their texture.

Pasta with Fresh Tomato Sauce

SERVES 4 / TOTAL TIME: 45 MIN

This summer dish is a good way to use an abundance of ripe tomatoes from the garden when they are all at peak flavor at the same time. And since you don't need to cook the sauce, it's perfect for a hot summer night.

For the sauce, in a large bowl, mix together:

4 to 6 ripe tomatoes, peeled, seeded, and chopped
1 small white or red onion, cut into small dice
1 large garlic clove, minced
¼ cup [5 g] slivered fresh basil leaves
2 Tbsp roughly chopped fresh flat-leaf parsley
⅓ cup [80 ml] olive oil
3 Tbsp balsamic or cider vinegar
Salt and freshly ground black pepper

To remove the seeds from the peeled ripe tomatoes, halve them first, then, one at a time, while holding the tomato half over a strainer set into a large measuring cup (to catch the juices), gently squeeze the seeds out. And save those juices!

Let sit at room temperature for at least 15 minutes and up to 1 hour.

Bring a large pot of water to a boil for the pasta. When it comes to a full boil, add:

A generous amount of salt (it should taste like sea water)
1 lb [455 g] your favorite dried pasta (I like fettuccini)

Cook until just tender and drain in a colander, reserving some of the pasta water to loosen the pasta if necessary.

Taste the tomato sauce for seasoning, and add salt and pepper as needed.

In a large bowl, toss the pasta with the reserved tomato juice and:

½ cup [15 g] grated cheese, Parmesan, romano, or Asiago

VARIATION: Having an abundance of our farmhouse chèvre we can afford to use a lavish amount tossed with pasta, and rarely feel the need for any other cheese.

Plate each serving, spoon on the tomato sauce, and sprinkle with more cheese.

Pasta with Asparagus & Preserved Lemon

SERVES 6 TO 8 / TOTAL TIME: 45 MIN EXCLUDING MAKING THE LEMONS

As an all-in-one meal, this was a favorite lunchtime offering during our Apple Farm weekends. It was also a perfect use for the preserved lemons we like to make and have on hand.

Bring a large pot of water to a boil for the pasta.

When it comes to a full boil, add:

A generous amount of salt
1 lb [455 g] dried pasta

Linguini, fettuccine, or pappardelle all work well here.

Cook the pasta until it is just tender. Remove and reserve a generous amount of the cooking water, and drain the pasta in a colander.

While the pasta is cooking, in a large skillet over medium heat, melt or warm:

¼ cup [55 g] butter or ¼ cup [60 ml] olive oil

Add:

1 bunch asparagus (1 lb [455 g]), trimmed and cut diagonally into 1 to 2 in [2.5 to 5 cm] pieces

Sauté until almost tender, but still crisp. Remove from the heat and let rest, uncovered.

Mince:

¼ cup [55 g] or more Preserved Lemons (recipe follows), including both the rind and pulp

You may rinse the lemon before you mince it to reduce the salt.

In a large bowl, toss the asparagus and preserved lemon with the pasta, adding a little of the reserved cooking water to loosen the pasta as needed.

Grate with a Microplane, or shave with a vegetable peeler (which makes such pretty curls):

A chunk of good Parmesan cheese

Sprinkle the cheese over the top of the pasta and serve at once with:

Fresh lemon wedges
A drizzle of your best olive oil

You may want to add a squeeze of fresh lemon juice at the end for extra zing.

PRESERVED LEMONS

There are many variations of these lemons, but this is my way of preparing them. I prefer to keep them simple and pure, with no other ingredients.

Wash and dry: **3 or 4 lemons**

Cut each lemon into eight wedges   **1 cup [160 g] kosher salt,**
and transfer to a medium bowl.   **preferably Diamond Crystal**
Toss with:

Pack into a ½ pt [240 ml] glass jar, pressing the lemons down into their juice
Cover and let stand at room temperature for 1 week, shaking occasionally.
Store in the refrigerator, where they will keep for up to 1 year.

To use, finely dice or slice the preserved rind.

Braised Pork with Cider and Apples

SERVES 10 TO 12 / PREP TIME: 1 HOUR / COOK TIME: 2 HOURS

When we made this at the Chutney Kitchen, we called it Normandy Pork, since the ingredients are all to be found in that northwestern region of France. I tend to use simpler names as the years go by; I'm not sure if it's a trend, or just me. At any rate, these flavors are very well suited to pork, and of course, it's only natural for us to use our own apple products at the Apple Farm.

Preheat the oven to 325°F [165°C].

Cut into 1½ in [4 cm] cubes:	**3 to 5 lb [1.4 to 2.3 kg] boneless pork shoulder roast**
Season well with:	**Salt**
In a large skillet over medium heat, melt:	**3 Tbsp butter**

In batches, brown the pork lightly and transfer to a casserole dish, preferably clay.

Add to the skillet and sauté until softened, about 10 minutes:	**2 medium onions, sliced lengthwise** **4 garlic cloves, sliced** **3 shallots, slivered**
Then add and bring to a boil:	**2 cups [480 ml] hard cider** **1 cup [240 ml] white wine** **1 tart apple, finely chopped** **3 Tbsp chopped fresh thyme**

Pour this over the meat in the casserole dish. Cover with a sheet of parchment paper or aluminum foil and put the lid on. Place the dish in the oven and cook until the pork is very tender, 1½ to 2 hours.

Meanwhile, place the skillet over medium heat and melt:	**3 Tbsp butter**

Recipe continues…

Add to the skillet:	**3 large tart apples, such as Jonathan or Fall Pippins, peeled, cored, and sliced** **1 cup [125 g] pearl onions (at least 2 per person), or 1 cup [48 g] sliced green onions (white and light green parts)**
Sauté until softened, about 10 minutes. Season with:	**3 Tbsp fresh thyme leaves** **Salt and freshly ground white pepper**

Try Sierra Beauty or Spitzenberg, but a Philo Gold (a variety of Golden Delicious) is lovely for a more aromatic apple flavor. Use what you have or can find. Late-season apples tend to keep their shape when cooked; early-season apples turn to sauce.

Cover and let the apple mixture rest until the pork is ready. When it's done, remove from the oven and lower the oven temperature to 200°F [95°C]. Pour the pork cooking juices into a large heatproof measuring cup, and skim off any fat that rises to the top.

Add the apple mixture to the pork and set aside, covered.

Pour the skimmed cooking juices into the skillet, place over medium heat, and add:	**1 cup [240 ml] heavy cream**
Simmer to reduce a little until slightly thickened, then add:	**2 oz [55 ml] brandy**

Taste for seasoning. Add salt and another grind of white pepper, if needed. Pour the sauce over the pork and apples and let rest in the oven at 200°F [95 °C] for about 1 hour to let the flavors meld.

To serve, spoon the pork and apples over:	**A cooked delicate small pasta, such as orzo or riso**
Serve alongside:	**Snap peas, gently sautéed**

At the French Laundry, our standard pasta to use, one we liked immensely, was the semi di melone ("melon seed") from De Cecco, but they have stopped making it, much to our dismay.

Open a bottle of hard cider and enjoy!

Spicy Fig & Almond Torte

SERVES 8 TO 10 / PREP: 35 MIN / COOK TIME: 1 HOUR 10 MIN

This is a beautiful dessert to serve when offering a brandy or liqueur, such as amaretto. It will be most appreciated in winter, when there are no fresh fruits available. And it tastes just as good on the second day.

Preheat the oven to 300°F [150°C].

On two small baking sheets, toast until just starting to color:

¾ cup [90 g] whole almonds (about 15 min)
½ cup [70 g] fine bread crumbs (about 10 min)

Grind toasted almonds minimally in a blender to make a coarse meal.
Raise the oven temperature to 325°F [165°C].

Generously butter a 10 in [25 cm] springform pan.

In a large bowl, combine the ground almonds and the bread crumbs with:

Zest of 2 oranges
12 dried figs, minced
1 tsp baking powder
½ tsp ground cinnamon
¼ tsp freshly grated nutmeg
¼ tsp ground allspice
¼ tsp ground cloves
1 Tbsp cognac

Separate into two large mixing bowls:

5 eggs

Add to the yolks:

¾ cup [150 g] sugar

With an electric mixer, beat the yolks and sugar for 5 minutes, until very thick. Stir in the crumb mixture by hand.

In a clean bowl, beat the egg whites until soft peaks form. Gently fold a quarter of the egg whites into the batter, and then carefully fold in the rest.

Pour or spoon the batter into the prepared pan. Give it a whack on the counter to settle the egg whites, but not too hard. Bake until it feels just firm to the touch, about 1 hour.

Let cool on a rack for 30 minutes and remove the sides of the pan.

Recipe continues...

Folding a little bit in first loosens the mixture, making it easier to fold in the rest of the egg whites. I like to use a slotted spoon.

Sift over the torte: **Powdered sugar**

Serve with: **Softly whipped cream**
                                        Toasted almonds, orange zest,
                                        or both

Either slice and serve immediately, or store, covered, for up to 2 days
at room temperature. It keeps beautifully.

Virginia Draper's Figgy Pudding

SERVES 8 TO 10 / TOTAL TIME: 1 HOUR EXCLUDING RESTING TIME

This unusual and wonderful recipe was given to me by the lovely Virginia
Draper with the admonition, "Now you owe me one!" I was meeting with
Virginia and her husband, Jerome, who were known in the Valley for their
vineyards, especially the Cabernet Sauvignon. We were planning a luncheon
for the San Francisco Food and Wine Society, and although we didn't end
up including this dessert, I loved serving it later at the Chutney Kitchen and
the French Laundry. It earned the nickname "figgy pudding."

Cut into small chunks and transfer to   **12 large, ripe figs (overripe**
a medium bowl: **and a little dry is fine)**

Chop: **8 oz [225 g] semisweet or**
                                            bittersweet chocolate

Add to the figs and stir in: **½ cup [120 ml] Kahlúa**

Let rest 1 hour or more so the flavors can meld.

When ready to serve, whip until   **1 cup [240 ml] whipping cream**
soft peaks form:

Gently fold the chocolate mixture into the whipped cream (or vice versa).

Serve in tall stemmed glasses and   **Shaved chocolate or cocoa nibs**
garnish with:

VARIATION: This is also
quite good made with dried
figs. If they are very dry,
steam them first to soften.
Then give them a longer soak
in the Kahlúa, about 2 to
3 hours.

Apricot & Cherry Clafoutis

SERVES 10 / PREP TIME: 30 MIN / COOK TIME: 30 MIN

This is a simple way of producing a fruit dessert very quickly, and it is altogether satisfying and delicious. Sour cherries are traditionally used for clafoutis in France, but since we only have sweet cherries locally, I decided to add apricots for some extra zing. In France, they don't pit the cherries, which probably makes them more flavorful, but it's safer to serve the clafoutis without the pits!

This is at its very best served warm from the oven. It will puff up dramatically, and then lose air while cooling. So if you want to show it off, be sure to present it to your guests right out of the oven. It is a perfect brunch offering as well as a lovely dessert.

Preheat the oven to 375°F [190°C].

In a small dish, combine:	**2 Tbsp sugar** **1 tsp ground cinnamon**

Set aside the cinnamon sugar. In the oven, warm a 10 in [25 cm] deep-dish pie plate or a cast-iron skillet.

In a large bowl, whisk together until smooth (or use a blender):	**3 eggs** **1 cup [240 ml] half-and-half or milk** **¼ cup [60 ml] melted butter** **1 tsp vanilla extract** **½ tsp salt**
Add gradually, while whisking (or with the blender running):	**⅔ cup [90 g] all-purpose flour**
To the warmed pie plate (or skillet), add:	**2 Tbsp butter**
Swirl the dish to melt the butter, and scatter over the bottom of the dish:	**3 cups [420 g] halved and pitted cherries** **2 cups [450 g] pitted and quartered apricots, preferably Blenheims**

VARIATIONS: Some of my favorite variations are plums, apples, or rhubarb.

Drizzle with: **A splash of brandy**

Return the pie plate to the oven. When the fruit is hot, after about 15 minutes, pour the batter over it and sprinkle with the cinnamon sugar mixture.

Bake until puffy and set, 25 to 30 minutes.

Serve, preferably very warm, with   **Apple cider syrup (see page 231)**
any of the following: **Vanilla ice cream or Cinnamon**
                                        Ice Cream (page 231)
                                        A dollop of whipped cream or
                                        sour cream

Caramel Apricot Rice Pudding

SERVES 10 TO 12 / PREP TIME 40 MIN / COOK TIME: 1 HOUR

This is best served while it is still warm from the oven. The components can be made ahead and combined, then popped into a slow oven for an hour. Try it for a special brunch treat or after a light supper.

Preheat the oven to 325°F [165°C].

Start with:
1½ cups [270 g] dried apricots, preferably Blenheims

If they are very dry, soften by soaking them in warm water for 20 minutes. Drain and set aside.

In a small bowl, mix together and set aside:
**3 Tbsp raw sugar, such as Demerara
1 tsp ground cinnamon
¼ tsp freshly grated nutmeg**

In a small saucepan, put:

⅓ cup [65 g] Arborio rice or another short-grain rice

Add enough water to cover by 1 in [2.5 cm].

Bring to a rolling boil. Turn down the heat as low as possible and cover. Cook for 20 minutes, uncover, and fluff the rice. Let cool.

In a 7 by 9 in [17 by 23 cm] baking pan, melt:

¼ cup [55 g] butter

Mix in:

½ cup [100 g] brown sugar

Spread out evenly over the bottom of the pan, and add the apricots in a layer. Set aside.

While the rice is cooling, in a medium bowl, mix together:

3 eggs, lightly beaten
½ cup [100 g] sugar
1 tsp salt
2 tsp vanilla extract

In a large saucepan, scald, or bring almost to a boil, and remove from the heat to cool a little:

3 cups [720 ml] whole milk or half-and-half

Pour the egg mixture into the milk very gradually, a little at a time while whisking, to avoid cooking the eggs.

Spread out the rice evenly over the apricots. Pour the custard gently over all and sprinkle with the cinnamon sugar.

Bake until the custard is set, 45 minutes to 1 hour.

While still warm, spoon into shallow bowls. Be sure to get the apricots and caramel in each serving. Serve with a pitcher of heavy cream.

Summer Pudding Inspired by Elizabeth David

SERVES 8 / TOTAL TIME: 40 MIN EXCLUDING CHILLING TIME

Having come across this recipe in Elizabeth David's classic *Summer Cooking* (1980), I kept it on my maybe-someday list for years. But whenever I looked at it, I remembered there was no cream and no butter, so, I wondered, how could it be a dessert? It wasn't until I was at the Apple Farm and faced with bucket loads of berries that I finally tried it out. It was a hit, both beautiful to look at and delightfully refreshing, especially on hot summer days.

In a large saucepan, over low heat, warm together:	**1½ lb [680 g] berries** **1 cup [200 g] sugar**
Cook until the berries break down and their juices flow, about 2 to 3 minutes. Then stir in:	**2 Tbsp brandy or a berry wine**
Meanwhile, remove the crust from:	**1 to 2 loaves firm white bread, sliced**

Line the bottom and sides of an 8 cup [2 L] soufflé dish or a bowl with plastic wrap. Next line it with some of the bread slices, fitting them snugly against the sides and bottom.

Pour half the berry mixture into the dish. Add a layer of bread, top with the remaining berry mixture, and finish with a layer of bread. Make sure to save any extra juice from the berries that has collected in the saucepan. You will want it later.

Weigh down the pudding. A small plate or saucer that just fits inside the soufflé dish will work. You then want something heavy on top of the plate to press the berries down. Refrigerate for at least 4 hours, or overnight.

When ready to serve, turn out the pudding onto a flat, rimmed platter, and pour the reserved juices over it. If there is any bread showing, use a pastry brush to paint the bare spots with the juices.

If you don't have enough juice, paint it with:	**A little raspberry or strawberry jam, thinned with water**
Cut into wedges and serve with:	**Softly whipped cream**
Garnish with:	**A few berry leaves or sprigs**

If you want to stay true to what Elizabeth David would have wanted, use black raspberries and red currants, if you can find them. But it's more important to use what is abundant and at the height of the season.

Raspberry wine goes wonderfully with this pudding and is worth searching for.

A good sliced cottage loaf works well. You don't want to use a loaf of brioche or challah, as they would be too rich for this recipe.

On Olive Oil

In my mother's pantry, we always had a bottle of Wesson oil and a tin of olive oil, which my mother bought from a local producer in the Central Valley. When I became a little more discerning, I threw out the Wesson oil in my own pantry. Mostly I used olive oil, but I played with other oils for a while. I tried a bottle of canola oil and vowed never to buy another. It just didn't have any flavor, and cooking for me is about building layer upon layer of flavor. The flavor of good olive oil is something I welcome, and now I use it for almost everything I cook.

At the Chutney Kitchen and French Laundry, I kept three grades of olive oil on hand. The lesser quality, which had a higher smoking point, I used for sautéing. The in-between, I used for salad dressings and most cooking tasks. I stocked a really good one to use for finishing off dishes such as my Turnip Soup with Fresh Mustard Greens (page 213).

I'm loyal to California producers, probably because I'm a California girl at heart. Early on at the Chutney Kitchen, I bought one of the first locally produced olive oils from Lila Yeager, who was one of the partners at Freemark Abbey Winery. And I also bought from Napa Olive Oil, in St. Helena. Visiting the old white barn, with its antique olive oil presses, was too wonderful to resist.

It's fun to try the many different olive oils available today, but I find it ridiculous to purchase olive oil from the Mediterranean when we are so capable of producing olive oil in our own climate. We have a long history of producing good olive oil. In the 1700s, Spanish Franciscan priests arrived in California with their cuttings and planted row upon row of olive trees. When the trees matured, the olives were harvested, crushed, and pressed into oil at Franciscan missions from San Diego to Sonoma. Now, some of the best olive oil in the world is produced here.

It's important to remember that the fresher olive oil is, the better, and shipping it from afar guarantees it won't be fresh. These days, unless I've received some special oil, usually as a gift or made by a friend, I have settled down to just one reliable brand, Sciabica, made on a farm in Modesto by a family that has been growing olives since 1936. I use it for everything. And at the Apple Farm, we buy it in 5 gal [19 L] drums and decant it into empty wine bottles. It keeps very well and we love the flavor.

A FEW TIPS: Use olive oil lavishly, as it works well with almost everything.

• Store it in a dark, cool place, such as a pantry or cellar. Light and heat are the enemies of good olive oil. You don't want to refrigerate it because it congeals the oil, but it won't hurt it.

• Use it up. It does not improve with age.

• If you buy a large amount, decant it into smaller bottles you can use more easily. Green glass wine bottles are great for keeping the light out.

• A combination of olive oil and cider vinegar will keep your wooden counter or cutting board in good shape. I use it often in my own kitchen. Mix 1 part olive oil with 4 parts vinegar. Rub the mixture into the wood, and buff the wood with a dry cloth.

Olive Oil Tart

MAKES 12 TO 16 SLICES / PREP TIME: 30 MIN / COOK TIME: 15 TO 20 MIN

This lovely savory tart was inspired by a photo in Roger Vergé's big, beautiful book *Entertaining in the French Style* (1986).

Preheat the oven to 400°F [200°C].

I like to serve this as very warm finger food, but be careful, the onions hold their heat!

In a large bowl, whisk together:

2¼ cups [315 g] all-purpose flour
½ tsp salt

In a small pitcher, whisk together:

¾ cup [180 ml] good olive oil
½ cup [120 ml] lukewarm water

Make a well in the flour and pour in the water oil emulsion. Beginning with the flour closest to the well, use your fingers to quickly stir the flour into the oil and water. Gather up the dough into a smooth ball. Transfer the dough to a baking sheet and, with your fingers, push it into two long rectangles. Crimp the edges, and with a fork, prick the bottom a few times. Bake until just set and starting to brown, about 15 minutes.

Do not knead. You want it to be tender.

The edges are important to hold the filling in.

In a skillet over medium heat, warm:

3 Tbsp olive oil

Add and sauté until almost softened and light brown, about 10 minutes:

2 white or yellow onions, slivered
Salt and freshly ground black pepper

Remove from the heat and transfer to a medium bowl.

In a small bowl, beat together:

2 eggs
¼ cup [60 ml] heavy cream

Drizzle the eggs and cream over the onions and stir to combine.

Spoon the filling into the crust, and distribute on top:

1 cup [140 g] Kalamata olives, halved and pitted

Return to the oven and bake until the filling is set and the crust is brown around the edges, another 15 minutes or so.

Sprinkle with:

A handful of fresh thyme, and some flaky salt

Sprigs are beautiful here.

Cut into wedges, and serve warm.

Big Parties

It all began with our oldest daughter, Kathy's wedding. She was nineteen when she married Bill Hoffman. He was her first date, and she made a good choice. I'm actually writing this on the week of their fortieth anniversary!

It was 1973, and we wanted to have a *party*, as opposed to a reception. We decided to break the rules: no formal reception line, no sit-down supper. Following the ceremony at the little church in Rutherford, we just darted back through the rain to Yountville to our kitchen at the Chutney Kitchen, and set out food for what turned out to be one big, wonderful party.

I was determined to stick to finger food, as I hated trying to juggle a plate and fork and napkin and wineglass all at the same time. Some people manage it gracefully, but my family isn't among that group. So we began by serving an array of nibbles, several of them passed around, and a few more beautifully arranged on a table.

That was the first large party we hosted. Then, as the years went by, we learned to handle bigger events—the type of parties that involved rented tables and chairs, so that people could sit down to eat a proper meal. But I still think the best sort of party is one where everyone is able to walk around, moving from one table to another, each one with a different array of foods. It tends to keep the party livelier because no one gets stuck in one place.

After passing around some finger food, we'd bring other food out in stages: When the shrimp was gone, we'd replaced it with platters of steak with all the fixings to make small sandwiches. Then we offered an array of cheeses and fruits, and there might be some dancing before we presented dessert. Coffee would be in the kitchen for those who needed it for the drive home. We liked to pass trays of Champagne to start with, and then let guests pace themselves by encouraging them to go to the bar to choose their drinks.

In those days, wedding cakes were always white, sugary, tasteless affairs, which all the guests nibbled at to be polite. But they were not real food! So for Kathy and Bill's wedding, we pulled out Aunt Polly's recipe for Angie's Spice Cake (page 278), which was full of fruits and nuts. I iced it with our favorite frosting, a granulated sugar and butter concoction that traditionally crowns a red velvet cake. The result was a three-tiered, buttery beauty, dense with dried fruit and nuts. It was a smashing success, and the prototype for many cakes to follow.

Through the years, there were many more weddings, for our family, for friends, employees, and even customers. The base for a wedding cake might be a chocolate pound cake, or a coffee sponge cake, or even a simple sponge cake, but never what I call "wedding cake white"! We played with the garnishes, using a pastry tube to make stars and dots and stripes, but usually there were fresh flowers on top, and the cakes all tasted as good as they looked!

opposite: At my grandson Joe's wedding in 2008, I got to take off my apron and join the party. Here I am, with my little sister, Kay.

I have always preferred round tables at these functions, so that more guests can gather around and reach the goodies.

I had a rule (which at least I tried to enforce): We avoided topping off glasses. It hopefully discouraged guests from drinking too much, and occasionally, a trip to the bar provided them with a good excuse for leaving a boring conversation!

Figaroles (Fig-a-Roles)

SERVES 6 / PREP TIME: 30 MIN / COOK TIME: 10 TO 15 MIN

In October 2002, I was told just before an event for Mendocino's resident professional opera company, Opera Fresca, that the theme was going to be—what else?—opera. They requested that the menu reflect the theme.

It was a challenge, but I managed to come up with a name for the first course, fig-a-roles. Then I had to dream up a dish to match. So I stuffed figs with a goat cheese mixture, and wrapped them in bacon slices. Thus "fig-a-roles."

Preheat the oven to 350°F [180°C].

Spread out on a rimmed baking sheet:

18 thin slices bacon or pancetta

Partially cook in the oven, until some of the fat has rendered, but the slices are still soft and pliable. Don't let the bacon get crisp and brown.

In a medium bowl, mix together:

8 oz [225 g] fresh goat cheese
1 Tbsp finely chopped
fresh chives
1 tsp chopped fresh rosemary

Season with:

Coarsely ground black pepper

On a work surface, arrange:

18 fresh figs

Cut a small slit lengthwise in each one. Stuff each fig with about 1 tsp of the cheese mixture and wrap with a strip of bacon. You may have to trim it if the ends overlap too much. Secure the Figaroles with either firm, woody rosemary sprigs, if you have them, or small skewers.

Arrange on a baking sheet and bake in the oven just until the bacon is crisp, about 10 to 15 minutes. Remove before the cheese melts.

These really are too messy for finger food, so serve them on small plates with knives and forks.

Pickled Shrimp

SERVES 20 TO 25 / TOTAL TIME: 40 MIN

We used to make these shrimp for almost every large party we hosted. They were set out on a round table, in a huge glass bowl. Surrounding them were three sauces for dipping, bowls of lemon water for refreshing fingers, piles of napkins, and bowls for the tails. This was finger food at its best, and the size of the crowd around the table didn't diminish until the last shrimp was gone.

Large shrimp prepared this way also go well with salads, the addition of citrus providing a wonderful refreshing quality.

Bring a very large pot of salted water to a boil.

Peel but leave the tails on: **5 lb [2.3 kg] large shrimp**

If you are cooking 1 lb [455 g] or less, remove the pot from the heat after you add the shrimp and let them cook in the hot water until done.

Add the shrimp to the water, a few at a time, and cook just until curled and pink.

Remove each batch from the boiling water with a slotted spoon, drain, and return the water to a boil before you add the next batch. Be careful not to overcook the shrimp, because they will toughen up. Pat them dry with a clean towel.

Transfer the shrimp to a large bowl, and add:

1 orange, quartered and thinly sliced
1 lemon, quartered and thinly sliced
1 lime, quartered and thinly sliced
1 white onion, slivered
¼ cup [60 ml] olive oil

Season with: **Coarse sea salt and coarsely ground black pepper**

Toss to combine well. This can be made up to 4 to 6 hours in advance and refrigerated. But you can also serve it right away. The flavor is better at room temperature, so be sure to take it out of the refrigerator and let it warm up a little before serving.

To serve, arrange in a large bowl, and surround by small bowls of any or all of the following:

Guacamole
Red Pepper Mayonnaise (page 79)
Green Mayonnaise (page 79), made with cilantro or chives and orange zest

Have small bowls available for washing fingers, and to put the tails in.

Bloody Mary Sorbet

SERVES 10 TO 12 / TOTAL TIME: 1 HOUR EXCLUDING CHILLING TIME

This festive, savory sorbet goes very well with Pickled Shrimp (page 272) or with cold sliced steak.

In a large bowl, stir together:

3 cups [720 ml] tomato juice
3 Tbsp fresh lemon juice
3 Tbsp fresh lime juice
1 Tbsp prepared horseradish
Salt and coarsely ground black pepper
½ cup [120 ml] vodka (optional, but would this be a Bloody Mary without it?)

Freeze as directed in your ice-cream maker. Transfer to a flat tray, cover, and put into your freezer to firm up to a scoopable texture, at least 1 hour.

To serve, put a scoop in each shallow bowl and if you like, add:

3 pickled or grilled shrimp

Garnish with:

A sprig of cilantro and maybe a scoop of guacamole

Raising the may pole at our 13th annual May Day Celebration, held in lower field at the Apple Farm. Going all the way back to our Yountville days, our family had a long tradition of ambitious themed celebrations. We love to set the stage for a great party. My granddaughter Sophia is the little girl in front, and my son Eric is in the yellow shirt raising the pole.

Smoked Trout Pâté on Apple Slices

SERVES 20 TO 30 / TOTAL TIME: 40 MIN

This came about when we were getting some wonderful smoked trout, which wasn't too dry, and we had Pink Pearl apples ripening on our trees. These pink-fleshed apples are the type that don't turn brown when exposed to air, and they have a wonderful tart flavor. I mixed the trout with our own homemade farmhouse cheese. The combination tasted perfect on Pink Pearl apple slices. A good fresh chèvre or a natural cream cheese will also do the job beautifully.

Carefully pick the bones from:

8 oz [225 g] smoked trout

Discard the skin. Break up the trout into pieces, transfer to the bowl of a stand mixer, and at low speed, mix the trout with:

8 oz [225 g] natural cream cheese or fresh chèvre, at room temperature
¼ cup [60 g] prepared horseradish (we like Tulelake brand)
Salt and coarsely ground black pepper

Mix just until combined. You should still have small pieces of the trout intact.

Serve the pâté on:

Slices of apple, preferably Pink Pearl

Top the pâté with:

Toasted salted walnuts (see Margin Note)

To make the toasted salted walnuts, warm about 2 cups [240 g] in a 300°F [150°C] oven. Then toss with 1 Tbsp of melted butter, a sprinkle of sugar, and a sprinkle of coarse salt. Toast for another 10 to 15 minutes.

Persimmon Pudding with Two Brandy Sauces

SERVES 16 TO 20 / TOTAL TIME: 30 MIN EXCLUDING MAKING THE CAKE

When life gives you persimmon trees, make persimmon pudding—and persimmon trees we have at the Apple Farm. So I dreamt up this winter dessert as a tribute to my Aunt Polly, who gave me the recipe for Angie's Spice Cake (page 278), and my Aunt Saidie.

This variation on the spice cake recipe is served warm, with the two brandy sauces that Aunt Saidie presented with her pudding at Christmastime.

Assemble and bake:	**1 recipe Angie's Spice Cake (page 278), omitting the frosting, and replacing the carrots with 2 cups [280 g] grated firm-ripe Fuyu persimmons**
Serve warm, and pour over each slice:	**Hot Brandy Sauce (recipe follows)**
And on the side, add:	**A dollop of Hard Sauce (recipe follows)**

Any leftover sauce will keep, covered, at room temperature for 1 day.

HOT BRANDY SAUCE

In a small saucepan over medium heat, warm:	**1 cup [120 ml] cognac, or another brandy** **1 cup [120 ml] apple cider syrup (see page 231)**

HARD SAUCE

In a medium bowl, with an electric mixer at medium speed, cream:	**½ cup [110 g] butter, at room temperature**
Gradually beat in:	**1½ cups [150 g] sifted powdered sugar** **½ tsp freshly grated nutmeg**
Add:	**3 to 4 Tbsp cognac, or another brandy**

Angie's Spice Cake

SERVES 12 / TOTAL TIME: 2 HOURS EXCLUDING COOLING TIME

While I was looking for an alternative to the usual, inane white wedding cake, I read that in England there was a groom's cake made with fruit and nuts. So for the wedding of my oldest daughter, Kathy, I dredged up my Aunt Polly's spice cake recipe.

In the little notebook where Aunt Polly kept her recipes, she called it Angie's Spice Cake. Angie was her longtime housekeeper, and I've had no reason to tweak her recipe, since Angie really knew what she was doing and deserves the credit here.

Preheat the oven to 350°F [180°C].

Butter a standard 10 in [25 cm] Bundt pan or tube pan.

In a large saucepan, combine and bring to a boil.

2 Tbsp butter
1⅓ cups [265 g] sugar
1⅓ cups [320 ml] water
2 cups [280 g] coarsely grated carrots
1 cup [140 g] golden raisins
½ cup [70 g] currants
2 tsp cocoa powder
¼ tsp ground cinnamon
¼ tsp ground cloves
¼ tsp freshly grated nutmeg

After 5 minutes, remove from the heat and let cool.

Meanwhile, in a medium bowl, sift together:

2 cups [280 g] all-purpose flour
1 tsp baking soda
1 tsp salt

Chop and add:

1 cup [120 g] walnut halves, toasted and cooled completely

Sir the dry ingredients into the cooled carrot mixture.

Fill the prepared pan with the batter. Bake until slightly browned and firm to the touch, about 1 hour. It won't hurt to let it stay a little longer in the oven if you're not certain, as it will sink in the middle if taken out too early. If in doubt, give it another 15 minutes. Remove the cake from the oven and allow to cool on a rack for 10 minutes. Invert onto a second rack and continue to cool.

Meanwhile, to make our favorite vanilla icing, combine in a medium saucepan:

3 Tbsp flour
1 cup half-and-half

Cook, stirring, over medium heat until thickened, about 5 minutes.

In a blender or food processor, whirl for 10 seconds until very fine: **1 cup [200 g] sugar**

With an electric mixer, beat until creamy: **1 cup [220 g] butter, at room temperature**

Add the blended sugar, along with: **1 tsp vanilla extract**

Continue beating until fluffy, and then add the thickened cream, a little at a time for a smooth spreadable consistency.

When the cake is cooled completely, turn out onto a cake platter. Ice the cake and serve. This moist cake keeps beautifully for several days if well wrapped.

below: Decorating a wedding cake with my daughter Karen in the dining room next to the teaching kitchen, ready to take it through the doorway to the wedding party outside.

Coffee Walnut Sponge Cake

SERVES 12 / PREP TIME: 1 HOUR / COOK TIME: 1 HOUR EXCLUDING COOLING TIME

This is a beautiful cake, not too sweet and with a strong coffee flavor. It is frosted with my favorite icing, but coffee-flavored. The cake goes well with a scoop of ice cream, especially vanilla or coffee.

Preheat the oven to 325° [165°C].

Melt:	**2 Tbsp butter**

Grease the bottom of an angel food cake pan (also called a tube pan) with some of the melted butter. Do not grease the sides, as you want the cake to have something to hold onto as it rises.

 Cut a piece of parchment to paper to fit snugly on the bottom of the pan, and grease the paper.

Toast in the oven for about 15 minutes until dry and fragrant:	**2½ cups [300 g] walnut halves**

Let cool and then chop. A nut grinder works well for this, but I prefer to chop them with a knife, as I like the larger pieces. Chop a small amount at a time to avoid getting them too fine. Set aside.

Stir together:	**2 Tbsp instant espresso** **1 cup [240 ml] brewed** **hot coffee**

Set aside to cool.

In a blender or food processor, whirl for 10 seconds until very fine:	**1½ cups [300 g] granulated** **sugar**
Sift together into a medium bowl:	**2 cups [280 g] all-purpose flour** **1 Tbsp baking powder** **½ tsp salt**
Separate:	**7 eggs**

In a medium bowl, beat the egg whites until they form soft peaks. Set aside.

In the bowl of a stand mixer, combine the sugar, egg yolks, and:

1 tsp vanilla

Beat at medium speed until the mixture is light and lemon colored. With the mixer on low speed, add the dry ingredients alternately with the coffee mixture, a third at a time.

By hand, fold in 1 cup [120 g] of the chopped toasted walnuts.

Give the egg whites a few whisks to bring them back together and gently fold them into the batter until blended, stopping as soon as there are no more white streaks.

Spoon the batter into the prepared pan. Bake until light brown and firm to the touch, about 1 hour.

Turn the pan upside down onto the neck of a wine bottle and allow to cool.

Meanwhile, make the coffee icing. Combine in a medium saucepan:

1 cup half-and-half
3 Tbsp flour
2 Tbsp instant coffee

Cook, stirring, over medium heat until thickened, about 5 minutes. Remove from the heat and allow to cool.

In a blender or food processor, whirl for 10 seconds until very fine:

1 cup [200 g] sugar

With an electric mixer, beat until creamy:

1 cup [220 g] butter, at room temperature

Add the blended sugar, along with:

1 tsp vanilla extract

Continue beating until fluffy. Add the cooled coffee mixture, a little at a time.

When the cake has cooled, remove carefully from the pan using a cake palette knife or sharp knife and transfer it to a cake platter. Frost the top and sides, and don't forget to do the center cavity. Cover with the remaining 1½ cups [180 g] chopped toasted walnuts. This can be tricky. I've found the easiest way to do it is to put a large baking sheet under the cake platter to catch any falling nuts, then tilt the cake at an angle so you have as horizontal surface as possible to sprinkle the nuts on. Pat the nuts into the frosting as you rotate the cake in order to cover all the surfaces.

To serve, cut the cake into slices. And don't forget the ice cream.

We Are an Apple Farm

We are rows upon rows of apple trees, old and young, with cover crops in between. We are a kitchen garden, surrounded by a picket fence and bordered by lavender; a hop arbor leading to the rose garden; goats hoping for visitors and a handout; two pigs growing fatter to become chops and sausage and lard for our freezers; and the horses and mule, frolicking through the orchard on their daily break. Tim is on his tractor, mowing or spraying compost tea; and brave workers perch precariously on ladders, pruning, thinning, or picking. Sometimes they also whistle or sing. And soon Tim is at his desk, taking orders and trying to juggle how many of which variety goes where. Our interns are taking charge of the cider press, clad in boots and aprons and gripping hoses. The chickens seem to be everywhere, but at the end of the day, they retire promptly, at an early hour, in their travelers' wagon coop.

We are a farm. With all the blessings and curses that go along with that right, we are a farm. Financially we've always known we were a little crazy, but so are most farmers. For the first ten years, the French Laundry (where Don and I continued to work) made it possible for the farm to weather the hard knocks. And it gave us enough time to become thoroughly hooked. Tim and Karen did the mucking out and began the slow recovery of a property that had been sorely abused. They began to farm organically, mostly for the protection of their children. Then, as their knowledge and conviction grew, they got into biodynamic practices. The place was alive with birds and bees.

You can feel the harmony of people, animals, and land here, everything working and living together. It's not all peaches and cream, though. Frustrations abound. Sometimes the reason is political, sometimes bureaucratic, sometimes just mother nature at work. The apples get an onslaught of worms; or the crop is very small; the goat dies; our tomatoes freeze. But we're now finishing up a good year, so it's hard to remember the bad things. It's the farmer's credo that next year will be the year! And through it all, there's the satisfaction of producing good, healthful food for our own family, and having enough to share with others.

I wrote this back in 2005, which seems such a long, long time ago with all that has been happening in the world. Still, it rings true. Even though much of the world is in trouble now, our farm life goes on.

Applesauce, of Course

MAKES ENOUGH TO FILL SIX 1 PT [480 ML] JARS / TOTAL TIME: 1 HOUR

I make a lot of applesauce. Often, I find a box of quite ratty-looking apples left for me outside my kitchen door by a family member. That's when it's time to gather my canning jars and plenty of apple juice.

I've confined my applesauce making to the early varieties, which shatter so nicely when cooked and have such a wonderful flavor. I used to stick exclusively to my favorite Gravensteins, until Tim introduced me to the Red Astrachans.

Later, when we had a bumper crop of Pink Pearls, I tried them as well. Their flavor turned out to be wonderful—they cooked up nicely, and they retained their beautiful pink hue. Pink Pearls turn ripe just after the Gravensteins, extending my applesauce-making season.

Peel and slice:

8 to 10 lb [3.6 to 4.5 kg] apples, such as Gravenstein, Red Astrachan, or Pink Pearl

Transfer the apples to a Dutch oven. You can pile them to the top. If there are too many, set aside a few to add to the pot when it has cooked down a bit.

Pour into the pot over the apples:

4 cups [960 ml] apple juice
1 cup [200 g] sugar
1 Tbsp salt

Bring it to a boil, and then turn down the heat to low. Cook the apples, uncovered, for 10 minutes. Stir and add:

Any leftover apples
¼ cup [55 g] butter

Continue cooking over low heat, stirring occasionally and making sure the applesauce remains at a simmer, until the apples are mostly shattered, at least 30 minutes more. I like to use a whisk to break up the large chunks that haven't shattered. Of course, you could cook it a little longer, so they break up on their own, but I am not bothered by a few lumps. It shows the applesauce was made with real fresh apples.

Cool the applesauce. Store what you plan to use soon, in jars, in the refrigerator for up to 10 days. Freeze the rest, covered, in plastic containers, for up to 6 months.

previous: Clockwise from top left: helping hands at harvest; our granddaughter Rita sorting in the packing shed; son-in-law Tim at the refreshment station; grandson-in-law Jerzy at the cider press.

My mother always said that the worms and birds know which apples taste best. So when I make applesauce, I use apples that were probably already sampled and simply cut around the bad parts.

Applesauce likes to boil over and spit a little, so I line the burners with foil.

I love my morning granola topped with my applesauce and cream. But better yet, applesauce can be a baby's first solid food.

Fresh Apple Salsa

MAKES 2 CUPS [260 G] / TOTAL TIME: 20 MIN

We consume a lot of salsas, so why not an apple salsa? This one is fresh and crisp, and is especially good with any grilled meat.

Core and cut into small dice, with peel on:	**2 tart apples**
Put in a medium bowl, and toss with:	**2 Tbsp [30 ml] fresh lime juice** **½ tsp salt**
Add and toss everything together:	**½ small white onion, finely diced** **A handful of fresh cilantro, coarsely chopped** **1 fresh serrano chile pepper, minced** **1 Anaheim or other mild chile pepper, finely chopped or slivered** **2 Tbsp slivered fresh ginger**
Right before serving, add:	**½ cup [60 g] toasted walnuts**

The salsa is best eaten fresh, while the apples are still crisp, but it will keep for up to 2 days, covered, in the refrigerator.

Sausages in Hard Cider

SERVES 8 TO 12 / TOTAL TIME: 40 MIN

My mother always cooked links of large sausages this way, but not having cider on hand, I think she just used water. You might want to serve these sausages with our Savory Apple Clafouti (page 293) for breakfast or lunch.

In a large skillet, place:

Four to six (2 to 3 lb) [910 g to 1.4 kg] fresh bratwurst or other uncooked sausages

Pour over them:

1 to 2 cups [240 to 480 ml] hard cider (or use or a mix of half apple juice and half white wine)

Bring to a boil over medium heat and cook the sausages, covered, for 5 minutes. Uncover, turn down the heat to low, and cook until the liquid is almost gone. Continue cooking, turning the sausages, as they brown. If the pan gets too dry, add another splash of cider.

When the sausages are a rich brown, transfer them to a platter. Pour into the pan:

1 cup [240 ml] more cider

With the heat off, use a pastry brush to dissolve the bits and pieces on the bottom of the pan in the liquid, then turn the heat on low and cook, stirring, until slightly thickened, about 3 minutes.

To serve, slice the sausages on the diagonal and pour the pan juices over them.

Duck Breasts with Peppered Apples

SERVES 4 TO 6 / TOTAL TIME: 45 MIN

A duck breast can be treated like a piece of steak or a chop: pan-fried, rested, and drizzled with pan juices. It's meant to be served rare or medium-rare.

Preheat the oven to 350°F [180°C].

On a work surface, place: **4 boneless duck breasts, skin on**

With your sharpest knife, make a few diagonal slices through the skin and fat, but don't cut into the meat.

Season generously with: **Salt and freshly ground black pepper**

Heat a large heavy skillet over medium-high heat until very hot. Place the breasts in the pan, skin-side down, and cook until richly browned, about 5 to 7 minutes. Turn skin-side up and brown briefly.

    Pour off the fat and reserve. Place the pan in the oven to finish the cooking, about 3 to 5 minutes more. (The whole cooking process should take no more than 15 minutes, and the duck breasts will be just firm to the touch. Using a meat thermometer, the internal temperature will be 125°F [52°C].) Transfer the duck to a platter and let rest at least 10 minutes, covered loosely with aluminum foil.

Pour into the pan: **3 Tbsp apple juice**
3 Tbsp good balsamic vinegar

Of course, we use our own apple balsamic vinegar.

With the heat off, use a pastry brush to dissolve the bits and pieces on the bottom of the pan in the liquid. Turn the heat to low and cook, stirring, until slightly thickened, about 5 minutes. Slice the duck breasts on the diagonal.

To serve, on each plate, make a bed of: **Bitter greens, such as arugula or chicory**

Fan the slices over the greens and drizzle with the juices.

Serve alongside: **Peppered Apples (recipe follows)**

PEPPERED APPLES

Peel and slice:

4 apples

In a large skillet over medium heat, melt:

¼ cup [55 g] butter

When the butter is bubbly, add the apples to the pan in one layer.

Sprinkle generously with:

**Freshly ground toasted black pepper
A sprinkle of salt**

Let the apple slices brown without stirring on one side, 2 to 3 minutes. Toss to distribute the seasoning, and brown the apples on the other side, 2 to 3 minutes more. Remove from the heat and let the apples rest until needed, up to 10 minutes. Serve warm with the duck and greens.

We love using our Philo Gold apples. We don't peel them because they have tender skins. Jonathans work beautifully for this, but have tough skins that need to be peeled. Any good apple though will be improved by this treatment.

In addition to serving the apples with the duck breast, we like them with Roast Loin of Pork (page 188) and Sausages in Hard Cider (page 289). Don and I also loved these peppered apples over our morning granola and yogurt.

Apple Farm Ice Cream Sundae

On the Apple Farm, we pour our apple cider syrup (see Margin Note, page 231) over a scoop of ice cream and sometimes add a sprinkle of toasted pecans. I especially like the syrup over Cinnamon Ice Cream (page 231) or the ginger ice cream (see Margin Note, page 231). Sometimes, though, it's really hard to beat plain old vanilla.

Savory Apple Clafouti

SERVES 6 TO 8 / PREP TIME: 30 MIN / COOK TIME: 30 TO 40 MIN

We like to serve this for brunch, coupled with Sausages in Hard Cider (page 289).

Preheat the oven to 400°F [200°C].

In a blender, mix until just combined:

1 cup [240 ml] milk or
half-and-half
⅓ cup [80 ml] melted butter
3 eggs
⅔ cup [90 g] all-purpose flour
½ tsp salt

In a large cast-iron skillet over medium heat, melt:

¼ cup [55 g] butter

Add:

5 cups peeled and sliced tart
apples
2 Tbsp brandy
A handful of fresh thyme leaves

Sauté the apples until hot. Pour the batter over the fruit and bake the clafouti until it is puffed and brown, 30 to 40 minutes. Cut into wedges and serve warm.

Our room with a view, upstairs from the main kitchen at the Apple Farm, overlooks our vegetable gardens and orchards.

Eggs

I have always loved eggs. When I was growing up, my mother made wonderful scrambles with a little sautéed green pepper in them. My Aunt Polly taught me to add a touch of water, not milk, while whisking the eggs. Water would make them more tender, she said. She was right. She probably didn't know the chemistry of it, but I later learned there was a definite reason, which has to do with the protein molecules binding together. Just add water to your scrambled eggs, and trust me.

When cooking for my young family early in my marriage, I found eggs to be a very affordable ingredient. I made all the usual things, from deviled eggs to soufflés. And to this day, when in doubt about what to have for dinner, we often settle for an omelet.

Once, when I was setting up the Chutney Kitchen, I raised my hand at an auction and bought a whole table full of miscellaneous pots and pans. Among them were seven small omelet pans made of heavy aluminum, which were very crusty, indeed. We set to work with a big carton of SOS steel wool pads, and after days—or was it weeks?—of work, we had beautiful, shiny pans that, when rinsed, had water beading up and running off the surface, as it should. There were a few other pans that we brought back to life, but the omelet pans were the most prized, and eventually got distributed among the family. I still have two of them hanging on my pot rack, more than forty-five years after rescuing them. I love them still.

We did brunch for a time at the Chutney Kitchen, and again when we opened the French Laundry. By then, my son Johnny was an expert with omelet pans, so I left him to man the stove while I did other things.

There have been times when eggs were out of favor, but thank goodness, those scary stories have been disproven and eggs have taken their rightful place in our diets. Thankfully, we are now passing up factory-produced eggs and returning to the old ways of raising happy chickens that produce eggs with good flavor and brightly colored yolks. I love the eggs we are getting locally, and though the price has gone up, they are still the best bargain to be had among food products.

These days, we put a lovely, soft-fried egg on top of a plate of hash, drop one into a bowl of soup, drape one over a mix of salad greens, and still have our eggs for breakfast with a clean conscience and much pleasure.

MY EGG TRICKS: I am now in my late eighties and have tried every egg trick to come along. These really work.

• Always cook them over low heat. I think browning them alters their taste and texture, and not to their benefit.

• Use butter or olive oil for the best flavor. Or use duck fat, if you are lucky enough to have some.

• When beating egg whites, use a whisk if you have one, and an unlined copper bowl, which has a stabilizing effect chemically. Except when making meringues, I take them to soft peaks, not stiff ones. This gives them more room to expand when they heat (as in a soufflé).

• Raise your own chickens for the eggs, or if you don't, buy them from a local small producer or a neighbor who has chickens. Don't try to save money on eggs—they are always a bargain!

• To make hard-boiled eggs, start them in cold water to cover. Bring them to a gentle boil, turn off the heat, and cover. Let sit for 15 minutes. Plunge the eggs into a bowl filled with cold water, and crack the shells all over (they should be tiny cracks) while the eggs are underwater. Let sit for 10 minutes or more. The water will seep between the shell and membrane, and they will peel easily.

Frozen Lemon Meringue Torte

SERVES 12 / PREP TIME: 1 HOUR / COOK TIME: AT LEAST 1 HOUR EXCLUDING
FREEZING TIME

For grand occasions, this dessert tastes as wonderful as it looks, and it can be
made 1 or 2 days ahead of time. It's simply a frozen concoction of layers of
crispy meringue, vanilla ice cream, and lemon curd.

First prepare the: **Lemon Curd (see page 214)**

Refrigerate in a covered container for at least 2 hours. It will keep, covered, in
the refrigerator for one week, so can be made well ahead of time.

Preheat the oven to 250°F [120°C]. Line a 12 by 17 in [30 by 43 cm]
rimmed baking sheet with parchment paper or wax paper.

To make your meringue, in
a blender or food processor, whirl
for 10 seconds until very fine:

1 cup [200 g] granulated sugar

This speeds up how evenly and quickly the sugar dissolves in the egg whites.

Set aside. Sift through a strainer to
remove any lumps:

1 cup [120 g] powdered sugar

In a large bowl, with an electric
mixer, beat on high speed to the soft
peak stage:

**¾ cup [180 ml] egg whites
(from about 6 eggs)**

Recipe continues…

Start adding the blended granulated sugar, 1 Tbsp at a time, beating just until the sugar is dissolved each time.

When all the granulated sugar is added, turn down the mixer speed to the lowest setting and add the powdered sugar, 1 heaping Tbsp at a time. Make sure it is well blended before adding the next spoonful. Keep beating until the egg whites are stiff and smooth.

Spoon the egg and sugar mixture evenly to fill the baking sheet. Bake until completely dry and crisp, 1 hour or more. I often just turn the oven off and leave it in there for an extra hour or so, or even overnight.

When your meringue is ready, use a sharp knife to cut it into rectangles that will fit into a loaf pan. An easy way to do this is to gently turn the loaf pan upside down onto the meringue and trace your rectangles with the tip of a knife before cutting. Be sure to save any extra trimmings to sprinkle over the top of each slice as you plate it.

From the freezer, take:

1 ½ qt [840 g] good store-bought vanilla ice cream

Unwrap the carton all the way, and cut slices about ¾ in [2 cm] thick to fit the loaf pan. You will have to patch it together, but that's okay.

To assemble the torte, line your loaf pan with plastic wrap, leaving the excess wrap hanging over the edges. This makes it easier to remove when it is finished. If the kitchen is too warm, pop each layer into the freezer as you go.

Start by spreading a layer of the lemon curd on the bottom, about ¼ in [6 mm] thick. The torte will look prettier when turned out if you start with the curd.

Add a layer of meringue, and then a layer of ice cream. Repeat the layers until the loaf pan is full. Depending on your pan, you will end up with two or three layers of meringue.

Store in the freezer, covered with plastic wrap, for at least 4 hours until you're ready for it. Amazingly, the meringue will stay crispy in the freezer. If you aren't having a big party, you can cut a few slices of the torte, serve, and pop the rest back in the freezer, well wrapped in plastic.

For the more adventurous, this dessert can take any shape, if you choose to build it up free form.

When ready to serve, drape a warm wet towel over the loaf pan to release the torte onto a cutting board. Use a hot, wet knife to slice it, and garnish each slice with:

Reserved meringue crumbs
Crispy Lemon Zest (page 215)
A few small citrus leaves

Chocolate Strawberry Meringue

MAKES 12 MERINGUE RINGS / TOTAL TIME: 2 HOURS

Preheat the oven to 250°F [120°C]. Line a baking sheet with parchment paper or wax paper.

Sift together:

1 ¼ cups [150 g] powdered sugar
¼ cup [20 g] cocoa powder

In a blender or food processor, whirl for 10 seconds until very fine:

¾ cup [150 g] granulated sugar

With an electric mixer, beat on high speed to the softly whipped peak stage:

¾ cup [180 ml] egg whites
(from about 6 eggs)

Add the fine granulated sugar, 1 Tbsp at a time, beating just until the sugar is dissolved.

Keep beating until the egg whites are stiff and smooth. With a whisk, fold in the powdered sugar and cocoa mixture by hand, whisking until very smooth.

Spoon the meringue into a pastry bag with a plain or star tip. Pipe onto the prepared baking sheet about twelve 3 to 4 in [7.5 to 10 cm] circles with open centers. Bake the meringues until they are completely dry and pale brown in color, about 45 minutes.

For the filling:

Rinse and remove the stems from:

2 pints [715 g] summer strawberries

Slice them from top to bottom into ¼ in [6 mm] slices so they have a pretty shape.

Toss with:

¼ cup [50 g] sugar

Whip until it holds a nice soft peak:

2 cups [480 ml] cold heavy cream

Place a small spoonful of whipped cream on the plate for glue, add the meringue ring, and follow with alternating spoonfuls of your strawberries and your whipped cream.

We like to drizzle with My Best Chocolate Sauce (page 224) or top with a sauce made of thinned jam or jelly.

FILLING VARIATIONS:

• Apricot Coconut: softened dried apricots, and toasted coconut folded into the whipped cream.

• Chocolate Chestnut: softened chestnut purée and coarsely chopped candied chestnuts (marrons glacés) folded into whipped cream.

• Other seasonal berries, such as raspberries, blackberries, or blueberries, with either whipped cream or vanilla ice cream or frozen yogurt.

• Kiwis sliced and tossed with sugar and a little lime juice. This is reminiscent of a pavlova.

If you don't have a pastry bag, cut off the corner of a plastic storage bag.

Making Jam

I grew up helping my mother prepare the fruit for her jams. This meant sorting, pitting, and rinsing whatever was ready to drop off the trees. She used to always say, "You cook it until it boils up, and when it boils down, it's done." It was good advice and I have heeded it ever since, bringing the pot to a boil, almost to boiling over, and then waiting for that moment when the fruit breaks down and folds back into itself, at which point it is ready for the jars.

I make jam using only fruit that we grow at the Apple Farm, or purchase from select farmers nearby, ideally at the height of their season. I really don't have any recipes for jams, because I like them to be a concentrated taste of each fruit flavor. There are some very nice combinations out there, but I prefer to keep the fruit flavor plain and pure.

HERE ARE MY FEW AND SIMPLE GUIDELINES

• Use only the best-tasting fruit.

• Use fruits high in acid, such as apricots, plums, strawberries, and brambleberries, which will balance the added sugar well.

• Use a properly shaped pan, one that is wider than it is deep, such as a confiture pan. The copper lining conducts heat better, and the wider bottom results in more even cooking, with the liquids evaporating faster.

• Make jam in small batches. My mother always said not to make more than two baskets of one fruit at a time.

• Do not overcook. You will lose color and freshness.

• When you combine the fruit and sugar, use proportions of 3 parts sugar to 4 parts fruit, and add a little fresh lemon juice to heighten the flavor and encourage the natural pectin, about 2 tsp for each 1 qt [960 ml] basket of fruit.

• Cook rapidly, and keep stirring to keep the mixture from sticking. If foaming is a problem, add a very small amount of butter to the pan.

• Cook the jam until the foam subsides and a gel begins to form. This usually takes 25 to 35 minutes.

• When finished, ladle hot into sterile jars. The jam will keep, covered, in the refrigerator for 3 to 4 weeks.

opposite: I discovered the ideal pan while visiting my son Johnny in France. Don and I were staying at the château where he was helping out, and that first morning, I woke up and came down to the kitchen to find a fire burning in the large fireplace there and several women already at work, cooking jam in a beautiful copper and brass-handled confiture pan. It was love at first sight, and I have had one in my kitchen ever since. Here we are making Santa Rosa Plum jam.

The Family Grows

The Apple Farm is a place, a family, a community, a farm, a garden, and a kitchen. It is also a statement of intent, an aesthetic and a hope. We have 32 acres [13 hectares] here hugging the Navarro River, and from the apple orchards we are able to look up at the towering redwoods on one side and oak-studded hills on the other. We're far enough away from the city to be a destination, but close enough to make it all work. Only thirty minutes in the car will take you to the gorgeous Mendocino coastline. Here there are foggy mornings and hot afternoons, which are perfect for apples and grapes. Looking up at the hills you might see sheep grazing, and you need to be careful of the wild turkeys in the roadways.

As for family, we are four generations here now. We started out under two roofs, but as the grandchildren gained independence, the old cottage, which served as a bathhouse, became a home for granddaughter Sophia. She moved on and built her own small home on the farm. That old bathhouse is now a snug little cabin where Rita and Jerzy welcomed their first baby over the winter, making the fourth generation in residence.

below: There are three colorful travelers' wagons for overnight guests and farmhands as well as a little cabin in the lower orchard, for summer overflow. The grandchildren come and go, from Maine to Chile, Mexico and India, but they all seem to be drawn back to the farm or settled nearby. Three new homes have risen up over this last year as family members have put down their roots. We are blessed to have this farm and the security and home base it has provided for our large family.

I am very proud of my family. None of them were college graduates, yet they are all leading successful, satisfying, creative lives. And they all love to cook and eat well. My daughter Karen and her husband, Tim, were the anchors, throwing their hearts and energy into the farm. None of us could, or would have, done it alone. If I thought I'd be sitting on the porch shelling peas in my old age, boy was I was mistaken! Karen, who taught with me in the Apple Farm kitchen for many years, is now teaching our classes with more of a farm-to-table emphasis.

My youngest, Terry, is an accomplished wood carver producing exquisite designs, which are incorporated into the handmade furniture of her partner, Debey Zito. My next youngest, Eric, builds some of the most beautiful homes in the Napa Valley. My oldest son, Johnny, who is third in line, is an accomplished chef in his own right and runs the Boonville Hotel, just down the road from the Apple Farm where he and Eric are building a home together. Kathy, my oldest, who worked in each of my restaurants, including picking and arranging the flowers for the French Laundry, continued doing this not just for Thomas Keller but also other restaurants and large events throughout the Napa Valley. She and her husband, Bill, have now retired and built a beautiful home in the woods of southern Oregon.

The ebb and flow of energy and youthful doings reminds me of our own children growing up in Yountville. All five of our children have worked for us in varying capacities over the years, occasionally heading off to Europe, returning to work a spell in the kitchen, then going off again for more excitement and experience. We watched them learn to do almost anything that was needed as they became adults, right before our delighted eyes.

Rum Cream Pie

MAKES ONE 9 IN [23 CM] PIE; SERVES 8 TO 10 / TOTAL TIME: 1 HOUR
EXCLUDING CHILLING TIME

For special dinners, this became my best shot at producing a dessert that looked fancy and tasted wonderful. Over the years, the recipe has caught the attention of younger generations. Our nephew Andy has presented this pie to his East Coast in-laws every Christmas for over ten years. Our grandson Joe turned out a fleet of these pies for Don's big eightieth birthday celebration. This concoction manages to be light, while delivering everything a special dessert should. The drizzle of chocolate on the top is very dramatic, but easy to do once you get the hang of it.

Recipe continues...

Preheat the oven to 325°F [165°C].

In a medium bowl, mix together:

2 cups [240 g] graham cracker crumbs (about 14 or 15 rectangles of graham crackers, crushed fine in a plastic bag with a rolling pin)
½ cup [50 g] sugar
½ cup [120 ml] melted butter

Press this mixture into a 9 in [23 cm] tart pan with a removable bottom or a pie pan. Use the palm of your hand to press it down on the bottom of the pan, and your fingers to press it up the sides. Bake until the sugar has caramelized, creating a crisp crust that has just started to brown, about 15 minutes. Be careful not to let the crust get too brown. Cool in the pan on a rack.

To make the chocolate sauce, in a small, heavy-bottomed saucepan over low heat, warm:

1½ oz [40 g] good bittersweet chocolate, such as Guittard
¼ cup [60 ml] water

As soon as the chocolate has melted, whisk in:

¼ cup [50 g] sugar

Bring to a boil and cook until the sugar is dissolved and the sauce is very smooth, 3 to 5 minutes.

Remove from the heat and add:

3 Tbsp butter
½ tsp vanilla extract

Whisk until smooth and set aside to cool.

For the filling, pour into a medium heatproof bowl:

¼ cup [60 ml] water

Stir in:

1 envelope gelatin

Let the gelatin sit and soften for 3 to 5 minutes, then add:

¼ cup plus 2 Tbsp [90 ml] boiling water

Let cool. Whisk together lightly in a metal bowl:

3 egg yolks
3 Tbsp [45 g]
sugar
¼ cup [60 ml]
light rum

Stir in the gelatin mixture. Set the bowl into a larger one with a few inches of cold water and cool the filling, stirring occasionally, until it just begins to thicken.

Meanwhile, in another medium bowl, with an electric mixer on medium speed, beat until soft peaks form:

1 ½ cups [360 ml] heavy cream

Gently fold the whipped cream into the gelatin mixture before it has set. Now comes the tricky part!

Pour the filling into the cooled crust. Using a plastic squeeze bottle or a pastry bag with a fine tip, drizzle the chocolate sauce back and forth over the filling in a steady, thin stream. Drag a table knife back and forth across the chocolate to make a chevron pattern.

left: My grandson, Joe, will probably be the one to carry this recipe to the next generation. He has taken it on as his own personal science project, and the holidays are not complete without it. He was even inspired to create this illustration.

Sixth: The Elk Cottage

A Kitchen for Two (2008 to 2016)

Cooking for Two

In 2008 Don and I truly retired. We moved from all the hustle and bustle at the Apple Farm to a quiet little cottage, which we had completely renovated, in the small town of Elk, about 30 miles [48 kilometers] northwest of the farm. Elk is on the Mendocino coastline, and we arranged it so my kitchen window looked out over the that beautiful, rugged Northern California shore. I had gone from cooking for fifty people at the French Laundry to twelve for the classes I taught at the Apple Farm. And now, finally, I was fixing meals just for the two of us. It was the first time in many, many years that I cooked for only two—really since we were first married, a half-century ago, before the children arrived.

So I had to downsize my pantry, and learn more about what to do with leftovers. We would have breakfast, which we never did when we ran the French Laundry. There, I started the day with a cup of coffee and went right to work, waiting until lunchtime to eat anything. When Don and I moved to Elk, we always ate breakfast, often eggs, and once or twice a week, granola, which I'd make myself or buy from Margaret Fox, who had started the Café Beaujolais in Mendocino.

I continued to read cookbooks and magazines, always *Saveur*, sometimes *Cook's Illustrated* or *Food & Wine*. I would get excited about cooking a recipe I came across, but nine times out of ten, I wouldn't like it. So I'd simply go back to my old favorites. Sometimes, though, I did find something new that was appealing and fit into my regular routine, or a new combination of flavors, or even a new way of cutting vegetables.

My restaurant years taught me to be prepared, and I carried this training over to my life at home. While washing the breakfast dishes, I liked to think through the food for the rest of the day, since I liked to have all my ducks in a row. If dinner was to be a meat from the freezer, I would take it out to thaw, salting it so it would taste better. Almost without thinking about it, I would do what I could ahead of time, so I could concentrate on the sautéing and the seasoning just before dinner. If we were going to have something with a cream sauce that night, I would make it early and keep it on the back of the stove. The salad I would prepare and keep covered with a damp paper towel in the fridge to keep it cool.

Back when I was in my restaurant kitchen, I learned to have things ready to serve at the same time, and always made sure the food was either very hot, or cold. It was only during these later years in my kitchen in Elk that I learned how many flavors actually peaked at room temperature.

I've also learned not to fixate on measuring much, unless I'm baking, of course. You can learn what a half teaspoon looks like in the palm of your hand by practice. My ingredients became simpler. I stopped, for example, playing around with so many varieties of salt, and kept just two by the stove, Diamond Crystal

previous: I loved my old Wedgewood stove, restored after I retrieved it from someone's garage. It is still in the family today, having been passed on to my granddaughter Rita.

I grew my herbs right outside the kitchen door. I have always kept three big pots of chives there, which I would harvest in rotation, so one was cut down, one had grown back halfway, and one was mature. I grew sorrel, so I could make sorrel sauce whenever we had salmon, and I loved to make sorrel soup. We had a beautiful bay tree right outside our gate, and parsley, cilantro, oregano, marjoram, and sage, all in raised beds, screened to make it difficult for the deer to eat. Mint grew wild everywhere.

kosher salt and Maldon sea salt flakes, which I could sprinkle on when I wanted a little crunch on top. I kept only one olive oil in the house, a really good one made in Modesto, and coconut oil for stir-frying. The only dried herb I used was Mexican oregano. For any other herb, I would just go out and pick what I needed. I almost always made my own stock, but kept a can in the pantry for emergency use. I also kept in my pantry rice, polenta, and pasta. My kitchen equipment was simple. No dishwashing machine, no garbage disposal, no microwave. But I had never had any of these in my home kitchen, so it was nothing new.

I never baked bread in my restaurants. I left it to the experts, who had the knowledge and equipment to do a good job. That didn't change when we moved to Elk. There were good bakers up the road in Mendocino and Fort Bragg, and I felt it was important to support them by buying their bread.

Inevitably, whenever I would see friends or former customers, they would always ask me, "Do you cook for yourself at all anymore?"

"Of course I do," I would say. "That's what I do." I can't imagine life without cooking.

below: I loved being able to cook just for the two of us during those sublime years we spent in our cottage at Elk.

left: The cove in Elk showing the whole sleepy town, population 200. A century before, with ten times the population, the town had ten hotels and fifteen saloons and a very bustling port due to the thriving lumber industry. From the wharf at the base of the cliffs, loads of lumber were put on a sling to be winched out to the ships that were moored safely offshore.

We made a weekly shopping trip, driving up the coast to Mendocino, or farther north to Fort Bragg, which both had very good markets. When there were thick-cut lamb loin chops, I would buy them for a treat, sprinkling them with salt and pepper, and cooking them on top of the stove. Sometimes I talked Don into buying mussels or clams, which we'd take home and steam. He would have preferred steak but ate them cheerfully. I'd serve them with a green salad and a fresh baguette to sop up the juices. Our neighbor from across the street, Kevin Joe, would sometimes go out fishing and bring us a cooked crab, still warm. We would pick the meat from the shells and devour it with one of my favorite mayonnaise concoctions. The freshness was astonishing.

Gingered Shrimp with Mustard & Chutney

SERVES 2 / TOTAL TIME: 30 MIN

We prepared this dish so often at the French Laundry and the Apple Farm that when Don and I moved to Elk, I completely abandoned it for several years. But then I found some wonderful fresh shrimp locally and made it again. We were so delighted with it, tasting it afresh, that we enjoyed it many times, as either an appetizer or a light lunch. Although you can use a different chutney if you like, I much prefer apricot with this dish.

In a small dish, stir together and set aside:	**3 Tbsp white wine** **2 Tbsp Dijon mustard**
In a medium saucepan over medium heat, melt:	**2 Tbsp butter**
Toss into the pan:	**2 to 3 tsp finely slivered fresh ginger** **2 garlic cloves, minced**
Sauté for 1 minute. Then add:	**8 to 12 medium shrimp, preferably fresh, shelled but not deveined**

Sauté just until they are turning pink and beginning to curl, about 2 to 3 minutes, and add the mustard and wine mixture.

Shake the pan over the heat to distribute the mustard evenly and cook until the sauce reduces a little and coats the shrimp. Add a little more wine if there isn't enough sauce or it is too thick.

Shaking the pan will actually turn over more shrimp as they cook than if you simply stir, so it's worthwhile becoming adept at this.

To serve, place on each of the two plates:	**A few fresh cilantro sprigs**
Arrange half the shrimp on each plate. Drizzle the sauce over the shrimp, and place alongside:	**A spoonful of apricot chutney** **A dab of Dijon mustard**

Cabbage Slaw with Toasted Fennel

SERVES 4 / TOTAL TIME: 40 MIN

This is the way I've always made slaw, with one slight change: One day, when I didn't have the usual celery seeds, I substituted fennel. It was so good that I've never gone back.

Using a mandolin or a very sharp knife, finely sliver:

½ head green or Savoy cabbage

Transfer to a large bowl and add:

1 bunch green onions (all the green and most of the white parts), slivered
1 poblano pepper, finely slivered

Toss the vegetables and immerse in a large bowl of ice water, tossing again with your hands until they crisp up.

Drain in a colander and pat dry. Set aside, covered with a wet paper towel.

For the dressing, stir together in a small bowl:

¼ cup [60 g] sour cream
¼ cup [60 g] mayonnaise
1 tsp Dijon mustard
2 Tbsp toasted fennel seeds, coarsely ground
Salt and freshly ground black pepper

Transfer the vegetables to a large bowl, add the dressing, and toss. Add:

¼ cup [10 g] chopped fresh parsley
¼ cup [10 g] chopped fresh mint or cilantro

Toss again, and let rest for at least 15 minutes to develop the flavor before serving. Leftovers will keep, in a sealed container, in the refrigerator for up to 2 days.

Panzanella, My Way

SERVES 2 TO 4 / TOTAL TIME: 40 MIN

I first tasted this classic many years ago, at Lissa Doumani and Hiro Sone's Michelin-starred restaurant, Terra, in St. Helena. When I exclaimed to Lissa about how wonderful it was, she said, "Just wait until we have really good tomatoes; we are rushing the season a little!" So wait until you can get really good tomatoes out of your garden or at a farmers' market. This makes a meal on its own, especially with a good bottle of wine.

Preheat the oven to 350° [180°C].

To make the croutons, cut or tear into bite-size pieces:	½ **baguette or Italian loaf**
Transfer to a large bowl and add a mixture of:	**2 to 3 garlic cloves, minced** **2 Tbsp good olive oil** **1 Tbsp butter, melted**

Toss thoroughly. Spread out the croutons on a baking sheet and toast until they're golden and crisp, 15 to 25 minutes.

While the croutons are baking, in a large bowl, combine:	**2 or 3 tomatoes, cut into bite-size pieces** **10 or 12 cherry tomatoes, halved**
To season, drizzle the tomatoes liberally with:	**Your best olive oil**
Add:	**8 to 10 fresh basil leaves, slivered** **Salt and coarsely ground toasted black pepper** **A dash of balsamic vinegar**

Toss well, and let the salad stand for at least 15 minutes to develop the flavor. Just before serving, add one handful of the croutons for each serving. Toss together well, and taste for seasoning. Add more salt or pepper, as well as more oil, if needed.

Serve at room temperature in flat soup bowls and garnish with:	**1 or 2 sprigs basil**

What makes this recipe special is the quality of the ingredients. (I have never seen real tomatoes in a supermarket!) I prefer Early Girls for the flavor base. Then I add a few Sungold and Sweet 100 cherry tomatoes, and maybe a green-striped tomato to vary the color. Be sure to use garden-fresh tomatoes, and do not refrigerate them.

You may have more croutons than you need, but they keep well in an airtight container for up to 1 week.

Provide soup spoons as well as forks, since the finished dish will have an abundance of wonderful juices.

Oxtail Terrine

SERVES 6 TO 8 / PREP TIME: 40 MIN / COOK TIME: 4 HOURS / EXCLUDING
CHILLING TIME

My favorite way to entertain in Elk was to have another twosome join us for
lunch. If the day was nice, we could sit outside on our deck and linger over
a simple plate and a bottle of wine. In the summer, when we had good
tomatoes from the farm, I would serve panzanella (see page 317). At other
times it might be this recipe, a terrine of oxtails on a bed of zesty greens,
which was one of my favorite offerings. It is simple, light, and substantial,
all at the same time. I like to cook the oxtails a day or two before serving.

On a work surface, place:	**1 to 2 lb [455 to 910 g] oxtails (you can cut them apart between the vertebrae to give you 2 in [5 cm] chunks, or buy them precut)**
In a Dutch oven or heavy-bottomed pot over medium heat, warm:	**2 Tbsp olive oil**

Add the oxtail pieces and brown well on all sides, about 10 minutes.

Add to the pot:	**1 onion, slivered or chopped**
Season generously with:	**Salt and freshly ground black pepper**
Cook until the onions start to color, and add:	**2 cups [480 ml] red wine** **1 cup [240 ml] chicken stock**

Add enough water to just cover the largest pieces of meat. Bring to a boil, and
adjust the heat for a very low simmer. Cook until the meat separates easily
from the bones, about 4 hours.

Remove the oxtails and set aside until cool enough to handle. Pull the meat
off the bones, breaking up the larger pieces and discarding large chunks of fat.
Put the meat in a large bowl.

Strain the cooking liquid into a 4 cup [960 ml] heatproof measuring cup,
and skim the fat off the top. Taste for salt and add more if needed. The liquid

Remember that oxtail is
really that, a tail. It's thicker
at one end than the other,
so there are larger pieces
and smaller ones. They are
made up mostly of bone
and cartilage, without much
meat. For a 1 qt [960 ml]
terrine, you will need one
full oxtail. Our butcher
offers a precut package,
which is about six to eight
pieces, ranging from large to
very small. You might have
to buy two packages of oxtail
to have enough large pieces.

should be very flavorful. If you have more than 4 cups [960 ml], pour it back into the pot and reduce over high heat.

There should be enough gelatin from the bones and cartilage to set up the liquid when cold. If in doubt, put a little bit into the freezer for a few minutes to see whether it gels. If it doesn't, dissolve 1 Tbsp gelatin in ¼ cup [60 ml] of cool water and let sit for 5 minutes, until it is all dissolved. Add to the cooking liquid.

Oil a 1 qt [960 ml] loaf pan. I use a Pyrex one with a lid, which is just right.

Pour the liquid over the meat and mix well. Taste for seasoning again. Let the mixture cool until it starts to gel.

Transfer to the prepared loaf pan, covered with your lid. If you don't have one, use a piece of aluminum foil or plastic wrap. The gelling juices will keep the meaty pieces suspended, so they don't end up on the bottom. Refrigerate at least overnight.

I have never had to add gelatin, but when I started making this, I invariably fretted over whether it was going to set up or not. It always did.

When ready to serve, make the horseradish sauce. In a small bowl, stir together:

1 cup [240 g] sour cream
2 to 3 Tbsp prepared horseradish
Salt and coarsely ground toasted black pepper

My favorite horseradish is the Tulelake brand, from Northern California.

Invert the loaf pan over a serving plate and remove the pan. Slice the terrine thickly with a very sharp knife.

To serve, on each plate, make a bed of:

Hearty greens, such as mizuna (Japanese mustard greens), arugula, or watercress

Place a slice of terrine on each bed of greens. Pass around the horseradish sauce and:

A little pitcher of balsamic vinegar
Coarse sea salt
A basket of good bread
A bottle of red wine

For just the two of us, I often doubled the oxtails and served them hot the first night over a bed of mashed potatoes or wide noodles. The next day I rewarmed the leftovers and proceeded with the terrine. We could stretch two oxtails into one dinner and two lunches if we were alone.

Just an Omelet

SERVES 1 / TOTAL TIME: 10 MIN

I never tire of eggs. I grew up loving my mother's good scramble, and later learned how to turn out a perfect omelet. Sometimes when Don and I had a day full of errands, or came home from a couple of days of partying, we would look at each other and say, almost simultaneously, "Let's just have an omelet for dinner." To us it was always a source of comfort, and we would sit back after our meal, totally satisfied, both physically and emotionally.

When we did brunch at the Chutney Kitchen, and then for a while in the early days of the French Laundry, if Johnny happened to be in the kitchen, I would turn the pans over to him. He had a certain touch, and his omelets were wonderful. He became known for his knack, both at home and when he traveled, taking his omelet pan with him. He turned out omelets on a yacht in the harbor of Cannes, and as a chef on a boat cruising the San Juan Islands, to name a few spots. When he came to Elk, I turned the stove over to him and just enjoyed watching him at work.

opposite: We still use our old, heavy-duty aluminum pans. They need to be scrubbed hard with an S.O.S soap pad if they aren't used frequently or have been used for some other purpose. The rinse water should bead up and roll off when the pan is ready to use.

In a small bowl, lightly beat with a fork:	**2 eggs**
Add:	**2 tsp water**
Season generously with:	**Salt and freshly ground black pepper**
Place an 8 in [20 cm] omelet pan over low heat and melt:	**2 Tbsp butter**

When the butter foams up, pour in the eggs. When they begin to set around the edge, in about 8 seconds, use a spatula or kitchen fork to scrape the eggs from the perimeter of the pan toward the middle. The uncooked parts will seep into the bare spaces. Repeat this until the eggs are almost set, but still a little runny.

| If you want to fill the omelet, remove from the heat and add any or all the following: | **A sprinkle of chopped fresh chives**
Grated cheddar cheese
Crispy bits of bacon |

Fold the omelet over the filling(s), roll out onto a warm plate, and enjoy. The outside should be smooth, shiny, and not at all brown.

Rhubarb Shortcake

SERVES 6 / TOTAL TIME: 1 HOUR

If you miss the elusive hothouse rhubarb that often appears fleetingly around Valentine's Day, your next opportunity is spring and early summer, when field grown rhubarb is at its peak. When we find it at the farmers' market, we look for firm, crisp stalks. I prefer bright red ones, though green ones from your garden are just fine, just less beautiful. I have always thought it odd that, though rhubarb is a vegetable, we treat it so much like a fruit, cooking it with sugar.

We have learned to bake the rhubarb pieces, rather than cook them in a saucepan on the stove top. In the oven, they don't lose their shape.

Prepare:

½ **recipe shortcakes (see page 43)**

When the shortcakes are done, preheat the oven to 350° [180°C].

In a roasting pan combine:

4 cups [400 g] rhubarb, cut diagonally into 1 in [2.5 cm] pieces
½ cup [100 g] sugar
Juice of 1 orange

If you make this for two, there will be too much rhubarb, so save the remainder for another use. We like having it with a little cream for breakfast, or on our morning granola.

Loosely cover the fruit and bake until the rhubarb feels tender when poked with a fork, 15 to 30 minutes. Do not stir.

If your shortcakes aren't fresh out of the oven, warm them up at the same temperature until they're crisp, 5 to 10 minutes.

To make the caramel sauce, combine in a saucepan over medium heat:

¼ cup [55 g] butter
¾ cup [150 g] brown sugar
2 Tbsp cream or water

Bring to a boil and remove from the heat.

Split the shortcakes in half. Place one of the halves on each dessert plate and spoon the baked rhubarb over it. Replace the top half and add more fruit.

Spoon over each serving:

¼ cup [60 ml] heavy cream
A healthy drizzle of the caramel sauce

As an alternative, try using sour cream. It makes a delightfully different combination of flavors.

Fresh Herbs

While growing up, we weren't big on garnishes or fresh herbs, except for parsley and mint. Looking back now, it seems strange, since we grew so many vegetables. But I don't remember growing any except parsley. They all came out of the little tins my mother kept in the cupboard.

I'm beginning to realize that my mother's cooking leaned mostly toward the good old South, without many of the French, Italian, or Spanish influences of California. I don't know just when a sprig of parsley on the plate first came into my life, but I do know that it gradually came to be replaced by a very liberal use of fresh homegrown herbs.

If you have room for anything, even just a big ceramic pot on your deck, grow a few herbs! Yes, you can now find fresh herbs in every grocery store, but they are usually greenhouse grown with a serious lack of flavor. Much better are the ones we can get from farmers' markets, all grown on a small scale.

Better still, grow your own! Start with a few. Parsley, chives, thyme, mint, basil, and cilantro are my basics. Marjoram, oregano, and sage can be added if they suit your cooking needs. I particularly like chocolate mint for desserts. Keep them close and easy to get to, ideally right near the kitchen door.

When rinsing herbs, keep in mind that their flavor is in their leaves. Too much washing can dilute those flavors. There are some exceptions where the stems have more flavor than the leaves—parsley and cilantro, for example. When chopping, you can remove the big stems, but keep the tender ones.

Do wash anything you get from the store; you can't be certain where it came from. If you're gardening without pesticides, and there is no sandy grit in the leaves, don't wash them. The best way to wash is to take your handful of herbs and let them sit in a big pot of warm water. Agitate them gently, and the grit will drift to the bottom.

Braised Chicken with Lemon & Thyme

SERVES 4 TO 8 / PREP TIME: 15 MIN / COOK TIME: 30 MIN

This is a quickie dinner. I often cook extra thighs so I have enough to warm up one or two the next day to add to a salad, or just to eat unadorned for lunch straight out of the refrigerator.

Good ingredients matter. I have always made a point of getting my poultry from a local source, as I didn't want those chickens raised in cages, pumped up with water and additives so there's no taste left, and bred to have such big breasts that they can't even walk around. I wanted flavorful chickens that were healthful to eat. So find a good local source! I like to serve the thighs with roasted vegetables, as they can share the same oven. Small potatoes, carrots, onions, and fennel work well, and should take about the same amount of time to cook as the chicken, but check to make sure.

Preheat the oven to 400°F [200°C].

Make a rub by combining in a small dish:	**1 Tbsp chopped fresh thyme** **1½ tsp freshly ground black pepper** **1 Tbsp lemon zest**
On a work surface, assemble:	**8 bone-in, skin-on chicken thighs**

Sprinkle lightly with salt. Sprinkle both sides with the thyme and lemon mixture, rubbing it in a little.

Let the thighs warm up a bit while the oven heats up.

Arrange the thighs on a rimmed baking sheet. Bake until they are nicely browned, with crispy skin, 20 to 30 minutes. You can check to see if they're done by taking a sharp knife and pricking the underside. If it's bloody, cook a few more minutes; when the juices run clear, it's done.

Place the chicken on a serving platter. Pour off the fat from the pan and pour in:	**1 cup [240 ml] chicken stock or white wine**

With the heat off, use a pastry brush to deglaze the pan. Transfer to a small saucepan, turn the heat to low and stir until slightly thickened, 2 or 3 minutes. Pour the pan juices over the chicken and serve.

At the French Laundry, the very first thing we did when we started renovating the old stone building was to lay out and plant an herb garden. We put it right outside the kitchen door, so we could gather herbs as needed for that night's menu. We grew parsley, chives, thyme (one of my favorites), marjoram, sorrel, oregano, cilantro, pineapple sage, and eventually even the Japanese herb shiso.

During those wonderful years, I would stroll outside when I wanted a break and pick what I needed for that night's menu, cutting just a few stems. And when I was making a large pot of stock, I would throw the whole stem, with the leaves, right into the pot. After the stock had simmered for 1 or 2 hours, the leaves would fall off, and I could simply take out the stems.

A Simple Bowl of Soup

For lunch, very often a simple bowl of soup is a meal. I make a lot of them. When I am out of everything else, I make garlic soup. I throw a handful of garlic cloves, unpeeled, into my homemade stock, add a couple of slices of lemon, and lots of black pepper. The trick is getting the seasoning right. Then I let the broth simmer for 15 to 20 minutes so the garlic cooks. When it's soft, I'll squeeze the cloves out of their skin, return them to the soup and let it simmer for a while. If it reduces too much, I add water. (There's no need to add stock, since what has boiled off is water.) Often, I'll float a piece of toasted French bread in the soup, and add a sprinkle of grated Parmesan, or drop an egg into it. I have a lot of versions.

I feel deprived if I don't have my own stock in the refrigerator. During my restaurant kitchen days, I made a lot of cream-based soups since I didn't always have enough stock. Now, I am able to play around a lot with stock-based soups, starting with what I call my clean-out-the-refrigerator stock. Although I usually use chicken or duck for the base, sometimes it's just vegetables. (I rarely use beef; I prefer chicken in most things, as it is more adaptable and softer in flavor.) If I am working with an already cooked meat, or a roasted chicken, I'll toss the bones right into the stockpot. Then I'll take a look in the refrigerator, find a carrot or two, a little celery, and always some onion. I choose not to put garlic in my stock, which can always be added later. That's about it. If I don't need a clear stock, I'll add any leftover vegetables from dinner. I'm pretty much a scrounger these days.

Making Stock

Making stock is easy. Simply fill a stockpot with bones and vegetables, and cover with water. Add some herbs. Place the pot, uncovered, over high heat and bring to a boil. Then adjust the heat so it's as low as it can go, ideally with one little bubble breaking the surface in the middle of the pot. If you don't already have a stockpot, buy the largest one you have room for, one taller than it is wide. That way, when it is simmering for a long time, you don't have to add water so often as it reduces.

I've been known to make a little stock just for myself from the scrapings of a dinner plate. While I'm cleaning the kitchen, I'll just toss the scraps into a pot, add water, and cook it down. Strained and cooled, it can sit in the refrigerator until a little splash of stock is called for.

HERE ARE SOME GUIDELINES

• When you're boning a chicken, use everything in your stock: the skin, bones, and fat. If the bones aren't already cooked, take the time to roast them first, adding your vegetables right in there with them, plus a little olive oil. It only takes about 30 minutes in a 400°F [200°C] oven to roast them until they are brown.

• For vegetables, I use an onion, roughly chopped, with the skin left on, which adds a beautiful color to the stock; a carrot (I don't like too many); a celery stalk; and any other vegetable peelings I have on hand. I always keep a bag of tops, peelings, and onion skins in the refrigerator until I'm ready to get the stockpot going. Don't peel the vegetables, but do scrub them.

• Don't salt the stock, since it might reduce down quite a bit, and salty stock can ruin a dish. But do add a few black peppercorns.

• Add some herbs, with their stems intact: a handful of parsley, some sprigs of thyme from the garden.

• Never stir the stock; it will become cloudy.

• Cook the stock, simmering gently, uncovered, for 3 to 4 hours. Add more water if necessary, to keep the bones generously covered.

• When finished, remove the pot from the heat and let the stock cool for at least 15 minutes.

• When cooled, gently lift out the bones and vegetables. Strain the liquid through a sieve into a large measuring cup. Do it slowly, cup by cup—don't try to strain all the stock at once, or you'll get the dregs from the bottom, and it won't be nice and clear.

• Cool completely, and pour into jars or containers with lids. Label the containers with the date, unless, like me, you will use it up quickly. The stock will keep in the refrigerator for up to 7 days and in the freezer for 6 months. If you freeze the stock, leave ¾ to 1 in [2 to 2.5 cm] room in your container for it to expand.

Chicken meat that is cooked a long time in a stockpot may become dry and tough. Save it for your favorite pet.

Creamy Mushroom Soup
with Tarragon

SERVES 4 / TOTAL TIME: 45 MIN

I like the flavor of the cremini mushrooms in this soup, which I make more than enough of so we can have some for lunch the next day. But don't try and save it any longer—because of the cream, it doesn't keep well.

Brush or wipe clean: **12 to 18 white mushrooms**

Thinly slice four of the mushrooms and set aside. Coarsely chop the rest.

In a medium saucepan over medium **2 Tbsp butter**
heat, melt:

Add: **2 large shallots, minced**

Cook until softened, and add the coarsely chopped mushrooms and a pinch or two of salt.

Sauté until softened and juicy, about **2 cups [480 ml] chicken stock**
5 minutes, then add: **1 cup [240 ml] water**
            ½ day-old baguette, torn into
            small pieces, with the darker
            parts of the crust removed
            1 Tbsp minced fresh tarragon
            1 cup [240 ml] heavy cream

Bring to a boil, lower the heat, and simmer for 5 minutes.

In a medium skillet over medium **2 Tbsp butter**
heat, melt:

Cook the reserved sliced mushroom until just softened, 2 or 3 minutes.
  To serve, fill two warmed bowls with soup, and scatter half the mushrooms on the top of each one.

Garnish with: **A sprinkle of whole fresh**
            tarragon leaves

Potato & Celery Root Soup with Herbed Butterballs

SERVES 6 / TOTAL TIME: 40 MIN

Despite its name, celery root isn't the root of the green celery stalk. It's actually a related variety called celeriac and looks like a brown, hairy turnip with a rough, knobby peel. Its taste though is quite wonderful, a bit like celery, but almost nutty with a hint of sweetness.

In a small bowl, mash together until well combined:

½ cup [110 g] butter, at room temperature
2 Tbsp chopped fresh thyme
2 Tbsp chopped fresh parsley
2 Tbsp chopped fresh chives
Zest and juice of 1 lemon

Using a spoon and your hands, roll into six or more ¾ in balls [2 cm]. Set aside until ready to use. Do not refrigerate.

For the soup; in a large soup pot, combine:

2 medium potatoes, peeled and sliced
4 cups [960 ml] weak chicken stock or water
2 Tbsp butter
Salt and freshly ground black pepper

Bring to a boil, lower the heat, and simmer uncovered until the potatoes are almost tender, about 15 to 20 minutes, then add:

2 knobs celery root, peeled and cut into small pieces

You'll need to peel the celery root, but peeling the whole bulb at one time doesn't work; it's just too awkward. A quick and easy way to deal with it is to cut the bulb crosswise into ½ in [12 mm] slices, and then, using a paring knife, remove the peel in one long strip from each slice.

Cook until tender, another 5 to 10 minutes. Let cool a little, transfer the soup in batches to a blender, and purée until smooth. Return to the soup pot and add:

2 cups [480 ml] half-and-half

Heat over low heat until warm, but do not allow to boil as it may curdle. Taste for seasoning, and add more salt and pepper if needed.

To serve, ladle the soup into bowls, and put one herbed butterball in each one. Do not stir the soup. The butterballs will start melting on their own, leaving a lovely pool of butter and herbs in their wake.

Reflections on Good Kitchens

My beginnings were of course in my mother's kitchen, which was nice enough, but typical of the times, with an electric stove and overhead cupboards that were out of reach. They were filled with our "good dishes," the ones we used only on holidays. At those times, my mother would call out, "I need a ladder!" and one of my tall uncles would rush to her side and unload the good china, which needed to be washed since it hadn't been used since the last holiday. After bumping my head on the corner of one of the cupboard doors left open, and having to clean into the far corners of each one, I vowed never to have overhead cabinets with doors in my own kitchen, and I never did.

I do have open shelves, and wall space for a painting, but no under-counter cupboards, either! I have found that with some organization and planning, drawers hold almost everything needed. A pantry with open shelves is ideal, so you can see your staples easily.

After we married, Don and I took off the doors of the overhead cupboards in the series of rental houses we lived in, and put them back on when we moved on to the next house. Don was in the Air Force during those early years, and we moved a lot. The kitchens were not memorable.

Neither was the kitchen in our first house in Fresno. At least, though, it had a gas stove, which to my surprise and pleasure worked very well. From then on, I was hooked on cooking with gas. We moved several more times, buying and selling homes as we went, and removing and then replacing the cupboard doors. I cooked my first goose in one of these kitchens, made stock for soups, perfected my cheesecake recipe, and baked pies and cookies galore. From a fig tree outside one of the homes, I made fig jam. It was playtime in the kitchen for me, and I began collecting good pots, pans, and kitchen tools, which I still have.

Then came our move to the small town of Yountville and the kitchen in the café at the Vintage 1870. It was there that I kicked the cook out the door and took over. My career as a chef was launched.

I was able to design four of the six kitchens in this book. The first one I designed was the open kitchen at the Chutney Kitchen, where I served lunch and the monthly prix fixe dinners. My favorite kitchen, though, the second one I designed, was at the French Laundry. Then it was with my daughter Karen that I designed the largest kitchen I've had, the teaching kitchen in the farmhouse at the Apple Farm. My last kitchen, the one I designed in the small cottage we restored, set above the rugged Northern California coastline, is where I had the immense pleasure of cooking just for the two of us.

I've cooked in many, many kitchens, but through my eighty-nine years, the kitchens that have mattered most to me are the six kitchens I have named in this book.

In all these kitchens, the things that mattered greatly to me were: light, air, color, warmth, real wood, a pantry, open shelves, drawers under the counter, wood floors, beautiful pottery and cookware, real silver, and good tools.

Most important to me is light and air. The room has to be colorful, full of light and air, and with a window over the sink looking out to the kitchen garden. The window should be able to open up to let the morning sun and fresh air inside, just like the one I had at the French Laundry, where I could look out and see my herb garden and think about what I wanted to cook that night.

I want plenty of texture and real surfaces that dispel that cold stainless-steel and granite look. I guess you would call it a country kitchen look, but without the clutter. I want plenty of real wood, a chopping block in the center that is big enough, so I can unload the weekly shopping or have enough room to butcher meat on. Ideally, this center-island chopping block can be kept clear enough to really work on, chopping and slicing vegetables, and even rolling out a piecrust. No finish is necessary if it is used constantly and wiped clean after every task. I chop garlic and roll out piecrust on the same work space; the secret is to keep it clean to prevent buildup of grease and odors. For that purpose, I use a favorite rough-linen dishcloth—not the sponge, which I reserve for dishwashing. A bar towel of rough terrycloth is also a good choice. Just keep it clean! I do use a small board on top when working with fish, carving rare meat, or cutting raw poultry, just to be extra safe.

My first choice for flooring would be wood planks, but not too perfect or highly polished. The only things I have to plug in are a toaster and a blender. Not only does this save counter space, but I like using a knife to chop, slice, and dice by hand. I see photos of kitchens with totally bare countertops in the magazines. I wonder if anyone actually cooks there, or if they just call in a caterer. I prefer tidiness, but I want the kitchen to look used and ready for action.

The sink is very important to me, as I prefer to live without a dishwasher. I like washing my pots, pans, and dishes by hand, as it centers me. Besides, it is part of the process of cooking and should be treated as such, not put off to the end. Use your knife, then wash it. Don't let your pans pile up. I like washing our favorite plates, burnishing our old silver, and polishing my favorite copper pan. It's all part of the cooking process. If I had the room, my first luxury would be a second sink for prepping vegetables.

I always work with a pan of hot soapy water to wash up as I go. I'm very happy with my old white porcelain sink with drainboards on either side, but I do rather covet the cast cement ones that our grandson Joe is producing. They have lovely soft colors and feel remarkable to the touch. Maybe in my next kitchen!

This book, like most of my life, is centered in and around my kitchens, both personally and professionally. I feel at home in the kitchen, more confident in my surroundings; being there with my family, friends, and staff—all of that has contributed to my happiness. I've been many years at the stove, sometimes repeating beloved old dishes, sometimes giving them an upgrade as a result of greater experience or new ingredients, or inspired by a wealth of good books and magazines.

Writing this book over a span of almost ten years has turned it into something more than I intended it to be. My original idea was to simply put down the family recipes and tell the stories behind them. Somehow, it has grown in scope and forced me to dig a little deeper.

I have always cooked farm-to-table, beginning well before I heard the phrase. Many people think I had a message to communicate, but really, my only impulse was to do what I do best, and help our family survive. It comes as a surprise to find that I am included among the chefs who introduced California cuisine to the public. Although I didn't have a mission, I greatly admired Alice Waters and others who had something to say, and the fortitude to say it. All in all, I really have done just what I loved to do, which has always been simply to cook good food for those I cared for. That's what mattered. That's all that mattered.

below: My daughter Karen, badgered me to take up the hand-sewing that I practiced while she was growing up. We purchased some fabrics and gathered scraps from old projects, and I created these patchwork potholders (left, on stove). I have now gifted pairs of these to most of my family and friends, and take them in for mending as needed (see pages 1 and 352)

Epilogue

As I sit here at the kitchen table over morning coffee, I watch proudly as the daily Apple Farm hustle and bustle goes by my window. Tim, my son-in-law, comes up on his tractor to deliver a load of apples to the cold storage, which sits between our remodeled apartment and the barn deck. Our granddaughter Rita emerges from the garden with a tub full of fresh vegetables to add to the farm stand, which our interns are busy tidying and restocking. Jerzy, Rita's husband, comes up the hill with buckets of still-warm goat milk, which will soon be turned into chèvre and feta. My daughter Karen appears and disappears from the scene, overseeing and balancing everything. Cruz Alvarado, our faithful employee, who during the twenty years she has worked with us has become like another family member, dashes across the driveway from the commercial kitchen to spoil me with a basket of cheese biscuits, which she has proudly prepared for our overnight guests.

I feel sort of useless, unable to help out in a physical way. But after all, I am well into my eighties, and everyone keeps telling me that I deserve to just sit here and enjoy watching the beehive of activity. After coming out of the hospital in 2008, where I had been recovering from a heart problem, which resulted in a stroke, I was ready to take off my apron and turn our cooking classes over to Karen. And she was more than prepared to be on her own after assisting me for so many years. So Don and I packed up and crossed the Mendocino Ridge to our much-loved Elk cottage, to rest and recover and simply enjoy life for more than eight years. Eventually, though, we decided it was time to be closer to the family again. The whole family helped us refurbish our quarters at the Apple Farm. Don and I were able to enjoy our new digs for well over a year before his health declined and he passed away. I am grateful for that time because we settled in at the farm again and established new patterns together, which will continue to guide me for the rest of my time here.

As I sit in my warm little nook and look out the window, I can't quite see the orchard, but I only have to take a short stroll down the driveway, past Rita and Jerzy's little cottage, to stand and survey the bulk of our property. From the crest, we can look over our lower orchards, which are down on the floodplain, and see across the creek to the Sierra foothills, where my sons Johnny and Eric plan to build a little escape, and across the river to the majestic old-growth redwoods of Hendy Woods State Park. Along the well-worn road that encircles the farm, there are hedges made of blackberry bushes that have grown thick with berries. We encourage them with a little pruning, so we can reach the fruit and use it to make our jam. (Here I am using the editorial "we," as these days, Cruz has mastered the jam making, and I do nothing except devour it on toast in the morning.)

The apples are Tim's domain. He knows the location of every tree and the care and attention each requires. He has his pets, which he usually prunes himself, and he always knows just when to harvest each of the more than eighty heirloom varieties he has grafted and cultivated over the years. When we are at the peak of harvest, our outdoor farm stand boasts rows of wooden boxes with labels describing the history and flavor, texture, and best use for each. It really is a lovely sight to behold, all of the different textures and colors and shapes lined up, ready for tasting and purchasing at our self-service stand, where we require basic math skills and respect for the honor code from our customers.

I first decided to write this book when one of my grandchildren asked me long ago, "Who was Aunt Polly?" I realized that while our next generation knows many of our family's stories, their children have probably never heard them. Of course, this provoked a flood of memories, which I have tried to edit to avoid boring my readers to death.

Food has always been a defining force in my life, so I have chosen to focus on the recipes and the stories that go along with them, and let them reveal the history of our family, the restaurants, and the food. As my sister Kay and I often say after trying to recall the details of a story, "There is nobody alive that can dispute it, so if we say it's true, it's true!"

ABOUT DON

We lost Don, who just dwindled away and died from a fall. We are thankful that it was quick. We were able to stay in our perfect "assisted living" quarters back at the farm for almost a year. During that time, it was sheer pleasure to be in on the activities and accomplishments of our ever expanding family.

Here I am, surrounded and comforted by my family. I find myself talking to Don's usual place across the table, sharing my thoughts and the small frustrations of everyday life in the midst of a large family. He would be so pleased to see this book finally in print. Without his support and help, it never would have happened.

My husband Don was a remarkable force in his own right. After serving in the Air Force, working in banking, and bringing our family to Yountville to take on Vintage 1870 and the Vintage Cafe, he started from scratch (working with me of course) our two successful restaurants. Beyond that, he spent thirteen years on the Yountville city council, serving four of those years as city mayor. In 1975, as mayor, he had the city hire noted designer Lawrence Halprin to collaborate with the community to develop a master plan to preserve the small-town atmosphere of Yountville. The plan dictated that businesses couldn't take up more than 6 percent of the town, and that street signs would be simple redwood posts with names carved on them and painted white. He was enthusiastic about preserving and nurturing the unique historic character of our town, and even had the old building that we bought, the French Laundry, listed on the National Register of Historic Places. Doing all this, he still worked hard every day at the restaurant, always being the last one to leave and lock the door. He is missed.

Sally's Pantry

There are certain things I've learned to keep on hand, but I've also learned that it's not just what you have, it's about how you cook.

By staying with what was in season, cooking with what I could find fresh and local, I've never needed to crowd my pantry with processed, packaged (so-called) foods. I do keep canned and preserved items in my pantry: things we've prepared in our own kitchen, such as jams, chutneys, and pickles. I also have some store-bought items: canned tomatoes, a backup can of chicken stock. But I stay away from those packaged concoctions industrially engineered to taste good.

Below I have listed the basic items I make sure to keep on hand, so I can cook what I want to cook.

CANNED GOODS

ALBACORE TUNA: Canned by Katy's Smokehouse, in the small Northern California town of Trinidad (katyssmokehouse.com).

BEANS: I stock black, white, and garbanzos.

CHICKEN STOCK: I prefer to make my own (see page 328), so I only keep a backup can of chicken stock for emergencies, a quality product made by a trusted brand with good flavor.

TOMATOES: When we run of our own in the freezer, I turn to cans of whole tomatoes, not chopped or crushed. For crushed tomatoes, I can always take out a tomato and squeeze it. But I do try to keep some tomato paste on hand.

JARS

CAPERS: I keep a backup jar in the pantry, but I am usually working out of an open one in the fridge. Make sure to keep them covered with plenty of their brine and they will keep very well.

JAMS AND CHUTNEYS: Homemade, of course. Why would I ever use store bought?

MAYONNAISE: I prefer Best Foods/Hellman's brands.

OLIVES: I love the large green Castelvetrano olives, but there are so many to choose from these days. They vary in flavor, color, texture. The oil-cured black ones are too salty for me.

PICKLES: I make my own (see page 27), but on the rare occasion when I run out, I'll turn to a good kosher dill, especially one from Sonoma Brinery (sonomabrinery .com).

DRIED INGREDIENTS

BEANS: We grow and dry our own black beans and large white Italian butter beans on the farm, and I know it's fall when I find myself sitting around shelling them. For the best heirloom beans, turn to Rancho Gordo (ranchogordo.com).

CHILES: My granddaughter Rita grows different kinds of chiles, so I usually have a changing rotation of types to try. But I'm quite partial to the good color and flavor of the guajillo. A good source for chiles is Tierra Vegetables (tierravegetables.com).

MY GO-TO STARCHES

BREAD: I love good bread, and today there are so many great local sources. I like having a baguette, as well as a sandwich bread and perhaps a loaf of sourdough handy. If anything becomes stale, I make Toast Rounds (page 176), croutons, or toast crumbs to sprinkle on what I'm cooking. Northern California bakeries we adore are Della Fattoria, in Petaluma; Acme Bread and Cheese Board, in Berkeley; Red Bird, in Cotati; Model Bakery, in St. Helena; Tartine and Josey Baker Bread, in San Francisco; and Bouchon Bakery, in Yountville.

COUSCOUS: It's made from semolina like most dry pastas, but it has a very different mouth feel. It adds a nice bit of starch to a plate to soak up juices. It can also be used to make a salad in place of bulgur.

PASTA AND NOODLES: Orzo or riso, since I can't get any more of the semi di melone ("melon seed") pasta I loved using at the French Laundry. I also keep linguini and spaghetti on hand, and I like the Italian artisanal brand Rustichella d'Abruzzo as well as De Cecco. I have also come to enjoy Japanese soba, somen, and udon noodles.

POLENTA: A coarser sifted cornmeal made from flint corn, so good with Southwest Pork (page 134) and in Poblanos Stuffed with Polenta & Cheese (page 132).

POTATOES: I like russets, reds, German Butterballs, and Yukon golds. They need to be stored in a cool dark place to prevent greening. They will turn oddly sweet in the refrigerator.

RICE: I use the organic rice raised by the Lundberg family, not far from us here in Northern California, especially their long grain jasmine and basmati varieties. Short grain versions work best for risotto and puddings.

ROLLED OATS: We mostly use these for our big trays of granola, and they are a great addition to cookies.

OILS AND VINEGARS

OLIVE OIL: I keep two grades of Californian olive oil on hand, both from Sciabica, in Modesto: a medium grade they call Marsala for almost everything, and save the good stuff, Sevillano, for drizzling and dipping. Make sure to store your oil in dark, tightly sealed glass bottles.

VINEGAR: We make a delicious raw, unpasteurized apple cider vinegar here on the farm. We also blend it with our apple cider syrup (see page 231) and reduce it to make a lovely apple balsamic. If we have lots of raspberries, we make raspberry cider vinegar. I also keep unseasoned rice vinegar on hand.

BAKING SUPPLIES

DRIED FRUITS: I like to have golden and black raisins, currants, dried Blenheim apricots, and our own dried pears.

EXTRACTS: I keep vanilla and almond on hand, though I rarely bake.

FLOUR: I stick with all-purpose flour, and keep the baking soda, baking powder, and cornstarch fresh.

NUTS: I love all nuts and try to have available walnuts, almonds, hazelnuts, pecans, and peanuts. The best almonds are from Massa Organics in Sacramento (massaorganics.com).

SWEETENERS: I have a good mild honey from a local beekeeper. I also keep in stock granulated and organic cane sugar, dark and light brown sugars, but not extra-fine sugar for baking, because granulated can be processed easily in a blender. I use blackstrap molasses, and, of course, the apple cider syrup we make on the farm (see page 231).

SEASONINGS

HERBS: I prefer fresh, but I do keep dried bay leaves and Mexican oregano, which tastes more authentic in Mexican

dishes than regular oregano. To grow it fresh, you need to be in a hot, dry locale, which we are not.

PEPPER: I keep Tellicherry black peppercorns, along with white, green, and pink peppercorns.

SALT: My go-to is Diamond Crystal Kosher Salt. For a finishing salt, I like to also have on hand either Maldon sea salt flakes or one of the lovely fleur de sels from France.

SPICES: I don't keep many around, just the usual suspects: small amounts of cinnamon, nutmeg, allspice, clove, coriander, ginger, and larger amounts of cumin and fennel, which I use more often.

IN THE REFRIGERATOR

CHEESE: A sharp white cheddar, a chunk of good Parmesan, and our homemade chèvre goat cheese, which we can't sell since we've never gone through all the necessary rigmarole.

EGGS: From our own chickens. When they're taking time off, we get eggs from our neighbors.

FRESH GINGER: Luckily, it keeps quite well for weeks in the refrigerator, so it's easy to have on hand.

MORE DAIRY PRODUCTS: Milk, half-and-half, sour cream, plain yogurt, and butter, always butter. I recommend Straus Family Creamery (strausfamilycreamery.com).

VEGETABLES: A bag of spinach, romaine hearts, green onions, a head of white cabbage, carrots, and yellow and white onions.

CONDIMENTS

ASIAN CONDIMENTS: Soy sauce, toasted sesame oil, and fish sauce. Find a brand you like and stick to it, as there are many inferior products on the shelves.

HORSERADISH: I like Tulelake Old Fashioned horseradish (beavertonfoods.com).

KETCHUP: In case I feel like a shrimp cocktail.

MUSTARD: There are so many mustards these days, and I enjoy trying them, but I always turn back to my tried and true Grey Poupon dijon.

NUT BUTTER: A small jar of peanut butter. Don didn't like nut butters, so I didn't have them on hand for the longest time. But I now keep peanut butter or almond butter around to use in a salad dressing, occasionally.

PRESERVED LEMONS: I make my own (see page 251).

IN THE FREEZER

BERRIES: Raspberries and blackberries, if we have any left after making jam and vinegar. I freeze the berries on a tray before putting them into the bags.

MEAT: Bacon, ham hocks, and other cuts of pork, after we butcher a pig. And often goat meat from one of our own goats. Sources for good meat: In Northern California, I highly recommend Fatted Calf (fattedcalf.com), Willowside Meats (willowsidemeatsllc.com), and Sonoma County Meat Company (sonomacountymeatco.com).

POBLANO PEPPERS: When my granddaughter Rita has a bumper crop. Before bagging them, I char them and strip off the skins.

STOCK: I freeze my homemade chicken stock (see page 328) in bags, too. Fatted Calf and other good markets now have good frozen stock.

TOMATOES: To freeze our home-grown tomatoes, which are so much better than store bought (especially when picked at the height of their ripeness), I cook them down on large trays in the oven and bag them. They make a delicious roasted tomato paste that is rough in texture and very versatile.

OUT AND ABOUT IN THE KITCHEN

GARLIC: Our own, grown at the Apple Farm, keeps well for months in a cool corner.

LEMONS: We have a few Meyer lemon trees in pots and a large one in the ground that produce most of what we need, but we always live in fear of the next hard frost. We also keep plenty of Eureka lemons around. They have much higher acid than Meyers, which can often provide the finishing touch to your cooking.

MUSHROOMS: When it rains, my grandson Willy heads out to gather black chanterelles. I relish having them available. Hedgehogs and golden chanterelles also often come our way from nearer the coast. There are some fairly local shiitake growers as well that we like to encourage. Sometimes I'll get some dried shiitakes, which are so good to add to a stew or soup. They are a perfect example of a pantry staple.

SHALLOTS: They first became widely available when I had the French Laundry. I now use them a lot, often instead of onions and garlic.

THINGS I DON'T KEEP

Anchovies. When I was younger, I didn't use them as I found them too strong for my taste, but in recent years, my son Johnny and my grandson Perry, at the Boonville Hotel, use them to enhance a dish with magical results. If I were to start all over again, I would probably use them more. Artichoke hearts, because they don't taste like artichokes. I don't like the taste of canned vegetable stock or canned fish stock, especially when it's so easy to make my own. I'm not crazy about canned beef stock, either. I don't like olives stuffed with things, or sweet mustards. I don't keep a so-called cooking wine, which often turns out to be rot gut. But I never throw away the last of an open bottle of good wine, because I can use a splash to deglaze a pan or top off a soup. Since I use fresh herbs, I don't need dried ones cluttering up my pantry. I don't keep maple syrup, as our delicious apple cider syrup (see page 231), made on our farm, more than fills the bill.

Acknowledgments

So many people have helped me along the way. My mom gave me confidence and knowledge, and taught me how to work! She was proud of her role as wife and mother, and encouraged me to be proud of my lifestyle. I was lucky to have very good high school teachers. They aimed me toward UC Davis, where I was mentored by Doris Heineman, the Dec Art Department chair. She was tall and stately with such a sense of color and style I could learn by just looking at her. Aunt Polly helped me polish my country girl ways. My kitchen staff and my family were always there, spoon in hand, and their opinions were crucial. Lorraine Jones, who became the backbone of the Chutney Kitchen, was a good friend, and later our partner in purchasing the French Laundry property. Lorraine and Geraldine Sommerfeldt moved with us to the French Laundry, sharing waitshifts with our children. Patty Grantham, a wine buff and friend of my son Johnny, joined our waitstaff and helped Don buy the wine. Joanne Blicker cleaned, helped me with the prep, and then donned her white embroidered apron to serve in the dining room. David Alosi worked with us for years as a waiter and gardener. Tom Overton kept our pots and pans polished to perfection. Through the years, Tom scrubbed my big aluminum pot that we cooked pasta in so hard that it eventually wore thin and wouldn't stand up when empty, the long handle outweighing the pot itself. I presented it to him as a keepsake when we closed our doors on the last night. Mickey Riva, an old friend and employee at the Vintage Cafe came in on closed days to make chutney and jam. My two stalwart helpers in the kitchen were Richard Carter and Laurie Malmquist. Richard did so well in the kitchen that I was never tempted to adjust a plate that he produced. He had an artistic eye and a good palate. We became more than employer and employee—he became part of my family.

Laurie was smart and good, and she and Richard held down the kitchen on the rare occasions when I was not able to be there. There were countless others who cooked alongside of me, making me a better cook from their suggestions and support. I did many caterings for the Napa Valley ladies. They taught me a lot about gracious dining. I picked up from them the lovely habit of serving a simple salad, along with a cheese plate, after the main course. They also gave me the awareness to think beyond "white wine with fish, red with beef." Faith Echtermeyer planted the seed of doing a book in the seventies. We even took a stab at it, but soon it dwindled as we focused on more realistic ventures. Dorothy Kalins also encouraged me to write a book. Her confidence in what we were doing was valuable. Brittany Davis and Polly Bates did much of the transcribing of my early pencil scratches. My three daughters, Kathy, Karen, and Terry, combed through every story, recipe and photograph with their keen eyes and palates to make sure we got it right. My grandson Byron, who runs his own graphic design company, and his brother Troyce, who traveled the world with his keen eye for photography light and composition, took on the full weight of the project, without contract, salary, or time out from their busy lives. Debey Zito, my daughter-in-law, had the brilliant idea of getting her friend Bruce Smith involved. When we put Byron and Bruce together, it gave me a much needed second wind; they were a perfect fit and a joy to work with. Bruce, through research and interviews patiently gathered a phenonimal amount of information and pulled it all together into a cohesive package; his subtle voice throughout the book provides the common thread. Lastly, but far from least, are all the many people that I have cooked for through the years. Your support has been my strength.

Index

Ben and Jerry's is a registered trademark of Ben & Jerry's Homemade, Inc.; Best Foods is a registered trademark of Conopco, Inc.; Better Homes & Gardens is a registered trademark of Meredith Corporation; Betty Crocker is a registered trademark of General Mills Marketing, Inc.; Bisquick is a registered trademark of General Mills Marketing, Inc.; Bouchon Bakery is a registered trademark of Shamus & Peabody, LLC; Bundt is a registered trademark of Northland Aluminum Products, Inc.; Cheerios is a registered trademark of General Mills IP Holdings I, LLC; Chemex is a registered trademark of Chemex Corporation Formerly International Housewares Corporation; Cook's Illustrated is a registered trademark of America's Test Kitchen Limited Partnership; Cost Plus is a registered trademark of Cost Plus Management Services, Inc.; Crisco is a registered trademark of B&G Foods North America, Inc.; Cuisinart is a registered trademark of Conair LLC; De Cecco is a registered trademark of F.lli De Cecco Di Filippo Fara S. Martin S.p.A.; Diamond Crystal is a registered trademark of Cargill, Incorporated; Fatted Calf is a registered trademark of Ryty Partners LLC; Folgers is a registered trademark of The Folger Coffee Company; Food & Wine is a registered trademark of Time, Inc.; Freemark Abbey is a registered trademark of Jackson Family Farms, LLC; Graffeo is a registered trademark of Graffeo Coffee Roasting Company, Inc.; Grand Marnier is a registered trademark of Marnier-Lapostolle Bisquit SA; Grey Poupon is a registered trademark of Kraft Foods Group Brands LLC; Guittard is a registered trademark of Guittard Chocolate Co.; Hamburger Helper is a registered trademark of General Mills Marketing, Inc.; Heath Ceramics is a registered trademark of Heath Ceramics Corporation; Hellmann's is a registered trademark of Conopco, Inc.; Jell-O is a registered trademark of Kraft Foods Group Brands LLC; Kahlúa is a registered trademark of The Absolut Company; Ladies Home Journal is a registered trademark of Meredith Corporation; Maldon is a registered trademark of Maldon Crystal Salt Company LLC; McDonald's is a registered trademark of Mcdonald's Corporation; Michelin is a registered trademark of Compagnie Générale Des Etablissements Michelin SCA; Michelob is a registered trademark of Anheuser-Busch LLC; Microplane is a registered trademark of Grace Manufacturing Inc.; MJB is a registered trademark of Massimo Zanetti Beverage Group; The Nut Tree is a registered trademark of the City of Vacaville; Peet's Coffee is a registered trademark of Peet's Coffee, Inc.; Procter and Gamble is a registered trademark of The Procter & Gamble Company; Pyrex is a registered trademark of Corning Incorporated; Rancho Gordo is a registered trademark of Rancho Gordo, Inc; Rustichella d'Abruzzo is a registered trademark of Rustichellad D'Abruzzo S.P.A.; S.O.S. is a registered trademark of The Clorox Company; Saveur is a registered trademark of Editions Hubert Burda Media SAS; Sciabica's is a registered trademark of Nick Sciabica & Sons; Sheetrock is a registered trademark of United States Gypsum Company; Starbucks is a registered trademark of Starbucks Corporation; Straus Family Creamery is a registered trademark of Straus Family Creamery Corporation; Sunset magazine is a registered trademark of Sunset Publishing Corporation; Tante Marie's Cooking School is a registered trademark of Risley, Mary; Tartine is a registered trademark of Tartine, L.P. Tartine Enterprises, Inc.; Time magazine is a registered trademark of Meredith Corporation; Tulelake is a registered trademark of Beaverton Foods, Inc.; Wesson oil is a registered trademark of Richardson Oilseed Products (US) Limited; White Mountain is a registered trademark of Sunbeam Products, Inc.

AUG 1 7 2022

AUG 1 7 2022